WHEN SMALL STATES MAKE BIG LEAPS

A volume in the series
Cornell Studies in Political Economy
edited by Peter J. Katzenstein

A list of titles in this series is available at
www.cornellpress.cornell.edu.

When Small States Make Big Leaps

Institutional Innovation and High-Tech
Competition in Western Europe

Darius Ornston

CORNELL UNIVERSITY PRESS ITHACA AND LONDON

Cornell University Press gratefully acknowledges receipt of a subvention from the Office of the Dean, School of Public and International Affairs, University of Georgia, which aided in the publication of this book.

First published 2012 by Cornell University Press

Printed in the United States of America

Library of Congress Cataloging-in-Publication Data

Ornston, Darius, 1978–
    When small states make big leaps : institutional innovation and high-tech competition in Western Europe / Darius Ornston.
      p. cm. — (Cornell studies in political economy)
   Includes bibliographical references and index.
   ISBN 978-0-8014-5092-1 (cloth : alk. paper)
   1. High technology industries—Denmark.   2. High technology industries—
Finland.   3. High technology industries—Ireland.   4. Corporate state—
Denmark.   5. Corporate state—Finland.   6. Corporate state—Ireland.
7. Industrial policy—Denmark.   8. Industrial policy—Finland.   9. Industrial
policy—Ireland.   I. Title.   II. Series: Cornell studies in political economy.
   HC360.H53O75 2012
   338.4'76094—dc23   2012004510

Cornell University Press strives to use environmentally responsible suppliers and materials to the fullest extent possible in the publishing of its books. Such materials include vegetable-based, low-VOC inks and acid-free papers that are recycled, totally chlorine-free, or partly composed of nonwood fibers. For further information, visit our website at www.cornellpress.cornell.edu.

Cloth printing   10 9 8 7 6 5 4 3 2 1

To Roxy

Contents

Acknowledgments

This book first began at Swarthmore College with the admittedly arbitrary decision to apply for a Fulbright scholarship in Finland in 2000. While my research into the politics of European integration yielded few concrete results, I was struck by the disjuncture between what I observed in Finland at the height of the dot-com bubble and what I learned as a doctoral student at the University of California, Berkeley, two years later. My experience with text messaging and electronic banking, and the broader structural transformation that they represented, fit poorly within the literature that I encountered in my graduate seminars. Literature on neo-corporatism, small states, social systems of production, and the "varieties of capitalism" all suggested that coordinated market economies like that of Finland should upgrade existing industries before entering new ones, particularly dynamic high-tech sectors. While the literature on competitive corporatism appeared to explain Ireland's big leap into high-tech markets, it did a poor job of characterizing the institutional changes that had taken place in Finland over the last two decades. This book represents my effort to resolve this puzzle, to identify how Finland and other historically neo-corporatist economies such as Denmark adapted neo-corporatist institutions to confront disruptive economic challenges.

I could not have completed this project without the assistance of several exceptionally committed and gifted faculty members. My professors Ken Sharpe and Bruce Morrison got me hooked on political science and European politics, respectively, tolerating and even encouraging my idiosyncratic interest in small states. At the University of California, Berkeley, Jonah Levy, John Zysman, and Nick Ziegler deserve special mention as the most involved members of a friendly and supportive community. I am also grateful to Andrew Janos, Erik Baekkeskov, David Collier, Bev Crawford, Rahsaan Maxwell, Dann Naseemullah, Abe Newman, Toby Schulze-Cleven, Laura Stoker, Sirpa Tuomainen, Mark Vail, Steven Vogel, Bart Watson, and Margaret Weir for sharing their time and wisdom on so many occasions.

In the field, I relied on the support of the Fulbright Program, which funded my initial visit to Finland, as well as the German Marshall Fund of the United States, which financed fieldwork in Denmark, Finland, and Ireland between 2005 and 2006. The American-Scandinavian Foundation and the Berkeley Department of Scandinavian also financed separate visits with smaller grants. This financial support would have been worthless were it not for the generosity of the hundreds of individuals who shared sensitive information and hours of their time. These individuals are too numerous to name, and many requested that their contribution to this project remain anonymous. Several individuals deserve special mention, however, for hosting my visit, providing office space, helping me to arrange interviews, inviting me to deliver presentations, offering critical feedback, and providing encouragement. In Finland, Ylä-Anttila, Petri Rouvinen, and Christopher Palmberg at the Research Institute of the Finnish Economy, together with Kari Lilja and Olli Rehn, not only hosted me but also offered friendship and mentorship. I am grateful for their active support. In Denmark, I could not have completed my research without Øve Kaj Pedersen at Copenhagen Business School, Erik Rasmussen at Mandag Morgen, and Bent Dalum at the University of Aalborg. Finally, I am indebted to Niamh Hardiman for taking an early interest in my research and providing a home at University College Dublin.

In transforming my research into a book, I benefited from insightful and encouraging feedback from Mark Blyth, Pepper Culpepper, Roger Haydon, Wade Jacoby, Peter Katzenstein, Rahsaan Maxwell, Abe Newman, John Stephens, Mark Vail, and multiple anonymous reviewers. I also was fortunate enough to work within an exceptionally collegial environment at the University of Georgia's School of Public and International Affairs. The late Chris Allen was an exceptionally enthusiastic and inspirational mentor, while Markus Crepaz, Shane Singh, Patricia Sullivan, Brock Tessman, and Dean Tom Lauth have continued to offer feedback and support. I am most indebted, however, to Danny Breznitz, who did all the hard work of a committee member without receiving any of the credit. Danny not only helped with fieldwork and provided feedback but facilitated my professionalization as a scholar, patiently forging contacts, dispensing advice, identifying priorities, and diffusing crises.

My family made the first and final contributions to this research project. If Ken and Bruce shaped my interest in European politics, my parents, Nick Ornston and Donna Parke, together with extended family members Bob and May Macnab, cultivated a broader sense of curiosity and a passion for ideas. While it was hard to appreciate this contribution while enduring marathon dinnertime conversations among four microbiologists, it is a gift that I have come to appreciate and will treasure for the rest of my life. My wife, Roxy, to whom this book is dedicated, and son, Eric, made the final and most important contribution by bringing the project to a happy and successful conclusion. They provided encouragement during hard times and inspiration during good times. I look forward to many long dinnertime conversations with them in the future (but preferably not about microbiology).

WHEN SMALL STATES MAKE BIG LEAPS

INTRODUCTION
Recasting Corporatism

This book was inspired by the puzzling ability of several western European states to compete in rapidly evolving high-tech markets. We would not expect continental European economies to succeed in such markets. European capitalism is more commonly associated with sluggish growth and mounting unemployment. Skeptics argue that cozy deals among trade unions, employer associations, and state agencies inhibit the redistribution of resources to new actors and activities. Even those who admire these cooperative economic arrangements suggest that neo-corporatist institutions are most effective in modernizing century-old low- and medium-tech industries such as food processing or forestry. European economies look as though they are uniquely vulnerable to radical innovation and the destruction of traditional niches.

Curiously, however, several traditionally low-tech European economies, including Ireland, Finland, and Denmark, have defied these trends. Furthermore, each has done so by entering precisely those dynamic high-tech industries in which they should be most disadvantaged. Ireland, which depended on footwear and textiles until the 1970s, redefined itself as a software and computer export platform. Finland and Denmark made an even more implausible transformation, moving from wood processing and food processing into knowledge-intensive research and design activities in a range of high-tech industries, from telecommunications equipment to biotechnology. These diverse pathways into new markets are particularly puzzling because they defy liberal market-oriented narratives. Ireland, Finland, and Denmark relied on similar bargains among state agencies and industry and labor associations to manage economic adjustment.

1

Rather than inhibiting the redistribution of resources, however, these deals appear to have accelerated restructuring.

How to resolve this puzzle? I argue that the ostensibly static institutions described above have changed over time. Historically, institutionalized cooperation in policymaking and production was perceived as conservative, protecting existing investments (Katzenstein 1984; Streeck 1992). Firms and employees relied on long-term loans, generous social benefits, and defensive industrial policies to defend established enterprises, occupations, and industries. These conservative deals supported incremental upmarket movement within stable low- and medium-tech industries in early postwar Denmark and Finland. As chapter 6 relates, this logic continues to yield important insights into several contemporary western European countries, such as Austria, Germany, and Norway.

Countries facing acute economic crises and new external constraints, such as EU-imposed restrictions on deficits and state aid, however, can use institutionalized cooperation to achieve very different objectives. Literature on "competitive corporatism" suggests that countries can adapt concertation, or institutionalized cooperation in policymaking, to advance market reform (Rhodes 1998). In the Netherlands, Ireland, Italy, Spain, and Portugal policymakers were strong enough to threaten societal actors, particularly trade unions vehemently opposed to pro-market reforms, but they were too weak to absorb the political costs associated with unilateral action. In this environment, policymakers struck deals with trade unions and employers, linking wage restraint to fiscal and social benefit retrenchment. In this book, I describe how countries such as Ireland used competitive corporatist bargaining among policymakers and how producer associations facilitated restructuring, entering cost-sensitive assembly activities within new high-tech industries. This strategy enabled Ireland to enter new high-tech markets, although it also rendered the country more vulnerable to cost competition and, eventually, economic crisis.

Competitive corporatism, however, is not the only way countries can adapt. Countries with a stronger pattern of coordination or cooperation in production, such as Denmark and Finland, have responded to economic crises differently. Policymakers in these countries also struck deals with vulnerable trade unions, but they were able to engage firms in sensitive domains such as human-capital formation and research. They thus used policy concertation to convert hitherto conservative patterns of coordination in production, adapting private-public, industry-labor, and interfirm collaboration to invest in disruptive new inputs such as venture capital, human capital, and R & D. These "creative corporatist" deals (Ornston 2013) supported very different economic trajectories. In contrast to conservative corporatism, such investments explicitly targeted new enterprises, occupations, and industries. Unlike competitive corporatism, high-quality investments supported more knowledge-intensive activities within high-tech industries, greater immunity to cost competition, and a stronger position in the 2007–9 financial crisis.

This tripartite distinction among conservative, competitive, and creative corporatism enhances our understanding of contemporary capitalism in three ways. First, in this book I defy descriptions of convergence based on a liberal economic model (Friedman 1999). In showing how institutionalized cooperation can be converted to assume an independent and offensive role in accelerating economic adjustment, however, I also transcend static accounts of capitalist diversity to demonstrate how it is changing over time (Hall and Soskice 2001). Significantly, change is not limited to incremental processes of layering, hybridization, or dualization. Instead, I identify room for institutional "conversion" (Streeck and Thelen 2005, 31), the process by which actors adapt old institutions to perform new functions, within highly coordinated economies. In so doing, I document and explain sweeping, nonliberal institutional change in contemporary capitalism. I also acknowledge the boundaries of institutional innovation, explaining why it is easier to create competitive corporatism than creative corporatism and why both are limited in their adjustment capacity.

Second, in exploring the circumstances under which countries convert economic institutions, I attempt to enhance our understanding of the different roles that policymakers, trade unions, and employers exercise in shaping economic adjustment. My argument supports literature on concertation, affirming that the state (and trade unions) matter (Hemerijck and Vail 2006; Molina 2006). Policymakers can trigger significant institutional reform by threatening trade unions, while even weakened trade unions can strike deals regarding the scope and speed with which this occurs. At the same time, the evidence confirms that employers play a significant, independent role in policymaking and production (Swenson 1991), determining whether institutional adaptation is confined to market reform or supports collective investment in new inputs. I thus bridge hitherto distinct state- and labor-centered literature on concertation in policymaking, on the one hand, and firm-centered research on coordination in production regimes, on the other. In doing so, I not only highlight the differences between concertation and coordination but illustrate what happens when the two phenomena coincide. More specifically, I illustrate that peak-level policy concertation can convert coordination to perform very different functions.

Finally, this insight reveals that these neo-corporatist reforms have had important and counterintuitive implications for economic adjustment. Most obviously, I resolve a significant theoretical and empirical puzzle in the literature on comparative politics and political economy by explaining how ostensibly incremental neo-corporatist economies can compete in rapidly evolving high-tech industries.

I thus challenge the long-standing link between institutionalized cooperation and incremental adjustment (Katzenstein 1984; Soskice 1999), as well as political and economic theories based on geopolitics, state size, or multinational corporations (Casper 2007; Dalum 1992; Leslie 2000).

In demonstrating that neo-corporatist economies can compete in high-tech markets, a rapidly evolving, disruptive field where they should be highly disadvantaged, I suggest that they may be able to adapt to a much broader range of challenges, including internationalization, the services transformation, and even climate change. Indeed, this helps explain why Denmark and Finland were less vulnerable to the consequences of the dot-com bubble and subsequent crash than ostensible high-tech leaders such as Britain, Ireland, and the United States. In identifying the specific mechanisms by which Denmark and Finland adapted to disruptive challenges, however, I identify important challenges and limitations that country-specific literature (Campbell and Pedersen 2007; Castells and Himanen 2002) has hitherto neglected.

I begin with the literature on neo-corporatism, tightly associated with incremental innovation with established industries and implying vulnerability to new information technologies. We have few tools to explain why ostensibly liberal countries such as Ireland turned to neo-corporatist bargaining to compete in high-tech markets, or why traditionally neo-corporatist economies such as Denmark and Finland assumed an even more impressive position in such markets. I resolve these puzzles by distinguishing among the three neo-corporatist subtypes: conservative, competitive, and creative. A specific constellation of stakeholder power and interests shapes each subtype, which in turn generates distinctive economic trajectories.

Before we examine reactions to high-tech challenges, we need historical context to characterize the level and nature of neo-corporatism in postwar Denmark, Finland, and Ireland. More specifically, Finland relied on extensive state-industry cooperation, Denmark relied on slightly less comprehensive industry-labor cooperation, and Ireland did not possess any significant form of cooperation. Their postwar economic performance seems to support the traditional neo-corporatist interpretation since Denmark and, particularly, Finland were among the lowest-tech and least research-intensive economies in western Europe. Conservative corporatist bargains reinforced these low-tech trajectories by providing long-term loans or "patient capital" to established firms, compensating workers, and defending vulnerable industries. Ireland, with its more liberal institutions, occupied a more competitive if problematic position. Institutional reforms enabled all three countries to assume significantly stronger (and unique) positions in new high-tech markets.

Finland went from being one of the least competitive and least innovative countries in the 1970s to being one of the most successful by the end of the 1990s. Restructuring reflected movement away from conservative corporatism, as vulnerable stakeholders dismantled ostensibly core deals in financial and labor markets and industrial policy. It also reflected new bargains on risk capital, skill acquisition, and research. Policymakers mobilized pension and insurance fund capital in early stage financial markets and expanded university output in bilateral negotiations with industry. Creative corporatism was most pronounced in innovation policy, in which stakeholders converted existing patterns of private-public and interfirm cooperation. Creative bargains in this domain dramatically increased investment in R & D. They enabled firms to assume leadership in a narrow range of technologically demanding fields such as mobile communications. This higher value-added position within high-tech markets reduced Finnish susceptibility to cost competition in the wake of the dot-com crisis and minimized the country's reliance on nontradable services such as finance and real estate. At the same time, the country has become dangerously reliant on a small number of high-tech activities, and firms have struggled in part because of the narrow emphasis on technological R & D.

Creative corporatist bargaining was not limited to Finland, of course. The Danish case is in some ways even more impressive, because the country's small and medium-sized industrial base appears to militate against involvement in high-tech competition. As in Finland, a center-right government pushed stakeholders into accepting financial liberalization, labor market deregulation, and fiscal austerity. Yet the same government also promoted new forms of cooperation in early stage financial markets, labor markets, and industrial policy. Creative corporatism was most pronounced in labor markets, where industry and labor enjoyed a long tradition of cooperation. Collectively, these measures supported a distinctive route into new high-tech markets, focusing on knowledge-intensive activities within a broad range of industries. As in Finland, this high value-added position insulated Denmark from cost competition and during the 2007–9 financial crisis. At the same time, producers face long-term challenges, as they struggle to scale activities in more capital-intensive and technologically demanding industries.

Ireland also turned to and benefited from neo-corporatist bargaining as it sought to compete in new industries. Vulnerable trade unions embraced neo-corporatist reform in 1987 for reasons familiar to their Danish and Finnish counterparts. Irish policymakers, however, could not draw on the same tradition of meso- and micro-level cooperation as their Danish and Finnish peers. As a result, they were most successful in achieving competitive measures, reducing government spending and taxation. This combination of cost containment and macroeconomic stabilization attracted a wave of foreign direct investment in high-tech industries such as computer equipment, telecommunications, and software. At the same time, Ireland struggled to develop resources such as risk capital, advanced skills, and research. As a result, Irish dominance in high-tech industry reflects relatively low-end assembly and customer service operations. Ireland, in fact, lags behind Denmark and Finland on several important dimensions of high-tech competition, which rendered it particularly vulnerable to cost competition in the wake of the dot-com crash, more dependent on nontradable services such as real estate, and more susceptible to the 2007–9 financial crisis.

Can we generalize this argument to other European countries? Creative corporatism is not, I suggest, limited to Denmark or Finland, and I document a similar shift to creative corporatism elsewhere in Northern Europe as well as East Asia. This emerging pattern of creative corporatism differs from conservative corporatism in Central Europe and from competitive corporatism in Southern and Eastern Europe. I use this expanded universe of cases to explain institutional innovation, emphasizing the interaction between policymaker and trade union capacity and employer preferences. I conclude by discussing the challenges that face all neo-corporatist subtypes, paying particular attention to the future of creative corporatist economies as they adapt to a new round of disruptive innovations.

THE PARADOX OF HIGH-TECH CORPORATISM

Traditionally, many western European economies relied on institutionalized cooperation among state actors and encompassing producer associations (industry and labor) to manage economic adjustment. This "neo-corporatist" approach to governance differs from the decentralized competition among individual firms and employees that prevails in liberal market economies such as Australia, Britain, Canada, the United States, and New Zealand and the hierarchical command-and-control structure that characterizes statist economies such as France. Neo-corporatist economies are instead characterized by voluntary cooperation rather than hierarchical state control, as policymakers actively consult and share responsibility with societal actors. Societal actors are organized into producer associations that transcend individual firms or employees such as employer confederations, industry associations, and trade unions.[1] Finally, cooperation among producer associations or "stakeholders" is institutionalized in routinized patterns of policymaking and production. Stakeholders, for example, are embedded in long-term relationships rather than temporary joint ventures or ad hoc lobbying networks.

The specific labels used to characterize "institutionalized cooperation among state actors and encompassing producer associations" have varied with time. Early literature on "neo-corporatism" (Schmitter 1974) bifurcated into two

---

1. Like the authors of earlier literature on neo-corporatism (Pempel and Tsunekawa 1979; Schmitter 1974), I argue that either labor or industry associations can be encompassing and engaged in institutionalized cooperation.

strands. The literature on concertation focuses on institutionalized cooperation in national-level policy formulation and implementation (Lehmbruch and
Schmitter 1982). The literature on coordination addresses peak- and lower-
level processes of institutionalized cooperation in production (Soskice 1990).[2]
While this distinction has introduced greater precision into neo-corporatist
studies, it has also obscured the ways in which peak-level policy concertation
impacts coordination in production at lower levels. In this book I retain the term
"neo-corporatism" to recapture the interplay between policy concertation and
economic coordination. At the same time, I build on earlier literature by distinguishing between policy concertation and coordination in production.

Initially conceptualized as a system of interest intermediation (Schmitter
1974), neo-corporatism was soon perceived as an excellent or even "superior" way
to regulate conflicting societal demands over output during the economic shocks
of the 1970s (Goldethorpe 1984; Pekkarinen, Pohjola, and Rowthorn 1992).
Most commonly applied to the labor market, encompassing neo-corporatist
trade unions were hypothesized to internalize the impact of their wage demands
on inflation and unemployment, moderating their claims, and securing superior or comparable economic outcomes relative to their liberal peers (Calmfors
and Driffill 1988). In practice, wage moderation was achieved through "political exchange," in which trade unions (and employers) received significant policy
concessions, including institutionalized influence over policy formulation and
implementation (Pizzorno 1978).

Neo-corporatist bargaining facilitated political exchange by enabling state
actors, trade unions, and employers to identify common objectives such as industrial peace, making credible commitments to refrain from industrial action,
and coordinating across different domains such as wages and social policy. This
shift from wage bargaining to political exchange is a key point of departure for
this book, which is less about wage restraint and industrial peace, a common ob-
jective across neo-corporatist countries, subtypes and scholarship (Goldethorpe
1984; Hassel 2007), than about the bargains that are struck to achieve it, which
vary considerably.

In early postwar Denmark, Norway, and Sweden—paradigmatic examples of
neo-corporatism—state actors, trade unions, and employer associations traded
wage moderation and industrial peace for more generous social benefits, expan-
sionary fiscal policies, and other redistributive measures (Scharpf 1984). Later

---

2. Additional labels include "social partnership" (O'Donnell 2001) and "social pacting" (Hassel
2009), related to concertation, and "negotiated" (Zysman 1983) and "organized" capitalism (Vogel
2003), related to coordination.

literature broadened the focus from labor market bargaining to other institutional domains, including finance and industrial policy (Landesmann 1992). This work revealed that central European economies relied on functionally equivalent institutions at the meso level to compensate organized societal actors during troubled economic times. For example, Swiss banks channeled patient capital to troubled firms and Austrian policymakers used state aid to modernize vulnerable sectors (Katzenstein 1984). Classical neo-corporatism in Scandinavia and functional equivalents in central Europe were thus perceived to make market adjustment possible by delaying the pace of economic change.

Literature on the "varieties of capitalism" has shifted attention to collaboration in production or "coordination," demonstrating how institutionalized cooperation among organized industry and labor associations at the peak, sectoral, and shop-floor level can constructively influence productive activity. More specifically, it argues that coordination facilitates investment in high-quality inputs such as physical equipment, human capital, and knowledge (Hall and Soskice 2001). The literature, however, emphasizes the same conservative bargains I have described. Long-term bank-based capital protects firm investments in highly specialized capital equipment (Streeck 1992). Bank loans are, in turn, reinforced by defensive public and industrial policies (Zahariadis 2002). Finally, patient capital, countercyclical public policies, and generous social benefits encourage workers to develop firm- and industry-specific skills by guaranteeing long-term employment and insuring workers against job losses (Pontusson 2005). These commitments to defend specialized investments are particularly effective in decentralized political systems, where constitutional constraints and power-sharing arrangements inhibit radical institutional reform (Wood 1997). As a result, this new literature does little to ameliorate the incremental orientation that characterized an earlier generation of scholarship on neo-corporatism.

On the contrary, the literature consistently links coordination and, by extension, nonliberal capitalism more generally to the incremental modernization of stable, mature industries. For example, firms are perceived to diffuse technologies rather than create new ones (Ziegler 1997), modernize production processes instead of inventing products (Edquist and Lundvall 1993), and improve existing products before developing novel ones (Soskice 1999). This combination of high-quality inputs, technological diffusion, and incremental innovation was highly successful during the early postwar period, defending niches such as Austrian steel (Katzenstein 1984), Danish agriculture (Edquist and Lundvall 1993), Finnish paper (Lilja, Rasanen, and Tainio 1992), German machine tools (Thelen 1991), and Swedish automotives (Porter 1990).

The Challenge of Rapid Innovation-Based Competition

Unfortunately, new information technologies threaten to undermine these institutional arrangements in several ways. New technologies transform the terms of competition in hitherto stable industries. More specifically, the ability to collect and transmit information enables competitors to master complex production processes, bypass traditional sales networks, and enter existing industries. Meanwhile, incumbents have used communication technologies to shift production to specialized subcontractors and lower-cost locations (Dossani and Kenney 2006). The ability to delegate and coordinate production processes across vast distances enables firms to "unbundle" integrated activities into global supply chains (Baldwin 2006). The resulting fragmentation of production is most visible in high-tech industries such as semi-conductors, where production has shifted from the United States to East Asia (Thun 2008). It extends to mature low- and medium-tech industries as well (Herrigel and Wittke 2004; Sturgeon 2003). Danish textile firms and Finnish forestry companies, for example, have sharply reduced their domestic production capacity since 1990.[3]

These developments challenge established industries and occupations, forcing firms and by extension countries to identify new products and activities. Growth is based less on the ability to defend an existing industry than the "experimental" search for different areas along the value chain, or the identification of new value chains altogether (Zysman 2006). In other words, new information technologies require countries to nimbly reallocate capital to entrepreneurial actors, flexibly redistribute labor across a range of activities, and quickly identify new roles in the global economy. In Denmark, for example, fashion and design have supplanted textile production.[4] In Finland, forestry firms have turned to packaging solutions and they are exploring new electronic media.[5]

Furthermore, new information technologies have emerged as important industries in their own right.[6] The demand for new high-tech products such as

---

3. Author interviews with former executive, forestry firm (31 October 2005, Finland) and representative, Danish Society of Engineers (9 November 2006, Denmark).

4. Author interview with representative, Danish Society of Engineers (9 November 2006, Denmark).

5. Author interviews with former research director, forestry firm (2 November 2005, Finland); former executive officer, forestry firm (10 November 2005, Finland); and research director, forestry firm (24 November 2005, Finland).

6. Of course, high-technology industries are not the only source of income and employment growth. They do, however, represent a critical case in which neo-corporatist countries are least likely to succeed. In demonstrating that neo-corporatist economies can compete in dynamic high-technology industries, I suggest that they can respond to disruptive developments in a range of low- and medium-technology sectors.

computers, telecommunication networks, and mobile phones has expanded exponentially since the 1980s, as consumers and businesses alike seek new ways to transmit, collect, and organize information. Growth opportunities persist, even in the wake of the dot-com downturn, as entrepreneurs identify new applications and link existing hardware to new knowledge-intensive services ranging from music to navigation. Information technology has thus retained its status as a growth industry, even in a sluggish postcrisis environment (Lim 2009).

As a result, economies that positioned themselves within these markets have enjoyed rapid growth. This transformation is most visible in emerging economies such as Hong Kong, Israel, South Korea, Singapore, and Taiwan, where analysts link successful development to high-tech competition (Hommen and Edquist 2008). Similar, if more muted, dynamics prevail in Europe. High-tech manufacturing and services generated impressive employment growth and income gains in Britain, Finland, and Ireland during the 1990s, in contrast to stagnant output and mounting unemployment in continental economies such as France and Germany (OECD 2005). High-tech markets have received even greater attention in the wake of the real estate bubble, as British and Irish policymakers seek a more sustainable source of growth and employment. Ireland's 2009 Smart Economy Taskforce, for example, has explicitly prioritized knowledge-intensive, export-oriented high-tech industries as an alternative to nontradable services (Department of the Taoiseach 2008).

Information technologies also represent an important source of innovation. The industries themselves are characterized by the rapid development of new products and related services. For example, Britain, Finland, and Ireland all enjoyed productivity growth, with gains concentrated in high-tech sectors (European Commission 2003a). High-tech industries are potentially even more valuable to the extent that innovation spills over into traditional industries. High-tech industries, in other words, have a potentially beneficial effect on other industries by diffusing communication technologies, identifying novel applications, and encouraging the development of new growth-oriented enterprises. They thus represent an important source of income, employment, and productivity, especially in a fragile postcrisis environment.

Neo-corporatist economies appear poorly equipped to respond to these challenges and opportunities. The same institutions that defended existing industries throughout the postwar period are perceived to inhibit the redistribution of resources to new activities. Patient capital and defensive industrial policies delay the redistribution of capital to new firms and social policies hinder job creation. At best, these policies encourage actors to upgrade existing capital equipment, skills and production processes. Meanwhile, information technologies continue to erode established niches. As a result, continental European economies are perceived to struggle in this "new" economy.

The Paradox of High-Tech Neo-Corporatism

Several neo-corporatist economies, however, have excelled in this disruptive climate. Denmark, Finland, and Ireland all experienced rapid economic growth and declining unemployment during the 1990s and 2000s. International benchmarking exercises regularly identify Denmark and Finland as among the most "competitive" economies in the world (World Economic Forum 2012). Even more surprisingly, these economies succeeded by entering fast-moving high-tech industries where they should be most disadvantaged. Ireland redefined itself as Europe's leading computer exporter, Finland emerged to dominate mobile telephony, and Denmark has quietly entered a diverse array of industries from biotechnology to software.

These developments can be viewed in comparative perspective by characterizing high-tech exports as a share of total exports, employment in high-tech manufacturing and services as a share of total employment, and the number of high-tech patent applications to the European Patent Office per million inhabitants in nine wealthy EU member states (table 1.1). The table uses data from 2007 because this was the most recent year for which patent data was available and it avoids a 2008 reclassification of high-tech industry that would complicate comparison with earlier years. Importantly, 2007 figures also capture high-tech competition at the beginning of the 2007–9 financial crisis, before figures were skewed by large shifts in income and employment.[7] Countries are ranked from least to most liberal, using data from Martin Höpner (2007, 14), and the top four countries in each category are shaded.[8] We would expect liberal economies at the bottom of this table, such as Britain, to perform strongly in this space, and neo-corporatist economies, such as Denmark or Finland, to occupy a much weaker position.

Export analysis would appear to support claims that liberal economies such as Ireland are best positioned to compete in high-tech markets. At the same time, liberal high-tech leadership is misleading in several respects. The most "successful" high-tech competitor, Ireland, experimented with very nonliberal strategies, including centralizing collective wage bargaining in 1987. Furthermore, traditionally neo-corporatist economies have also assumed a surprisingly competitive position in this space. Finland, for example, ranks second only to Ireland in the share of high-tech exports, surpassing paradigmatic liberal market economies such as Britain.

Finally, high-tech exports provide an incomplete picture of high-tech competition, particularly as developed countries outsource manufacturing operations

---

7. Chapters 3 through 7 discuss how countries responded to the financial crisis and its aftermath, albeit with revised measures of high-tech employment and exports.

8. Höpner's index of "organization" combines corporate ownership, employee codetermination, employer federation density, and trade union density.

TABLE 1.1 High-Tech Competition in Western Europe

COUNTRY	HIGH-TECH EXPORTS / TOTAL EXPORTS, 2007	HIGH-TECH EMPLOYMENT / TOTAL EMPLOYMENT, 2007	HIGH-TECH EPO PATENTS / MILLION INHABITANTS, 2007
Austria	11.1	3.94	33.6
Finland	17.5	6.71	86.3
Sweden	13.6	5.93	84.0
Germany	13.0	5.18	38.9
Netherlands	18.3	4.88	45.1
Denmark	11.7	5.27	40.1
Belgium	6.6	4.67	32.1
Ireland	25.7	6.20	17.7
Britain	16.7	5.30	18.9

All data from Eurostat (2011).

to lower-cost locations in eastern Europe and East Asia.[9] Measures of high-tech exports fail to distinguish between innovation-intensive competition and low-end assembly activity within nominally high-tech activities. For example, the countries that ranked most highly in the share of high-tech exports such as Malta (47.8%), in western Europe, and the Philippines (51.4%), at the global level, are not known for rapid innovation-based competition (Eurostat 2011). Table 1.1 thus provides figures on the share of high-tech employment. Surprisingly, neo-corporatist countries perform quite strongly here. Finland ranks first in the share of high-tech employment. Denmark also defies its common classification as a low-tech economy (Edquist and Lundvall 1993), rivaling Britain in the share of high-tech employment. Finnish and Danish strength in high-tech industries reflects their heavy reliance on high-tech services, representing over 4 percent of the labor force (Eurostat 2011).

This service activity is significant because it generates value that is not always reflected in physical exports. This is evidenced in figures on high-tech patenting activity, where we would expect liberal market economies to dominate their neo-corporatist counterparts. In fact, a neo-corporatist country, Finland, ranks first both in per capita high-tech patenting and in the share of high-tech patents (34.0%). Denmark also occupies a strong position in this space. While Denmark generates relatively little revenue from high-tech exports, it leads the European Union (and Europe more generally) in per capita biotechnology patent applications. More market-oriented economies such as Britain and Ireland, by contrast, perform quite poorly on measures of high-tech patenting and high-tech patenting share. While inventors in these countries might be more inclined to file in the

---

9. Finland and Denmark ranked even higher in the share of high-tech exports at the height of the dot-com boom (Eurostat 2011).

United States, Britain (11.4) and Ireland (11.6) also trailed Denmark (13.2) and Finland (46.4) in per capita–adjusted high-tech patent applications to the United States Patent Office in 2005 (Eurostat 2011). This represents an important challenge for Ireland as it seeks to compete in high-tech markets.

The capacity of Denmark, Finland, and, to a lesser extent, Ireland to enter new high-tech markets is puzzling for several reasons. First, all three countries are small states, which are perceived to operate at a disadvantage in high-tech industries. Scholars have long maintained that large economies occupy a privileged position in high-tech markets by virtue of their ability to finance capital-intensive R & D (Kristensen and Levinsen 1983). This helps explain Britain and Germany's relatively strong position in high-tech industries (seen in table 1.1). The capital-intensive aerospace industry, closely tied to defense spending, represents 30 percent and 14 percent of their high-tech exports respectively (Eurostat 2011). In this light, however, Danish, Finnish, and Irish achievements are even *more* impressive. With fewer than six million citizens, these countries are all but excluded from certain capital-intensive and security-related markets. For example, aerospace accounts for less than 3 percent of these states' high-tech exports.

Other authors contend that high-tech neo-corporatism can be traced to established multinationals and their ability to defend stable, specialized subsectors (Fagerberg and Jørgensen 1988). This might explain the enduring success of Siemens in Germany. Finland, however, was dominated by pulp and paper multinationals until it entered the mobile communications industry in the 1990s. Furthermore, chapter 4 of this book reveals that Denmark broke into the biotechnology and telecommunications equipment industries despite, rather than because of, its modest-sized multinational enterprises. Denmark and Finland's strong performance (seen in table 1.1) is thus particularly impressive, because it represents movement into fundamentally new industries and, in several cases, by fundamentally new firms.

Other scholars suggest that neo-corporatist countries can compete in high-tech industries by focusing on stable subsectors that are less vulnerable to competency-destroying innovations (Casper 2007, 141). Finnish telecommunication firms, however, compete in the market for mobile handsets, one of the most dynamic and unstable segments in the telecommunication equipment industry (Steinbock 2000). Meanwhile, Danish pharmaceutical firms occupy a similarly strong position in the radically innovative market for therapeutic drugs (Okamoto 2010). In other words, these countries have not only engineered big leaps into new high-tech industries but also entered radically innovative subsectors within those markets.

As a result, many scholars conclude that European economies such as Denmark or Finland can only compete in high-tech markets by becoming less neo-corporatist. In other words, successful countries must have dismantled neo-corporatist deals (Glimstedt and Zander 2003), layered market-oriented reforms on top of traditional institutions (Lange 2009), or escaped neo-corporatist constraints by acquiring financial capital and skilled labor abroad (Herrmann 2009). Indeed, Denmark and Finland appeared to dismantle traditional neo-corporatist bargains, including their bank-based financial system, generous unemployment benefits, and defensive industrial policies, during the 1980s and 1990s (Andersen et al. 2007; Henrekson and Jakobsson 2003).

This liberal narrative, however, is problematic for two reasons. First, the 1980s and 1990s witnessed more rather than less cooperation in important domains such as risk capital, skill acquisition, and research. Denmark and Finland's leading position in risk capital reflects intense neo-corporatist bargaining among policymakers and financial stakeholders such as industry associations, banks, and social insurance funds (Andersson and Napier 2005). Denmark experienced increasing collaboration among trade unions, employer associations, and state agencies in human capital formation (Martin and Thelen 2008). In Finland, trade unions, employer associations, and state agencies struck peak-level deals converting traditional industrial policies to promote private-public and inter-firm cooperation in research (Ornston and Rehn 2006). The existing literature sheds little insight into why stakeholders turned to neo-corporatist bargaining, why these deals did not inhibit restructuring, and why Denmark and Finland surpassed their liberal peers in certain knowledge-intensive activities.

Moreover, ostensibly liberal economies such as Ireland employed similar strategies in managing economic adjustment during the 1990s. While Ireland ranks at the bottom according to traditional neo-corporatist measures such as patient capital or local labor bargaining, policymakers, trade unions, and firms turned to centralized collective wage bargaining to manage labor market adjustment after 1987. Centralized collective bargaining was in turn linked to an increasingly complex and wide-ranging collection of policy domains from taxation to finance (O'Donnell 2001). Far from inhibiting restructuring, Ireland was considerably more successful in cultivating high-tech foreign direct investment and indigenous innovation after 1987 (Ó Riain 2004). In other words, neo-corporatist institutions enabled Ireland to capitalize on its considerable advantages. At the same time, Ireland lagged behind Denmark and Finland in more knowledge-intensive activities such as patenting and was more susceptible to cost competition in the wake of the dot-com crash and more vulnerable to the 2007–9 financial crisis.[10]

---

10. While Ireland's deteriorating cost competitiveness and subsequent reliance on nontradable services was exacerbated by an appreciating euro, membership in the common currency area did not have the same impact on Finnish high-tech industry.

I resolve each of these puzzles, explaining how neo-corporatist countries enter high-tech markets and why they appear to occupy such different positions within otherwise similar industries.

Institutional Innovation and Economic Restructuring

Neo-corporatist performance in high-tech industry varies because institutionalized cooperation can be used to achieve very different objectives. More specifically, I distinguish among a traditional literature on "conservative" corporatism, more recent work on "competitive" corporatism, and a new species of "creative" corporatism. Each engages state agencies, industry associations, and labor unions in the process of economic adjustment. Institutionalized cooperation facilitates adjustment in three ways. Actors can rely on powering (threats and side payments) and puzzling (dialogue) to generate a consensus regarding appropriate behavior and objectives; institutionalized cooperation facilitates implementation by persuading or pressuring actors to support objectives, as well as monitoring and sectioning noncompliance; and institutionalized cooperation can help coordinate activities among state agencies, trade unions, and industry associations and individual members within those groups.

If conservative, competitive, and creative corporatism thus rely on similar processes and mechanisms to achieve economic objectives, the objectives themselves vary. All three seek to achieve some degree of wage restraint but differ in the types of political deals they strike to achieve it. In brief, conservative corporatism seeks to delay restructuring by insulating actors from market competition; competitive corporatism seeks to accelerate restructuring by increasing market competition; and creative corporatism promotes restructuring by investing in disruptive new inputs.

Each neo-corporatist subtype possesses distinct, easily observable characteristics, governing the allocation of capital, labor, and knowledge. Conservative corporatism relies on patient capital, passive labor market policies, and defensive industrial policies to mobilize resources around existing actors. Competitive corporatism uses tax reductions, labor market deregulation, and fiscal austerity to promote market competition. Creative corporatism invests in disruptive new inputs such as risk capital, human capital, and R & D to mobilize resources around emerging actors and industries. The argument can be summarized by disaggregating neo-corporatist governance into three institutional domains: financial markets, labor markets, and industrial policy, which govern the allocation of capital, labor, and knowledge respectively.

In contrast to claims about institutional complementarities or coherence, I am not claiming that we should observe equal or similar levels of cooperation across different institutional domains. On the contrary, the varieties of capitalism literature has been criticized for its insensitivity to variation across different institutional arenas (Crouch 2005; Jackson and Deeg 2005). I avoid this error by examining developments within three separate domains, financial markets, labor markets, and industrial policy. Doing so not only increases the number of observations within each national case but also illuminates an important, if often overlooked, source of variation among otherwise identical conservative, competitive, or creative corporatist economies. For example, I challenge literature on the "Nordic model" that links successful competition to a social democratic welfare state (Andersen et al. 2007; Kristensen 2011). While this is true for Denmark, chapter 3 reveals that social policy played a more limited role in Finland. Institutional innovation and economic restructuring instead reflected state-industry and interfirm collaboration in R & D. Within-case variation simultaneously enables me to identify cases of "failed" adjustment within otherwise successful economies. Before doing so, however, it is important to first characterize each neo-corporatist subtype in greater detail.

Conservative Corporatism and Incremental Upmarket Movement

As noted, European economies traditionally relied on conservative corporatism to mobilize resources around existing actors. The earliest literature on neo-corporatist political exchange described how centralized collective wage bargaining traded wage restraint for Keynesian fiscal policies to promote full-employment (Scharpf 1984). More recent work on coordination has shifted attention from macroeconomic policy to microeconomic institutions, but it continues to emphasize functionally equivalent measures such as generous social insurance policies that encourage and protect investment in firm- and industry-specific skills (Pontusson 2005). Financial markets and industrial policy are characterized by similar deals. In the former, new and old scholarship focuses on the willingness of financial intermediaries to extend large long-term loans, often in exchange for institutionalized influence over their various holdings (Goyer 2006; Zysman 1983). The state, in turn, provides long-term patient capital to the universal banks, using investment or employment grants to protect and upgrade established firms and industries (Landesmann 1992; Zahariadis 2002).

These conservative deals have predictable consequences, defending existing industries rather than facilitating movement into new sectors (Streeck 1992). Banks target stable, often low- and medium-tech, industries that are less vulnerable to competence-destroying innovations. Patient capital enables firms to invest in and upgrade physical and human capital within these niches. Finally, reactive industrial policies protect and modernize entire industries. These conservative deals are not intrinsically problematic. Conservative corporatism was highly "competitive" in its capacity to defend low-tech niches such as Danish agriculture or Finnish paper. It remains relevant today in explaining how countries such as Germany defend established industries. In fact, Germany's capacity to upgrade traditional medium-tech niches such as infrastructure and capital goods reduced its reliance on nontradable services during the mid-2000s and its vulnerability to the economic crisis that followed (Elanger 2010; Ewing 2010).

Literature on conservative corporatism, however, sheds little light on how countries react to competence-destroying economic shocks such as the loss of a traditional market or the abrupt decline of an established industry. In fact, their adaptive capacity appears sharply circumscribed. These policies are most common within incremental political systems where societal actors can use their institutionalized influence to block or ignore reforms (Wood 1997). While the literature on conservative corporatism does not necessarily claim that conservative corporatist economies never change, institutional innovation occurs at the margin, circumventing rather than engaging traditional stakeholders. For example, literature on Germany emphasizes incremental processes of layering, dualization, or hybridization (Crouch 2005; Palier and Thelen 2010). Without denying the important role that these dynamics play in Germany and other countries, in this book I identify an alternative in which state agencies, trade unions, and employers strike national-level deals to modify neo-corporatist institutions to perform radically different functions. In doing so, I construct a more dynamic theory of capitalist adaptation and diversity.

Competitive Corporatism and Market-Led Adjustment

Literature on competitive corporatism has already illustrated how neo-corporatist institutions can adapt to these challenges by shifting attention away from coordination in the act of production to concertation in policy formulation (Rhodes 1998). This literature suggests that European countries facing competence-destroying economic shocks can use neo-corporatist institutions to increase, rather than reduce, market competition.[11] This is particularly true when

---

11. This characterization extends to related work on social partnership (O'Donnell 2001) and social pacting (Hassel 2009).

policymakers are pressured by external actors such as the European Union (Sala 1997). In fact, the European Union has played an indirect but significant role by limiting recourse to conservative corporatist instruments such as deficit spending, cartelization, and state aid. In so doing, the European Union enabled policymakers to more effectively confront neo-corporatist stakeholders, most notably trade unions, with the prospect of unilateral liberalization.

At the same time, policymakers are keen to diffuse the costs associated with controversial reforms, particularly when presiding over an unstable coalition government (Hassel 2007, 58). Trade unions, which are most directly threatened by pro-market reform, are the most likely actors to confront governments, although employers may also resist liberalization. Faced with significant resistance, governments may attempt to buy off trade unions, granting them the opportunity to shape reforms in exchange for their political support. This strategy enables trade unions (or employers) to avoid more sweeping market reform (Baccaro and Lim 2007).

The result is competitive corporatist bargaining in which institutionalized cooperation can be used to expand rather than limit market competition (Rhodes 1998).[12] Competitive corporatism closely resembles neoliberalism in its reliance on market-oriented reform but varies in the way that it is implemented and the fact that market signals are delimited by stakeholder negotiations. This strong market orientation is evident in the types of policies that distinguish competitive corporatist economies from their conservative (and creative) peers.

While the literature on competitive corporatism, like its conservative counterpart, is primarily focused on the labor market, and wage restraint in particular (Culpepper 2008; Hassel 2007; Perez 2000), the political exchange that is used to achieve it is quite distinct. Instead of exchanging wage restraint for full-employment guarantees or social-benefit protections, societal actors agree to a range of market-enhancing measures, including reduced government spending, less generous social benefits, and the expansion of part-time or irregular contracts (Baccaro 2002; Visser and Hemerijck 1997). Competitive corporatism can be extended to other policy domains as well. For example, stakeholders may agree to reduce government spending by dismantling defensive industrial policies. They may also facilitate the redistribution of financial capital by cutting corporate and personal income taxes.

These pro-market reforms have radically different consequences for how countries compete. Like liberalization, competitive corporatism accelerates the

---

12. This is not to suggest that concertation is competitive corporatist in nature. Institutionalized cooperation in policy formulation and implementation can be used to increase or protect social protection. The literature on competitive corporatism suggests that *vulnerable policymakers facing weak unions* will use concertation to advance market-oriented reform rather than social protection.

redistribution of capital and labor from declining firms to new growth-oriented enterprises. Not surprisingly, competitive corporatist economies were perceived to enjoy significantly stronger economic growth and lower unemployment throughout the 1990s, moving into a range of new industries, including high-tech markets (O'Donnell 1998; Visser and Hemerijck 1997). At the same time, the decision to prioritize market-enhancing reform limited investment in resources such as human capital or R & D. As a result, high-tech competition was more likely to revolve around basic manufacturing or assembly operations rather than knowledge-intensive services such as research, design, and development. Competitive corporatism, and by extension market-based strategies more generally, rendered these countries more vulnerable to cost competition in the wake of the dot-com bubble, more reliant on nontradable services to sustain growth and employment, and more powerfully affected by the financial crisis that followed in the late 2000s. Nor can their vulnerability to the ongoing financial crisis be attributed exclusively to low interest rates or a strong euro. As I describe, other euro members, such as Finland, adjusted very differently to the dot-com crash.

The concept of competitive corporatism yields important insights into how neo-corporatism can adapt to competence-destroying economic challenges. It is particularly prominent in countries with a weak or conflicted tradition of neo-corporatist governance, including Ireland, Italy, the Netherlands, Portugal, and Spain (O'Donnell 2001; Perez 2000; Royo 2002; Visser and Hemerijck 1997). Yet the literature on competitive corporatism remains problematic in several respects. First, it says relatively little about how policy concertation shapes production, and coordination in production in particular. While wage setting and market-based reform certainly influence production, they do not directly engage state, labor, or other industrial actors in the process of designing and assembling products and services. The literature on competitive corporatism, and concertation more generally, thus says surprisingly little about the relationship between economic policymaking and economics.

Consequently, research on concertation does not explain how historically neo-corporatist countries such as Denmark and Finland responded to competence-destroying crises. These countries struck similar peak-level deals but extended cooperation to address a much wider range of (productive) functions, including aggressive investment in risk capital, human capital, and research. These historically low-tech countries also assumed a very different position in international markets, relying on more knowledge-intensive activities such as design and development. The following section resolves both puzzles with reference to a new species of corporatism, creative corporatism.

Creative Corporatism and Knowledge-Intensive Competition

Countries with a strong pattern of neo-corporatist cooperation react to competence-destroying shocks by striking different deals. Like competitive corporatist countries I have described (and in contrast to conservative corporatist ones), policymakers grappling with competence-destroying economic shocks and identical EU-imposed constraints can effectively threaten to implement structural reforms. At the same time, policymakers confronting encompassing trade unions (and other special interests) in multiparty systems may seek to diffuse the cost of reform. Trade unions respond to the plausible, if uncertain, threat of radical liberalization by ratifying negotiated measures. Countries can thus enact significant institutional reforms, dismantling conservative corporatist hallmarks such as the universal bank, generous unemployment benefits, and state aid. In contrast to competitive corporatism, however, institutional change is not synonymous with liberalization. Stakeholders can instead "convert" coordination to invest in new actors, activities, and industries.

Such strategies are most appealing to trade unions, which not only avoid more comprehensive liberalization but can also assume a more active role in directing and administering new investments. In subsequent chapters I document significant benefits associated with investment-oriented policies, such as the expansion of continuing education in Denmark. Industry agreement is more problematic, however, as firms weigh market- and investment-oriented approaches. Here, the literature on competitive corporatism and related phenomena, such as concertation and social pacting, offers little insight. Partly because of its emphasis on wage bargaining and market-oriented social benefit reform, the literature pays relatively less attention to the role that employers play in institutional adaptation (Molina 2006; Royo 2002). To the extent that employers do play a role, they embrace pacts to secure wage restraint and market-oriented reform (Baccaro and Lim 2007; Culpepper 2008; Perez 2000). This is understandable because, while competitive corporatist agreements have significant distributional consequences and demand compliance and require effective monitoring, the outcomes associated with such strategies are relatively clear and the costs of committing are relatively low.

Collaborative investments in inputs such as risk capital, human capital, and research, by contrast, are characterized by significantly greater uncertainty and much higher costs. It is not immediately obvious that state agencies, trade unions, and other firms can do a better job of supplying resources than the market, or that those resources will be useful. Their success in doing so is predicated in part on each firm's capacity to coinvest scarce resources and its willingness to share valuable information about their products and production processes. Sharing this information with rival firms and trade unions, however, is a risky proposition. Stakeholders with different preferences and rival producers can leverage this information to undermine managerial autonomy, enhance their bargaining position, or appropriate sensitive technologies and production processes. Firm preferences are thus likely to vary with the institutional environment in which they operate (Woll 2008). More specifically, firms will be more likely to value such resources and more willing to participate in their collective investments when they have a legacy of constructive cooperation with state agencies, trade unions, and other firms in the realm of production.

The capacity to convert established patterns of coordination gives historically neo-corporatist countries a much broader menu of options as they navigate new crises and constraints. More specifically, countries can rely on "creative" corporatism (Ornston 2013), or institutionalized cooperation in the construction of disruptive new inputs. These investments are disruptive in the sense that investments are explicitly designed to promote the establishment of new enterprises, the acquisition of new skills, and the creation of new industries. The experimental search for new products, firms, and markets represents a significant departure from traditional conservative corporatist measures. At the same time, creative corporatism facilitates restructuring by relying on collective investment, in contrast to the market-based deals that characterize competitive corporatism.

Like its conservative and competitive peers, creative corporatism can be identified and measured by its distinctive content. In the labor market, creative corporatism is characterized by weaker employment protections and less-generous unemployment benefits but greater cooperation in human capital investment. In other words, peak-level deals target human capital formation, and we observe high and increasing levels of participation by industry associations, firms, and trade unions in local training. Those human capital investments are in turn focused on transitional workers or general skills, facilitating the redistribution of labor to new enterprises. While "flexicurity" and labor market activation has already received considerable attention (Campbell and Pedersen 2007), creative corporatism is not limited to social policy.[13] Policymakers, industry associations, and trade unions have struck similar deals in financial markets. Here, the universal bank no longer provides patient capital, but stakeholders continue to collaborate in early stage risk capital markets. More specifically, creative corporatism uses social insurance funds which were originally designed to protect asset-specific skills to invest in new enterprises. Finally, creative corporatism has jet-

---

13. In contrast to literature on the Nordic model (Andersen et al. 2007; Castells and Himanen 2002), I find little evidence of social-policy reform in Finland.

tisoned traditional industrial policies, including investment grants, employment grants, and reliance on state-owned enterprises. At the same time, policymakers, industry associations, and trade unions strike tripartite deals to promote investment in research and we observe increasing interfirm cooperation in product development. Research is reoriented toward the development of new enterprises and industries rather than modernizing established ones.

Creative corporatism facilitates investment in disruptive new inputs through the three mechanisms described. Peak-level bargaining generates a broad consensus supporting investment by persuading key stakeholders and making side payments. Industry and trade union associations play an important role in communicating shared understandings to individual members. Peak- and lower-level institutionalized cooperation also enables actors to coordinate investments, not only making larger and more complex investments, but tailoring resources to employers' needs. Finally, lower-level institutionalized cooperation pressures actors to mobilize resources as nonparticipation becomes more visible and carries reputational costs. By extension, it can also more effectively monitor and punish cheating, shirking, or other opportunistic behavior. In doing so, neo-corporatist bargaining helps stakeholders invest more aggressively and appropriately in new inputs.

These investments, in turn, support very different growth trajectories. New investments in venture capital, human capital, and R & D are more explicitly targeted toward the creation of new enterprises, activities, and industries and less vulnerable to capture by established actors. Those resources in turn create opportunities for firms to enter new high-tech industries, channeling risk capital for experimentation, which enables growth-oriented firms to acquire labor and supports diversification into expensive and complex new markets, products, and technologies. These inputs simultaneously permit movement into more knowledge-intensive high-tech activities by furnishing skilled labor and underwriting production design and development.

Creative corporatist economies can thus assume a distinctive position in high-tech markets relative to their low- and medium-tech conservative corporatist peers and their comparatively low value-added competitive corporatist rivals. This position is by no means unassailable, as subsequent chapters demonstrate, however, it did reduce vulnerability to cost competition. Danish and Finnish high-tech industries were less dependent on low-end assembly activity and less affected by the dot-com crash of 1999–2001. By extension, these economies did not rely as heavily on nontradable services after 2001 and were less vulnerable to the financial crisis of 2007–9.

Countries such as Denmark and Finland have invested more aggressively in disruptive new inputs such as early stage venture capital, continuing education, and R & D than conservative corporatist countries, such as Austria, Belgium, and Germany, competitive corporatist countries, such as Ireland and the Netherlands, and liberal countries, such as Britain (see table 1.2).[14] Those investments are remarkable because they are theoretically puzzling and historically unprecedented. Britain's large equity markets have always yielded unparalleled exit opportunities for venture capitalists, while Germany has always invested approximately 2.5 percent of GDP in R & D because of its capacity to support capital-intensive research. Denmark and Finland, by contrast, possess significantly smaller equity markets and financial resources. Indeed, historically, they did not prioritize investment in venture capital, human capital, or research. Denmark relied heavily on passive labor market strategies, such as early retirement, until the 1990s. Finnish expenditure on R & D was well below the OECD average at 1.2 percent of GDP in 1980. And both countries possessed diminutive venture capital markets (Eurostat 2011).

In the remainder of the book I analyze each step in the causal chain outlined above. First, I provide specific examples to illustrate how conservative corporatism inhibited competition in new high-tech industries until the 1980s. Within each case, I document and explain neo-corporatist adaptation in multiple policy domains. More specifically, I highlight the interaction between a policymaker's capacity to threaten societal actors (often enhanced by economic crisis and external constraints); the capacity of societal actors, most notably trade unions, to resist unilateral liberalization; and employer preferences regarding neo-corporatist

TABLE 1.2 Investment in Risk Capital, Skill Formation, and Research

COUNTRY	EARLY STAGE VENTURE CAPITAL INVESTMENT / GDP, 2007	PARTICIPATION IN TRAINING AND EDUCATION / TOTAL POPULATION, 2007	R & D EXPENDITURE / GDP, 2007
Austria	0.01	20.6	2.52
Finland	0.04	33.9	3.47
Sweden	0.07	26.6	3.40
Germany	0.02	17.4	2.53
Netherlands	0.02	26.8	1.81
Denmark	0.05	40.2	2.48
Belgium	0.03	10.4	1.86
Ireland	0.02	10.8	1.25
Britain	0.02	25.0	1.78

All data from Eurostat (2011).

---

14. Because transfer pricing by U.S. multinationals inflates Irish GDP by up to 20% (O'Hearn 1998), this table understates Irish investment in early stage venture capital and R & D. That said, Ireland still invests considerably less in early stage venture capital and research than Denmark and Finland do, and the discrepancy is even more striking when one uses non–GDP denominated statistics such as participation in education and training.

content (as influenced by the level and type of coordination). I explore the specific mechanisms of consensus building, commitment monitoring, and coordination by which stakeholders can achieve new objectives such as market-oriented reform or investing in disruptive new inputs. Finally, I link market-oriented reform and new investments to different patterns of high-tech competition, examining how individual firms utilized resources from neo-corporatist bargaining to experiment, grow, and diversify within new high-tech markets. I also demonstrate how the *absence* of neo-corporatism and collective investment hindered their ability to compete in these sectors.

The Evidence: Rapid Restructuring in Denmark, Finland, and Ireland

Analysis is based primarily (but not exclusively) on three case studies: Denmark, Finland, and Ireland.[15] Each is particularly puzzling in that it was highly unlikely to succeed in new high-tech markets. All three were small, historically low-tech economies. While Ireland's "special relationship" with the United States enabled it to capitalize on high-tech foreign direct investment, this does not explain why it lagged behind Denmark and Finland in certain aspects of high-tech competition. Collectively, this focus on small, historically low-tech countries thus controls for and eliminates alternative theories of high-tech competition. Furthermore, while it appears that I am analyzing three "success" stories, this characterization masks significant variation along several dimensions.

First, the three cases exhibit considerable cross-national and longitudinal variation in economic governance and high-tech success. As a result, I can compare episodes of liberalism, conservative corporatism, competitive corporatism, and creative corporatism, as well as different patterns of high-tech success and failure. For example, I use Finland's transformation from one of the most conservative corporatist economies in Europe to one of the most creative to explore the circumstances that drive institutional conversion as well as the relationship between different neo-corporatist subtypes and economic trajectories. In other words, I illuminate the sources of Finnish *failure* until the 1980s as well as its subsequent success. I analyze similar developments in Denmark to demonstrate that institutional conversion and economic restructuring is not limited to Finland or individual firms within Finland.

---

15. The conclusion generalizes to a broader universe of European cases. This includes an extensive and well-established literature on incremental institutional change and economic adjustment in Germany.

I also exploit cross-national variation, contrasting Denmark and Finland to Ireland. Ireland's transformation from liberal capitalism to competitive corporatism not only illustrates the transformative power of competitive corporatism but enhances our understanding of creative corporatism in two ways. It highlights the political dynamics that shape creative corporatism, and it more directly engages the most compelling alternative hypothesis, liberalization. The Irish case thus illustrates how creative corporatism differs from more market-oriented approaches, both in terms of its content and its implications for economic adjustment.

Finally, I exploit variation among different institutional domains to compare creative corporatist economies (Denmark and Finland) to each other. Denmark and Finland developed quite distinct patterns of neo-corporatism during the late nineteenth and early twentieth century. While both countries were nominally tripartite during the 1960s, Danish neo-corporatist was based on strong cooperation on the peak level, sectoral level, and the shop floor between industry and labor, and Finnish cooperation privileged peak- and sector-level cooperation between state and industry.[16] While Denmark and Finland struck creative corporatist bargains in all three domains, creative corporatist bargaining was most robust in Danish labor markets and Finnish industrial policy, and surprisingly limited in Danish industrial policy and Finnish labor markets.[17] I take advantage of these differences to more clearly illuminate the important role that neo-corporatist legacies play in influencing creative corporatist bargaining, as well as the importance of creative corporatist bargaining in promoting investment in disruptive new inputs and how these resources shaped high-tech competition. Variation across these domains also explains why ostensibly successful economies such as Denmark and Finland continue to face formidable challenges.

Although I increase the number of observations by analyzing developments in different policy domains, I ultimately rely on detailed within-case analysis to link causes to outcomes.[18] I trace the specific processes by which economic crises

---

16. This distinction builds on earlier, but since neglected, work differentiating between corporatism and corporatism without labor (Pempel and Tsunekawa 1979) and later work on liberal versus social corporatism (Katzenstein 1985).

17. Chapter 6 identifies a country, Sweden, in which creative corporatist bargaining is most pronounced in finance.

18. My analysis draws on secondary literature, quantitative indicators, archival research, and 253 semi-structured interviews conducted with policymakers, stakeholders, and industry representatives in Denmark, Finland, and Ireland between 2005 and 2006. Interview subjects were selected through a process of top-down snowball sampling and a separate, nonrandom group of state agencies, stakeholders, and industry representatives. Because many subjects, particularly industry representatives, requested anonymity, I identify interview subjects by position, date of interview, and country only. I do not list interviews, because doing so would expose interview subjects who were speaking from multiple positions or affiliations.

shaped economic reform or nonreform in financial markets, labor markets, and industrial policy, with particular attention to the preferences and actions of policymakers, trade union leaders, and industry representatives. I also explore the specific mechanisms by which peak-level bargains and lower-level cooperation did or did not enable stakeholders to achieve key objectives such as fiscal austerity or investment in disruptive new inputs. Finally, I examine whether or not those resources had an impact on economic adjustment by analyzing how companies did or did not successfully compete in new high-tech markets. In doing so, I illuminate and repeatedly test the mechanisms that link stakeholder power and interests to different neo-corporatist subtypes and different neo-corporatist subtypes to different resources and different resources to high-tech competition.

Before demonstrating how stakeholders adapted neo-corporatist institutions to compete in new high-tech markets, however, I first characterize postwar adjustment in Denmark, Finland, and Ireland. As noted, this analytic move illustrates how neo-corporatist bargaining historically constrained competition in high-tech industries and identifies the specific crises that sparked institutional innovation. It also introduces the very different patterns of private-public, industry-labor, and interfirm coordination that could or could not be converted to manage adjustment during the 1980s and 1990s.

2

THE CRISIS OF LOW-TECH PRODUCTION IN DENMARK, FINLAND, AND IRELAND

To the extent that Denmark, Finland, and Ireland relied on neo-corporatism before 1980 it was conservative in nature. In financial markets, banks issued large long-term loans to firms in exchange for ownership stakes and used their institutionalized influence to support interfirm cooperation within production cartels and marketing consortia. In industrial policy, policymakers relied on state aid or competitive devaluations to protect and upgrade established industries during economic downturns. And, in labor markets, stakeholders relied on centralized collective wage bargaining, generous social benefits, and employment protections to protect investments in specialized skills, and workers more generally.

Of course, the level and locus of neo-corporatism varied, influenced by distinctive responses to nineteenth century industrialization and state building. Neo-corporatism was most extensive and encompassing in Finland, where rapid industrialization in capital-intensive industries encouraged close cooperation between industry and the state. The universal bank exhibited a pervasive influence over Finnish society, monopolizing postwar finance, organizing firms into encompassing industrial families, and underwriting price-fixing cartels. Labor was largely marginalized, particularly following the civil war of 1918. While incorporated into collective wage bargaining with progressively more generous social benefits from the 1960s onward, industry-labor coordination in production remained limited.

Although Denmark was also neo-corporatist, industrialization in less capital-intensive industries limited national-level cooperation in financial markets and industrial policy. Although a robust cooperative movement supported local collaboration in production, private-public and interfirm cooperation was more limited than in Finland. Institutionalized cooperation instead reflected autonomous negotiations between industry and a more cohesive labor movement, which struck a collective agreement as early as 1899. Industry and labor agreed to expand social benefits in the early postwar period and collaborated within a wide array of forums on the peak, sectoral, and shop-floor levels.

Neo-corporatist bargaining was least developed in Ireland, which was influenced by its proximity to and direct subordination to Britain. As a result, Ireland was characterized by decentralized equity markets, acrimonious labor relations, and arms-length competition between individual firms. Although Ireland turned to centralized collective wage bargaining at various points during the postwar period, labor market bargaining was inconsistent and had little impact on policy formulation or coordination. Meanwhile, robust industrial policies largely reinforced Irish dependence on "impatient" foreign capital, and did relatively little to engage organized industry or labor associations.

To characterize traditional economic institutions, neo-corporatist bargaining and high-tech competition appeared to be inversely related before the 1990s. The country that relied most heavily on institutionalized cooperation among organized actors, Finland, was the least competitive in new high-tech industries. In Finland, neo-corporatist bargains supported entry into and upmarket movement within low- and medium-tech industries such as forestry but militated against the redistribution of resources to emerging firms and industries. Experiments in rapidly evolving high-tech industries failed dramatically, with the consequence that Finland was the least specialized in high-tech industries. High-tech exports represented only 4.7 percent of total exports in 1985 (OECD 2011).

In Denmark, decentralized financial arrangements and industrial policies created more space for small and medium-sized entrepreneurs to enter specialized niches in electronics and other high-tech industries. Denmark thus occupied a modest position in radios, telecommunications, and televisions in the 1980s. High-tech products, for example, represented 9.7 percent of Danish exports in 1985 (OECD 2011). At the same time, generous social policies undermined the industry's competitiveness on international markets by encouraging labor market exit and increasing nonwage costs.

Finally, Ireland, where neo-corporatist bargaining was least extensive and encompassing, was the country most specialized in high-tech markets, with the share of high-tech exports reaching 12.9 percent in 1985 (OECD 2011). Here, multinational capital and limited labor market regulations facilitated the rapid redistribution of resources from low- and medium-tech industries such as food processing and textiles into electronics, software, and pharmaceuticals. The rest of this chapter develops this relationship in greater detail, identifying the mechanisms by which patient capital, investment grants, and generous unemployment insurance schemes inhibited high-tech competition.

In illustrating how neo-corporatism was inversely related to high-tech competition, the evidence in this chapter would appear to confirm existing literature on neo-corporatism and incremental upmarket movement. As subsequent chapters relate, however, this interpretation is problematic for two reasons. First, while Denmark and Finland were ill-equipped to grapple with competency-destroying economic shocks, liberal Ireland suffered problems of its own. More specifically, the decentralized, arm's-length competition characteristic of liberal capitalism failed to secure the fiscal restraint, wage moderation, and industrial peace that sustains multinational investment. By the 1980s, capital flight had devastated traditional manufacturing industries and threatened emerging high-tech industries.

Furthermore, countries responded to these challenges not by abandoning but rather by adapting neo-corporatist institutions. More specifically, Denmark, Finland, and even Ireland embraced new and unprecedented patterns of institutionalized cooperation among trade unions, industry associations, and state agencies. These new competitive and creative corporatist bargains had different implications for economic adjustment. All three countries dramatically improved their hitherto modest positions in high-tech markets. Indeed, the countries switched places, with the most centralized and encompassing neo-corporatist country, Finland, making the greatest strides in new high-tech industries and the most liberal country, Ireland, experiencing the most trouble in knowledge-intensive activities.

The following analysis thus provides a foundation for the rest of the book by demonstrating how conservative corporatism (and liberalism in Ireland) inhibited high-tech competition. I also identify the nineteenth-century legacies that support and constrain contemporary institutional innovation. In Finland, stakeholders adapted a tradition of private-public and interfirm cooperation to increase expenditure on R & D. Denmark pursued a different creative corporatist strategy, leveraging industry-labor cooperation to invest in skill formation. Ireland, which lacked a strong tradition of private-public, interfirm, or industry-labor cooperation relied more heavily on "competitive" market-based reforms, including fiscal retrenchment and tax concessions. Before chronicling twenty-first-century innovation, however, it is first necessary to characterize the institutions that shaped twentieth-century economic adjustment and their nineteenth-century origins.

Finland: Conservative Corporatism and Low-Tech Industrialization

Neo-corporatist bargaining was arguably most centralized and encompassing in Finland. Neo-corporatism was based on extensive peak- and local-level private-public and interfirm cooperation in financial markets and industrial policy, with organized labor playing a subordinate role until, and even after, its incorporation into centralized collective wage bargaining in 1968. Rapid industrialization and socialist geopolitical threats encouraged centralized labor exclusionary bargaining among banking blocs, industry associations, and state agencies. Although neo-corporatist bargaining in financial markets and industrial policy facilitated movement into new industries, Finland was also more dependent on stable low- and medium-tech products than any of its western European peers. Forest and metal-based products alone accounted for nearly two-thirds of Finland's exports as recently as the 1970s (Lilja, Rasanen, and Tainio 1992, 139). Finland's failure to diversify away from forestry and other low-tech industries rendered the country increasingly dependent on the Soviet Union and vulnerable to the latter's collapse in 1991.

Financial Markets: The Universal Bank and the Origins of Finnish Corporatism

The Finnish financial system, and indeed Finnish neo-corporatism more generally, revolved around the universal bank (Ali-Yrkkö and Ylä-Anttila 2003, 251). The universal bank was a common response to the challenges of late industrialization (Gerschenkron 1963), particularly for countries competing in capital-intensive industries such as forestry. During the late nineteenth century, few entrepreneurs possessed the resources to construct a timber-processing facility, much less a pulp or paper mill (Mjøset 1987, 108). Individual entrepreneurs were also poorly positioned to weather a downturn in the notoriously volatile forestry industry. These constraints were even more acute in an underdeveloped economy (Krantz 2001, 35). In this environment, industrialization was dominated by foreign entrepreneurs such as the Norwegian-owned Gutzeit forestry firm and the Scottish-owned Finlayson textile mill (Schybergson 2001). Indigenous entrepreneurship was dominated by Swedish-speaking elites, who established private-sector banks to finance industrial activity. Finnish nationalists responded by establishing the National Share Bank and its flagship forestry firm, Repola, in 1889 (Fellman 2008, 149–50).

The Finnish- and Swedish-speaking banking blocs both mobilized individual savings from across the country and issued large long-term loans to their clients. In exchange, they received the right to place representatives on the supervisory board (Ali-Yrkkö and Ylä-Anttila 2003, 254). Supervisory board representation, in turn, enabled universal banks to influence firm investment. It also permitted banks to coordinate activities across their various industrial holdings. For example, the Finnish banking bloc commonly drew on its other investments to subsidize its flagship forestry firm, Repola, during cyclical downturns (Hakkarainen 1993).

During the interwar period, the banking blocs that organized intra- and intersectoral cooperation among their holdings sponsored cooperation outside of their industrial families. Paper companies from all banking blocs established the Central Laboratory in 1916 to support research in pulp and paper production (Sabel and Saxenian 2008, 34). The Central Association of Finnish Wood Processing followed shortly thereafter, after the collapse of the lucrative Russian export market in 1918. New syndicates in paper (Finnpap), chemical pulp (Finncell), and mechanical pulp (Finnboard) facilitated recovery by coordinating output during the 1920s (Schybergson 2001, 144). By the postwar period, the Finnish economy was heavily cartelized, with associations responding to cyclical downturns by manipulating production and pricing (Fellman 2008, 179–80).

By the postwar period, the universal bank dominated Finnish finance and society more generally. Within Europe, only Austrian and Portuguese firms exhibited a greater dependence on bank loans relative to equity financing during the 1980s (Hyytinen et al. 2003, 388). Public policies increased Finland's dependence on highly centralized patterns of bank-based finance. Import restrictions and heavy taxation reduced the scope for internal financing, with the result that Finnish firms were among the most dependent on external finance in the OECD (Hyytinen et al. 2003, 398). Nor could firms turn to foreign capital, as Finland restricted foreign ownership in strategic industries in 1939 and discouraged foreign investment during the postwar period (Fellman 2008, 176).

The cooperative movement, which played an influential role in constraining Danish neo-corporatism, was an extension rather than exception to this pattern of highly centralized financial control and collaboration. Although postwar cooperative membership in Finland rivaled that of Denmark (Marshall 1958, 227), the two cooperative movements were radically different. Pellervo, the Confederation of Finnish Cooperatives, was not founded by smallholders in the Finnish hinterland but established in the capital by Finland's social elite. Its founding members included twenty-five university professors and eleven senators, alongside civil servants and prominent industrialists (Kuisma 1999, 12). In the postwar period, the cooperative movement was closely linked to the Agrarian Union political party and, by extension, Finland's most influential politician, Urho Kekkonen. The cooperative movement was thus a direct participant within and beneficiary of postwar neo-corporatist bargaining, supporting industrial investment for generous agricultural subsidies. Indeed, the Finnish cooperative movement formed its own banking bloc that spanned multiple regions and sectors (Fellman 2008, 145).

Industrial Policy: Private-Public Cooperation in Postwar Industrialization

The Finnish state intervened in concert with the universal banks and complemented their industrial interests. The state invested in complementary infrastructure throughout the second half of the nineteenth century. National independence and the ensuing civil war between the Soviet-backed Reds and German-backed Whites resulted in an even broader state role, as policymakers aspired to promote economic development and self-sufficiency. The government nationalized the Norwegian-owned forestry giant Gutzeit in 1918. At the time, Gutzeit was the second-largest forest owner after the state. Like the major banking blocs, the government channeled long-term capital to Gutzeit to transform the firm from a timber processor to a pulp and paper producer (Schybergson 2001, 121–22). The state also took over the loss-making Outokumpu copper company in the early 1920s (Fellman 2008, 160). Nationalization and public entrepreneurship continued after World War II, with the state establishing its own investment bank under Postipankki and a broad range of industrial holdings (178).

By then, the state had assumed an even more dominant role in the national economy. Finland's defeat in World War II amplified concerns about national development, while in-kind reparations payments to the Soviet Union taxed the country's industrial capacity. To meet reparations payments, Finland not only established state-owned national champions but also directed private-sector investment (Fellman 2008, 168–70; Sabel and Saxenian 2008, 35). Although reparations payments ended during the 1950s, bilateral trade with the Soviet Union continued to absorb a significant share of Finnish output into the early 1980s (Economist 2000, 21). This trade was instrumental in supporting movement into new low- and medium-tech manufacturing industries such as cables, foodstuffs, textiles, and transportation equipment, effectively insulating exporters from foreign competition and disruptive technological innovations (Fellman 2008, 181).

Bilateral trade was embedded within a more encompassing system of state aid known as credit rationing. The government used high taxes to channel capital to industry at subsidized rates. Subsidized credit not only allowed the government to provide industry with cheap, long-term capital but also enabled policymakers to determine which enterprises received credit (Fellman 2008, 177). In practice, the government allocated quotas to individual banking groups. State intervention thus empowered the banking blocs, giving them privileged access to capital and offering them greater discretion in credit allocation (175–76).

Policies toward foreign investment reinforced bank influence. Finland placed restrictions on foreign ownership in 1939, and it discouraged foreign investment during the postwar period. These restrictions gave policymakers greater leverage in determining which firms could internationalize and under what conditions (Fellman 2008, 176–77). The government also used the currency as an adjustment instrument to restore competitiveness during economic downturns. Rather than relying on fixed macroeconomic objectives or negotiating with trade unions, however, policymakers turned to the banking blocs and their industrial associations. The "pulp cycle" became an important, even primary, instrument for protecting established resource-extractive firms (173).

The fact that devaluations were determined by centralized negotiations between civil servants, bankers, and industry associations reflects the tight nexus between state and industry in postwar Finland. In contrast to other countries such as France (Schmidt 2002; Zysman 1983), state intervention reinforced neo-corporatist bargaining rather than undermining it. State-owned enterprises sought to develop complementary industrial inputs or infrastructure, credit-rationing increased the universal bank's leverage over its industrial holdings, and restrictions on foreign ownership forced Finnish firms to rely on domestic financial firms. Meanwhile, financial intermediaries and firms, particularly forestry, played a central role in determining whether Finland required another competitive devaluation (Fellman 2008, 173). Indeed, this consensual, nonhierarchical confluence of private and public interest spilled over into other aspects of postwar Finnish society, including a tendency to form supermajority coalitions in parliament (Raunio and Wiberg 2008, 590); self-censorship in the media (Salovaara-Moring 2009, 215); and collaboration in economic councils (Fellman 2008, 187), educational courses (Knight and Routti 2011, 137), and informal roundtables.[1]

Labor Markets: Civil War, Industrial Unrest, and Belated Incorporation

Organized labor was conspicuously absent from Finnish neo-corporatism until the late postwar period. The labor movement was nearly destroyed by the 1918 civil war between Soviet-backed Reds and German-backed Whites. Membership losses were exacerbated by the resulting division between Socialist and Communist trade unions, with the Confederation of Finnish Trade Unions succumbing to an internal schism in 1949. Meanwhile, the Finnish Employers' Confederation was reluctant to engage organized labor after a bloody civil war and the assassination of the Finnish Employers' Confederation's former president. Employers refused to cooperate with the Confederation of Finnish Trade Unions and

---

1. Author interview with roundtable secretary (20 October 2005, Finland).

expressly forbade their members from collaborating with trade unions' lower levels (Bergholm 2003, 17). The civil war, labor fragmentation, and industry-labor conflict thus militated against labor market cooperation.

During the interwar period, managerial autonomy was limited only by public regulation (Fellman 2008, 163–64). The government attempted to improve labor market relations by legislating Nordic-style collective wage bargaining during the interwar period, but these efforts failed when employers refused to participate (Bergholm 2003, 18). In its place, the state standardized employment contracts and introduced social reforms (17). Union influence remained limited, however, and was most visible in European-leading levels of industrial unrest. Industry-labor distrust and trade union fragmentation fueled strike activity, which was by far the highest in Nordic Europe (Stokke and Thornqvist 2001). Labor market cooperation, to the extent that it existed, reflected state-industry negotiations in human capital formation. For example, the government established new faculties in forestry, wood, paper, mining, and chemistry in consultation with industry representatives during the interwar period. As in other policy domains, however, organized labor did not play a significant role (Lemola 1994, 185; Raumolin 1992, 331).

Organized labor was not consistently integrated into Finnish collective bargaining until the 1960s, decades after Nordic peers such as Denmark. The newly elected Social Democratic Party–led coalition government turned to the trade union movement to secure wage restraint following a competitive devaluation in 1967. The resulting Liinamaa agreement traded economic and social-policy measures for wage restraint (Fellman 2008, 182). The government viewed a consolidated social democratic confederation as a bulwark against Communist influence and actively promoted trade union membership by making dues tax deductible (Bergholm 2003, 53). The government also gradually moved to integrate Finnish trade unions into the councils, committees, and policy courses that I have described.

Meanwhile, trade unions utilized their increasing size and formal participation in collective wage bargaining to press for more generous social benefits. The government expanded social protections, increasing unemployment replacement rates in 1985 (Kiander and Pehkonen 1999, 100) and extending the length of notice in 1988 (Vartiainen 1998a, 44). Spurred by peak-level agreements, strike activity fell sharply during the 1970s and 1980s. By the 1980s, the Finnish labor market more closely approximated that of Nordic neighbors such as Denmark and Sweden, relying on employment protections and generous social benefits to protect established occupations and industries (Fellman 2008, 182).

That said, "successful" macrolevel concertation obscured limited coordination. While some Finnish firms had developed a shop steward system in the

1940s, paternalistic attitudes continued to dominate the shop floor until the 1960s (Lilja 1997, 124). Employee representation within individual enterprises was not fully institutionalized until the 1980s, and even afterward workers exercised limited influence over firm strategy (Kasvio 1994, 63). Employees exercised little influence over managerial decision making concerning strategic issues such as training or technological change, even within these new forums (64). Training, for example, was conducted within public schools in consultation with the state, rather than within enterprises in collaboration with trade unions (60). Limited coordination in production constrained Finland's capacity to adapt social and labor market policies during the 1990s and 2000s. In the meantime, however, conservative corporatist bargaining in finance, labor markets, and industrial policy generated even bigger problems.

Economic Adjustment: Low-Tech, Capital-Intensive Industrialization

Although these bargains enabled Finland to enter new industries, adjustment revolved around stable low- and medium-tech, scale-intensive goods. The universal banks of the late nineteenth century focused on timber processing, paper manufacturing, and mining, sectors where they could depend on mature technologies, stable clients, and predictable markets. Banks and their clients did not have to worry that competency-destroyed innovations would threaten their investments in specialized equipment and skills. A similar pattern prevailed in the postwar period. As Finland moved into higher-technology industries such as cables, textiles, and transportation equipment, bilateral trade with the Soviet Union provided a stable outlet for established industries (Fellman 2008, 172–73).

Once established, Finland's neo-corporatist bargains defended established firms and existing industries. Universal banks extended capital during tough economic times, defending and modernizing vulnerable firms. Meanwhile, the banks coordinated activities across their industrial holdings, reducing production to maintain profitability during downturns (Schybergson 2001, 140). Public policy reinforced this pattern of protection and modernization. Finland's exchange rate regime protected profitability in established export-oriented and resource-extractive industries during economic downturns (Fellman 2008, 174), while the state played an even more direct role in transforming the timber firm Gutzeit into a pulp and paper producer (Schybergson 2001, 121–22) and modernizing the ailing Outokumpu copper firm (Fellman 2008, 160).

In protecting established investments, however, these conservative bargains inhibited the formation of new firms and industries. Growth-oriented firms such as Nokia, a forestry and rubber conglomerate, entered electronics because banking effectively prohibited competition with incumbent firms. In the words of one historian, "The big boys were in the forest industry. . . . The two main banks had their firms in the forest sphere, so they did not allow Nokia to grow in these spheres. Electronics was young and small. It was left over. There was no interest by the major banks. It was a little playground, and [Nokia] could play there."[2] While Nokia was permitted to grow in this space, it received little support from banks or the states. Other electronics companies encountered similar resistance as prominent industrialists argued that Finland should export "nothing smaller than a horse."[3] As a result, one electronics entrepreneur noted that it was virtually impossible to secure external capital to finance operations, even during the 1980s.[4]

Industrial policies exacerbated this orientation toward established low- and medium-tech industries. The undervalued exchange rate that sustained Finnish competitiveness during the 1970s punished emerging industries such as electronics by raising the costs of their imports. Financial regulation also favored capital-intensive industries such as forestry and mining, which required massive outlays in large-scale capital equipment. Policymakers' attempts to promote diversification into new industries after World War II by establishing state-owned companies were most successful in low- or medium-tech industries with stable markets and high barriers to entry such as steel and chemicals. Efforts to move into new high-tech markets were less successful. For example, the state-owned company Televa never achieved profitability in communication equipment markets during the 1970s. The establishment of a national champion in television-tube manufacturing was marked by even larger losses and, together with a related corruption scandal, effectively ended the state's career as an industrial manager (Sabel and Saxenian 2008, 61).

Collectively, the bank-based financial system, complementary public institutions, and labor market policies reinforced Finland's established position in capital-intensive resource-extractive industries and metal-based engineering activities. Pulp and paper products represented over one-third of Finnish exports in 1970s, with another quarter based on wood products and basic metals (Koski and Ylä-Anttila 2006, 19). This reliance on low-tech, often energy-intensive industries rendered Finland increasingly vulnerable to cost competition and fluctuating commodity prices. Finland avoided the oil crises of the 1970s, but only with recourse to bilateral trade with the Soviet Union (Honkapohja et al. 1999,

---

2. Author interview with professor, Department of History, University of Helsinki (10 November 2005, Finland).

3. Author interview with former chief executive officer, electronics firm (10 November 2005, Finland).

4. Author interview with founder, electronics firm (20 November 2006, Finland).

405). By the early 1980s, policymakers and industrialists alike recognized that these developments were unsustainable.

The abrupt collapse of the Soviet Union, Finland's largest trading partner, confirmed Finnish vulnerability to economic shocks. The resulting 70 percent drop in exports transformed a severe financial crisis into an economic catastrophe (Honkapohja et al. 1999, 405). By 1993, economic output had fallen by 14 percent, the steepest decline in the history of the OECD (401). While the immediate cause of the downturn was a lightly regulated lending and real estate bubble, conservative corporatist institutions were perceived to compound the crisis by delaying restructuring and increasing costs (Tainio, Pohjola and Lilja 2000). In addition to the industrial and financial policies described above, labor market bargains and social concessions had generated inflationary pressures during the 1980s and directly contributed to ballooning fiscal deficits, as social payments rose during the early 1990s. Government debt as a percentage of GDP had climbed from 15 percent of GDP in 1990 to 59.6 percent of GDP by 1994 (European Commission 1999, 27). Payroll taxes to finance social benefits had also increased (Sinko 2002, 16). Meanwhile, doubling the terms of notice, more generous replacement rates, and other protections inhibited labor market mobility when pressures to restructure became most acute. By 1994, unemployment exceeded 15 percent (Honkapohja et al. 1999, 401). Nor does this capture the full scope of the crisis, as conservative bargains encouraged early retirement and other forms of labor market exit (Lehtonen et al. 2001, 114). Traditional neo-corporatist institutions appeared to offer few tools for managing these developments. Instead, they appeared to make them even worse. In fact, neo-corporatist institutions appeared to inhibit adjustment in Denmark as well.

Denmark: Conservative Corporatism and Niche-Based Competition

Denmark also relied on neo-corporatist institutions over the course of the twentieth century, although the level and locus of cooperation varied. Neo-corporatism was more limited in finance and industrial policy, as local cooperative movements were able to enter less capital-intensive industries without national-level, private-public, and interfirm coordination. Institutional cooperation, instead, revolved around the labor market, where industry engaged a comparatively unified trade union movement at the peak, sector, and shop-floor levels. This slightly less extensive and centralized pattern of neo-corporatist bargaining (particularly as it relates to finance and industrial policy) created more space for small and medium-sized producers to enter high-tech industries such as radio and telecommunication equipment. Denmark thus enjoyed a favorable position in high-tech markets relative to Finland. High-tech production remained modest, however, and producers struggled to compete with new rivals during the 1970s. Neo-corporatist labor market bargains compounded their difficulties by increasing labor market exit, pushing up taxes, and undermining cost competitiveness. As a result, Denmark's economy, like Finland's, slipped into crisis, with policymakers and firms faulting traditional (conservative) neo-corporatist institutions.

Financial Markets: National Fragmentation and Local Cooperation

Like Finnish finance, Danish finance can be defined in relation to the universal bank of the late nineteenth century. A similar movement developed in Denmark, spearheaded by three Copenhagen banks. Privatbanken was the most prominent of the three by virtue of its role in managing Carl Fredrik Tietgen's far-flung industrial empire. A Danish analogue to the Swedish industrial magnate Andre Oscar Wallenberg and his descendants (Stråth 2001, 77), Tietgen played an integral role in rebuilding Denmark following its humiliating military defeat by Prussia in 1864. Tietgen's industrial investments extended from food processing (De Danske Sukkerfabrikker and Tuborg) to telecommunications (Store Nordiske) and heavy industry (Burmeister and Wain shipyards). Privatbanken channeled large amounts of credit to these enterprises over long periods of time.

Yet Tietgen's influence was temporary, and Privatbanken was confined to Copenhagen. Even in its heyday, Tietgen's industrial empire was less cohesive than those of his Nordic peers (Stråth 2001, 77). Privatbanken and its Copenhagen-based rivals were weakened by internal competition (Hoepner 1999, 113; Kristensen 1996, 143). More important, the three banks were also undermined by a successful cooperative movement on the Danish mainland (Hoepner 1999, 113). By 1930, banks were legally prohibited from owning or sitting on the boards of companies (114). This measure formalized existing institutional barriers to the types of dense industrial families that characterized Finland.

As a result, firms were able to draw on other, less centralized forms of finance such as equity markets (Edey and Hviding 1995, 62) and internal finance (Hoepner 1999, 128; Hyytinen et al. 2003, 398). For example, many of Denmark's largest firms (Carlsberg, Danfoss) and virtually of all of its pharmaceutical companies (Novo Nordisk, Novozymes, Lundbeck, and Leo) remain independently controlled, most commonly through a tax-advantaged foundation (Rose and

Mejer 2003, 337). Although banks played an important role in the Danish financial system, they did not assume large, controlling stakes in their clients' companies. Only 5 percent of loans lasted more than five years at the beginning of the
1990s (Hoepner 1999, 128), with the result that universal banking was limited to
a few firms.

The universal bank was supplanted by a powerful cooperative movement. This
cooperative movement was inspired by Nikolaj Frederik Severin Gruntdvig, a
pastor, nationalist, and social activist who emphasized local self-help. The cooperative movement spread as rural Danes mobilized against what they perceived
to be an illegitimate government during the mid-nineteenth century (Kristensen
1996, 139). The Danish agricultural producer organizations represented the most
visible face of the cooperative movement. These cooperatives modernized agricultural production during the late nineteenth century by pooling resources to
diffuse expensive new technologies such as the cream separator (Edquist and
Lundvall 1993, 269). In so doing, they protected Danish agriculture from the
universal bank and consolidation more generally.

This same cooperative movement also created space for individual entrepreneurs. The producer cooperatives themselves represented an important market
for agricultural equipment and related machinery. The self-help movement also
supported local craftsmen by establishing cooperatively owned financial institutions. These institutions permitted a more heterogeneous array of financing
strategies by providing short-term loans and supplementing self-financing. In
other words, the Danish financial system created opportunities for smaller Danish producers to enter market competition, even if their modest size constrained
expansion (Hoepner 1999, 114).

The Gruntdvigian self-help movement also supported novel forms of local
cooperation. The same firms that formed and relied on financial cooperatives
collaborated in training and the diffusion of technology. Craftsmen founded
local vocational institutions following the collapse of the guild system in 1862
and established a network of local schools during the late nineteenth century
(Iversen and Andersen 2008, 275). These same actors also founded the first "au-
thorized technology service institutes" in 1907 (Bengtsson and Soren 2000).
These GTS (Godkendte Teknologiske Serviceinstitutter) institutes diffused the
latest technologies within local firm networks by offering educational activities,
consulting services, and technical assistance.[5] Local cooperatives, however, effectively blocked the cross-regional and cross-sectoral collaboration that characterized Finnish financial markets.

---

5. Author interview with director, Danish Technological Institute (24 November 2005, Denmark).

Industrial Policy: Political Constraints on Private-Public Cooperation

Nor did the state assume a significant role as a coordinating agent (Mjøset 1987, 444). This laissez-faire ideology could be attributed to Denmark's status as an early industrializer in small-scale food processing and related industries (Gerschenkron 1963). In addition to this, the state was bound by the same institutions and processes that blocked the universal banks. As noted, the cooperative movement was initially inspired less by the specter of centralized corporate control than the perceived illegitimacy of the Danish central state during the mid-nineteenth century (Kristensen 1996, 139). Once established, these institutions disrupted the tight nexus between leading exporters, universal banks, and policymakers that prevailed in Finland.

As a result, public-sector intervention was never explicit as in Finland, where the Bank of Finland fixed credit at artificially low levels. Although the Bank of Denmark possessed instruments to manipulate overall credit supply, this was viewed as a countercyclical instrument rather than a form of credit rationing. Interest rates were considerably higher in Denmark than in Finland, reflecting the former's deeper integration into the international financial system (Mjøset 1987, 431). Despite the country's large public sector, Danish policymakers also did not rely on state-owned enterprises to diversify into strategic industries such as heavy metals or chemicals, as Finland did.

While Danish grant aid was broadly similar to that of Finland during the early 1980s (Carlsson 1984, 225), industrial policies differed in several respects. First, industrial policies were governed by partisan dynamics rather than negotiations among the social partners, shifting with every change in the Danish government (Mjøset 1987, 451). Second, there was no effort to link sectors or regions in the kinds of national projects that characterized Finland. To the extent that one observes any continuity in Danish industrial policy, it involved subsidizing the locally administered GTS institutes and their efforts to diffuse new technologies to established enterprises and industries.

This is not to suggest that the Danish state played an insignificant role in postwar adjustment. In some respects, it was even more significant than in Finland. Budgetary surpluses were consistently lower in Denmark than in Finland (Huber and Stephens 1998, 363), partly reflecting the state's own status as the largest single economic sector (Pederson 1996, 557). State intervention, however, was more closely reflected in redistributive bargaining in labor markets than in direct collaboration in productive processes. In other words, state intervention privileged social-benefit expansion, employment creation, and Keynesian demand management rather than nationalization or state aid. To understand this dynamic, we must shift our attention to the true locus of postwar Danish neo-corporatism, which was bilateral bargaining between trade unions and industry associations in the labor market and related domains.

Human Capital: Labor Markets as a Locus of Cooperation

While Denmark's status as an early industrializer might appear to fragment the Danish trade union movement, labor was never divided by the fierce ideological and national divisions that characterized Finland and Ireland. As a result, a formidable trade union movement proved very effective in challenging Danish employers during the late nineteenth century. Vulnerable firms sought to combat leapfrogging and the domino strike by merging into the Danish Employers' Federation (DA) in 1896. Trade unions followed suit, forming the Danish Trade Union Confederation (LO) in 1898 (Lubanski et al. 2001, 31). The newly established LO was able to coordinate their actions to devastating effect during the industrial conflict of 1898.

Increasing industrial unrest led employers to sign the watershed September Agreement of 1899. Trade union representatives, employer representatives, and even corporate executives continue to cite the collective agreement, Europe's first, as an example of Danish labor market cooperation.[6] The September agreement effectively integrated Denmark's various craft-based unions within a gradually more centralized and encompassing system of collective wage bargaining. Employers accepted a labor court and state mediation in 1910 as an instrument for extending collective wage agreements to Denmark's fragmented unions. Centralized collective wage bargaining was reinforced when the coalition government embraced new welfare policies (Campbell and Hall 2006, 27) and a more robust State Conciliation Board (Lubanski et al. 2001, 34) during the 1930s. These two institutions established a foundation for peak-level two-year wage agreements during the postwar period.

The interwar bargain that traded wage moderation for social benefits created a framework for postwar collective wage bargaining and industrial adjustment more generally. Social expenditures increased significantly during the 1950s and particularly during the 1960s. Spending on health and welfare rose from 6 percent of GNP in 1952–53 to 16 percent of GNP by 1972–73 (Iversen and Andersen 2008, 312). A national pension scheme was introduced in 1957; a supplementary

---

6. Author interviews with economist, Danish Employers' Confederation (15 November 2005, Denmark); former director, Danish Employers' Confederation (15 November 2005, Denmark); and secretary, Danish Confederation of Trade Unions (17 November 2005, Denmark).

pension scheme followed in 1963; and unemployment replacement rates were increased to 90 percent of earnings by the end the 1960s, often as part of an overarching wage agreement (Iversen and Andersen 2008, 312; Mjøset 1992, 161).

Although Danish employers fiercely resisted any employment protections as an encroachment on their right to manage, the welfare state emerged as an alternative way to insure firm and industry-specific investments. The state displaced agriculture as Denmark's leading economic sector (Pederson 1996, 557). While policymakers launched the first labor market policies in the late 1960s, social protection revolved primarily around an increasingly encompassing early retirement and disability insurance scheme. Early retirement, sickness insurance, and related schemes thus protected workers who did not find employment in the expanding public or sheltered sectors (Torfing 1999, 13). In other words, Danish labor markets, and Danish political economy more generally, closely resembled the conservative corporatist model described in chapter 1, with stakeholders agreeing to protect established employees, occupations, and, by extension, industries from economic shocks.

Although Denmark and Finland possessed superficially similar social policies by the end of the 1980s, Danish neo-corporatism was different in that it involved extensive coordination at the sectoral and shop-floor levels. For example, Denmark's comparatively low levels of industrial unrest not only reflected centralized collective wage bargaining but also the early twentieth-century institutionalization of a shop steward system. The Danish shop steward system created a framework for addressing employee concerns, implementing collective wage agreements, and negotiating the introduction of technology and the reallocation of labor (Lubanski et al. 2001, 34). Trade unions were also incorporated into the cooperatively managed vocational and educational institutes. Unskilled workers created their own training facilities to compete with the specialized craft-based institutes, while the vocational training system as a whole emerged as an increasingly important forum for cooperation between labor and industry. These institutions played a peripheral role as stakeholders bargained over national health insurance and retirement schemes during the 1960s and 1970s, but they would support a creative response to labor market reform in later decades.

Economic Adjustment: Gradual Upmarket Movement in Specialized Niches

As in Finland, cooperation among employer associations, trade unions, and individual firms promoted gradual upmarket movement within establish industries, most notably agriculture. The Danish producer cooperatives allowed small and medium-sized producers to invest in costly new equipment such as the cream separator (Edquist and Lundvall 1993, 269). This pattern of cooperatively backed technological diffusion continued into the 1980s, as the Agricultural Advisory Service diffused best practices and new technologies to established producers, facilitating movement into progressively more efficient and higher value-added agricultural activities. Gradual upmarket movement in agriculture meanwhile created a market for local enterprises to enter directly related industries such as pumps, cooling technologies, heating systems, and stainless steel (276).

Danish manufacturers relied on a similar constellation of institutions to defend and modernize their position within these low- and medium-tech industrial niches. Cooperatively owned financial institutions could not cross-subsidize their industrial holdings or organized producer cartels, but subcontracting networks allowed firms to rely on producers in other niches to expand production or subcontract labor when they experienced soft markets (Kristensen 1995, 265). Meanwhile, producers relied on their own GTS institutes to facilitate long-term upmarket movement. An industrial analogue to the Agricultural Advisory Service, these publicly subsidized but independently managed institutes spread best practices in training, technology, and management by providing consulting services to local producers (Gergils 2006, 49–53). Diffusion-oriented industrial policies complemented and directly subsidized these activities (Christiansen 1988, 235). Vocational institutes and subcontracting networks (Kristensen 1995, 265; Kristensen 1996, 145–46) simultaneously safeguarded investments in specialized niches. The postwar Danish welfare state provided additional insurance, compensating vulnerable workers through a combination of generous unemployment benefits, disability insurance payouts, or early retirement schemes.

Because cooperation was more decentralized than in Finland, it created more space for individual entrepreneurs to enter electronics, and radio communications in particular, during the early twentieth century. Early twentieth-century inventions in acoustics enabled a constellation of small and medium-sized firms to enter radio manufacturing (Edquist and Lundvall 1993, 277). Danish competencies in acoustics in turn supported movement into radiotelephone equipment in the early postwar period. One producer, Storno, was established to construct a closed-circuit radio to the Copenhagen fire department in 1947. The startup was acquired by Great Northern, a Copenhagen-based industrial conglomerate. By the 1960s, Great Northern had developed the subsidiary into the fourth-largest mobile communication producer in the world, with a 30 percent market share in Europe (Iversen 2005, 47). Small and medium-sized entrepreneurs throughout Denmark entered related niches, including televisions, maritime communications, and hearing aids (Dalum, Faberberg, and Jørgensen 1988). Denmark thus occupied a more favorable position in high-tech markets, as the country's more decentralized institutional framework created space for individual entre-

preneurs to enter new industries, upgrading skills and equipment within established niches.

These niches proved problematic during the 1960s and 1970s, however, as
Denmark grappled with new cost-competitive rivals, including Japan, Korea, and
Taiwan (Kristensen and Levinsen 1983). Cost competition was not limited to
resource-based industries like agriculture and food processing but also extended
to medium- and high-tech industries such as radios and televisions. The Danish radio and television industry experienced a wave of bankruptcies during the
1970s.[7] Nor was communications immune from the turmoil. Great Northern
sold its radiotelephone subsidiary Storno to General Electric in 1974 because
the conglomerate was unable to tolerate increasing costs and volatility in the
radiotelephone industry (Iversen 2005, 149). Radio producers in North Jutland,
which had grown by outfitting yachts and other vessels, were also affected, in this
case by the decline of Danish shipbuilding (Dahl, Pedersen, and Dalum 2003, 13).

Danish producers could have responded by moving into new higher value-
added activities, but they struggled in their efforts to do so. Small and medium-sized
producers could not mobilize the capital to compete within increasingly research-
intensive high-tech industries. Indeed, they could not compete in their own niches,
as smaller enterprises were characterized by lower expenditures on research and
limited investment in new technologies (Amin and Thomas 1996, 266; Pedersen,
Andersen, and Kjær 1992, 1124). Denmark appeared to exemplify all of the limitations of small states described in chapter 1 (Kristensen and Levinsen 1983).

Neo-corporatist bargains compounded these challenges. The GTS institutes
specialized in diffusing established technologies to existing firms within mature
industries (Edquist and Lundvall 1993, 296). Policymakers promoted diversification by expanding grant aid and loans (Mjøset 1987, 427), reaching 5.3 percent
of value added in mining and manufacturing by 1982 (430). Funding, however,
was concentrated in established industries. Instead of facilitating diversification,
interventions delayed it at considerable cost (Christiansen 1988; Morris 2005).

Labor market bargains exacerbated declining cost competitiveness. Centralized collective wage bargaining proved increasingly incapable of sustaining wage
moderation (Lubanski et al. 2001, 39–40). Although policymakers attempted
to contain labor costs by offering progressively more generous social-insurance
schemes (Torfing 1999, 13), these measures created long-term problems. Unemployed workers were absorbed by the public sector or transferred into unemployment, disability, or early retirement programs. Workers enrolled in Denmark's

---

7. Author interview with former chief executive officer, electronics firm (16 February 2006, Denmark).

generous social programs had few incentives to move to new high-tech firms, thus reducing labor supply and increasing costs. Meanwhile, increasing reliance on unemployment, disability, early retirement, and public employment burdened industry with higher social contributions, further undermining cost competitiveness. Public-sector efforts to meet fiscal obligations through borrowing created large budget deficits and macroeconomic uncertainty.

By the 1980s, economic growth had stagnated and unemployment approached double digits. More important, Denmark's fiscal position appeared increasingly unsustainable. An International Monetary Fund bailout appeared likely, and one government minister proposed an outright default to avoid compromising national sovereignty. The acute crisis discredited traditional neo-corporatist bargains. The coalition government led by the Social Democrats that had presided over the expansion of Danish neo-corporatism collapsed in 1979, and the ensuing minority government led by the Social Democrats abdicated three years later (Mjøset 1992, 336). The incoming Conservative People's Party–led coalition government entered with a mandate to dismantle Danish neo-corporatism, and indeed it eliminated traditional neo-corporatist institutions, including centralized collective wage bargaining and full-employment policies, during the 1980s.

Ireland: Liberal Capitalism, High-Tech Competition, and Economic Crisis

Ireland was the most liberal economy of the three cases under consideration, with virtually no cooperation in financial markets, weakly embedded industrial policies, and inconsistent recourse to collective wage bargaining. The Irish financial system was dominated by multinational capital, and industrial policies relied on tax concessions to attract foreign direct investment, while labor markets were characterized by light regulation, decentralized bargaining, and outright conflict. Capital and labor mobility facilitated movement into a wide range of industries from footwear and textiles to computers and pharmaceuticals. Ireland in fact led Denmark and Finland in the share of high-tech exports and high-tech employment in 1985. Irish "leadership" in high-tech markets remained modest, however, lagging behind larger countries such as Britain, the United States, and even Germany and Japan (OECD 2011). It was also tenuous, as decentralized market competition failed to provide the macroeconomic stability, wage restraint, and industrial peace that multinational investors craved. By the 1980s, Ireland experienced an economic crisis that was just as acute as the one plaguing neo-corporatist rivals Denmark and Finland. As a result, the Irish case raises questions about the relationship between liberal capitalism and high-tech competition.

Finance: Decentralized Equity Markets and Multinational Capital

Ireland was controlled by the United Kingdom during the late nineteenth century, with the result that financial intermediaries emulated the liberal model of decentralized and arm's-length finance that prevailed in Britain, even after independence. Irish equity markets were smaller than those in large liberal countries such as Britain or the United States, but they were also considerably deeper than those in Denmark or Finland. With over fifty publicly listed firms by the early 1930s, the Dublin stock exchange represented an important source of finance for indigenous entrepreneurs (Casey 2000, 7). The Irish banking system was organized along similar lines. The British institutions that dominated early twentieth-century Irish finance adopted the same liberal arm's-length, short-term relationships that they relied on at home. Meanwhile, Irish banks were criticized for mobilizing deposits and investing them in London (Ó Grada 1997, 231). To the extent that they did invest domestically, they modeled their activity after their British counterparts (176), eschewing the model of long-term finance that characterized Finland. Irish banks instead preferred to launch an initial public offering on the British or Irish stock exchange (Casey 2000, 6).

In contrast to Denmark and Finland, the Irish cooperative movement did not function as a coordinating agent at the local or national level. The cooperative movement developed more slowly in Ireland than in Denmark because of the political, religious, and economic cleavages associated with British colonization. Large, predominantly Protestant landowners had their own distribution channels in Britain and little incentive to join the nascent cooperative movement (Mjøset 1992, 243). Smallholders were divided along religious lines. By the time Horace Plunkett, a Protestant, had merged thirty-three dairy cooperatives into the Irish Agricultural Organization Society in 1894, more than one-third of Danish farms were involved in dairy cooperatives (Mjøset 1992, 243). The cleavage between large businesses and smallholders was even more pronounced in other industries (243). Irish cooperatives also failed to expand to financing, technical consulting, and training, instead focusing on food processing (244). Indeed, the Irish cooperative movement was less cohesive than its Danish or Finnish counterparts and was characterized by fragmentation and intense competition between local branches (Mjøset 1992; O'Rourke 2006).[8] The Kerry Group, Ireland's most successful cooperative group, underscoring the country's liberal

---

8. This point was confirmed in author interviews with professor, Department of Food Business, University of Cork (12 June 2006, Ireland) and former secretary general, Department of Agriculture (15 June 2006, Ireland).

orientation, was listed on the stock exchange in 1985 (Kennelly 2001, 226). Other producer cooperatives, such as Glendale, quickly followed suit (246).

In fact, Ireland relied on an even more liberal source of finance in the form of foreign direct investment. Policymakers aggressively recruited foreign investment after 1958 (Ó Grada 1997, 50). This more mobile and volatile source of capital differed sharply from the local or national supply of patient capital that epitomized Danish and Finnish finance. Multinational corporations did not link, and were not linked to, domestic financial intermediaries, Irish enterprises, trade unions, or each other. Indeed, foreign multinationals were characterized by the striking lack of forward or backward linkages to the domestic Irish economy (Ó Grada 1997, 116; Mjøset 1992, 277). Although they were represented within the Irish Business Employers Confederation, they did not cooperate within the national-level industrial families or the local subcontracting networks that characterized Danish and Finnish industry. U.S. multinationals were also staunchly antiunion.

Collectively, this pattern of decentralized equity-based finance and foreign direct investment limited the prospects for neo-corporatist cooperation. The Irish banks followed the English lead in eschewing long-term ownership stakes in their industrial interests. The Irish cooperative movement was more notable for its fierce local rivalries than its advisory, technical, or training functions. Finally, multinational capital reproduced these arm's-length relationships by introducing foreign actors into the Irish economy, with few linkages to neighboring producers. Indeed, neo-corporatist bargaining was equally limited in industrial policy and labor markets.

Industrial Policy: The Developmental State and Foreign Direct Investment

Ireland embraced an active industrial policy from independence, as the nationalist Fianna Fail party sought to eliminate Ireland's dependence on Britain (Ó Grada 1997, 104). Import substituting industrialization, however, faltered in a market with only three million consumers. Two decades of economic stagnation and massive emigration led stakeholders to embrace free trade in 1958 (50). Policymakers eased the transition to free trade by introducing tripartite adjustment committees (51) and distributing generous adaptation grants (Ó Grada and O'Rourke 1996, 402). By the 1980s, however, Irish industrial policies were significantly different from the neo-corporatist measures that characterized Finland. While Irish expenditure on state aid was significantly higher at 5 percent of GDP during the 1980s (412), industrial policies differed from those of Finland in three respects.

First, Irish industrial policies were oriented toward multinational investment, particularly after the initial transition to free trade during the 1960s. The same 1958 deal that liberalized trade also gave a domestic agency, the Industrial Development Authority, a mandate to use tax concessions and subsidies to lure foreign investment to Ireland. The IDA sought to exploit Ireland's comparative advantage as a low-cost, low-wage producer by attracting investment in textiles, clothing, plastics, light engineering, and food processing (O'Sullivan 1995, 387). Critics suggested that the IDA was focusing almost exclusively on multinational capital at the expense of indigenous Irish entrepreneurs (O'Hearn 1998, Ó Riain 2004). By 1974, foreign industry represented over 60 percent of industrial production (Haughton 1995, 37), reinforcing the arm's-length relationships and undermining any nascent interfirm or cross-sectoral cooperation.

Second, Irish policymakers employed different policies. While the IDA offered investment and employment grants, as well as the direct leasing of land and office space to prospective multinationals (Mjøset 1992, 268), Irish industrial policy privileged tax concessions over direct public investments. Tax concessions accounted for almost half of the state aid that was issued during the 1980s (Ó Grada 1997, 54). Most notable among these tax concessions was the Export Profit Tax Relief Act of 1956. The act offered multinational manufacturers a full tax remission on any export-based profits from its revision in 1958 until the 1990s (Mjøset 1992, 272).

Finally, and most important for the purposes of this book, state aid was weakly embedded within neo-corporatist bargains. The IDA itself functioned as an independent agency with no formal connection to organized industry or labor. Its decision to prioritize foreign direct investment widened the gulf between the state and societal actors. Indigenous entrepreneurs criticized the IDA for discriminating against indigenous entrepreneurs (Ó Riain 2000, 179) and continue to this day to express skepticism about Irish public policy.[9] Although Ireland constructed explicitly neo-corporatist institutions to distribute modernization grants to domestic industries during the 1960s (Ó Grada 1997, 51), these side payments were reduced once trade had been liberalized, and they paled in comparison to the tax concessions, property leases, and employment grants of the 1970s and 1980s (Mjøset 1992, 272).

As a result, ambitious industrial policies were weakly connected to and did little to support organized economic actors at the national, sectoral, or local level. The multinational corporations that were lured through tax concessions formed

---

9. Author interviews with former director, Irish Software Association (19 May 2006, Ireland) and former director, National Software Directorate (31 May 2006, Ireland).

relatively weak relationships with other subsidiaries, local municipalities, employer associations, or local firms. To the extent that multinationals did rely on local infrastructure or training relations were often organized exclusively through the state rather through or with other firms. Even connections to domestic suppliers were limited, as foreign multinationals sourced comparatively few inputs from their indigenous counterparts. In many cases, foreign companies imported finished or semifinished components from abroad, relying on Ireland as an assembly and export center (Ó Grada 1997, 116; Mjøset 1992, 277).

Labor Markets: From Liberalism to Limited Neo-Corporatism and Back Again

Cooperation was marginally more developed in Irish labor markets. Trade unions were divided among numerous craft-based trade unions and suffered a precipitous decline in membership in the wake of the Irish civil war. While tensions between the Irish trade union movement and Irish employers were less acute than in post–civil war Finland, the trade union movement was internally divided between rival Irish and British confederations. This division remained a source of tension throughout the interwar and postwar period, with the two unions assuming diametrically opposed positions on whether or not to cooperate with the government. Employers faced little incentive to strike a deal with Irish labor, while the dominant center-right Fianna Fail government sought to contain and marginalize trade union influence. State intervention was instead characterized by wage freezes, standstill orders, and a controversial reorganization of the labor movement that introduced new political divisions (Ó Grada 1997, 99–100).

As a result, the Irish labor market more closely resembled liberal economies such as Britain or the United States. This liberal, lightly regulated structure facilitated the rapid redistribution of resources from troubled industries, such as footwear or textiles, to emerging sectors, such as computers or pharmaceuticals (Clinch, Convery, and Walsh 2002, 41). This decentralized framework, however, was also vulnerable to industrial unrest. Rapid restructuring during the 1960s fueled significant gains in trade union membership and mounting discontent. By the end of the decade, trade union density approached 50 percent and the number of days lost to industrial disputes had quadrupled (Ó Grada 1997, 100; Sexton et al. 1997, 96). The maintenance men's strike of 1969, which halted a third of production (Durkan 1992, 352), was an important watershed in Irish industrial relations.

Stakeholders responded by experimenting with neo-corporatist labor market policies to secure industrial peace. Employers and labor signed bipartite labor market agreements in 1970, 1972, 1974, and 1975, while the government entered collective wage bargaining with Keynesian tax concessions and spending increases in 1979 and 1980 (Durkan 1992, 352–57). Yet policy concertation did not rival that of Denmark, or even Finland. Social benefits remained modest. Unemployment and disability-benefit replacement rates were among the lowest in western Europe, exceeded only by Britain (Pontusson 2005, 192). Nor, more important, did the social partners play any significant role in administering those social benefits.

Coordination in production was even more limited. In fact, labor's right to organize was a problematic issue in Ireland long after the issue had been settled through basic agreements in Denmark and Finland. Irish efforts to recruit foreign direct investment limited trade union recognition, as U.S. subsidiaries were reluctant to embrace Irish trade unions (Gunnigle 1998). This explicit preference for operating within a nonunion environment was even more pronounced among more recent arrivals, particularly high-tech firms. This fragmented union structure and historically acrimonious labor market relations inhibited efforts to reach a viable agreement during the 1970s. The result was that a modest reduction in strike activity was purchased through progressively more generous wage increases and public spending (Durkan 1992, 367). By 1981, employers had withdrawn from collective wage bargaining altogether, further cementing Ireland's status as a liberal market economy in the area of labor relations (Hardiman 1988).

Economic Adjustment: High-tech Competition and Economic Crisis

Ireland's more liberal economic institutions appeared to support more rapid restructuring relative to Denmark or Finland during the 1960s and 1970s. While Ireland could not rely on the universal bank to support scale-intensive industrialization or cooperative financial institutions to modernize indigenous enterprises, foreign direct investment represented a far deeper source of capital. Public policy created an attractive framework for foreign direct investment, offering export-profit tax relief and generous grant aid. To the extent that such activities constrained firms or crowded out other activities, the burden fell primarily on domestic firms that were not eligible for the export-profit tax credit. Ireland quickly shed employment in less competitive low- and medium-tech industries (Mjøset 1992, 278).

These policies did not constrain foreign enterprises, however, which were quick to locate to Ireland during this period (Ó Grada 1997, 114). An affordable English-speaking workforce, limited labor market regulation, and a nonunionized environment were an additional draw, and flexible labor market institutions facilitated the rapid redistribution of human capital to new multinational subsidiaries and emerging industries (Clinch, Convery, and Walsh 2002, 41).[10] Growth was particularly rapid in new high-tech industries such as computer equipment and pharmaceuticals, where U.S. producers sought a foothold in heavily protected European markets (Mjøset 1992, 273). Digital Equipment, Ericsson, and Motorola each opened manufacturing facilities during the 1970s. By 1985, the Irish share of high-tech exports (12.9%) was 33 percent higher than Denmark's and 275 percent higher than Finland's (OECD 2011).

Irish "leadership" in high-tech markets, however, remained modest. The share of high-tech manufactured exports, for example, trailed that of large countries such as Britain, Germany, Japan, and the United States (OECD 2011). Furthermore, high-tech production was concentrated in relatively low value-added activities such as assembling or imported computer components or packaging software (O'Sullivan 1995, 387; Sterne 2004, 21). Irish reliance on labor costs, grant aid, and tax concessions reinforced this "low-end" orientation. For example, multinational producers that were attracted by Ireland's low corporate tax rate were reluctant to invest in R & D. Those cost-intensive activities reduced corporate profits and, by extension, the opportunities for tax arbitrage that influenced their initial investment.[11]

Furthermore, this low-cost, low-tax strategy appeared increasingly unsustainable within a voluntarist arm's-length political system. Employers faulted collective bargaining for failing to contain wage growth and government spending during the 1970s, but the alternative proved even worse. Wages increased rapidly under decentralized collective bargaining from 1981 to 1987 (Thomas 2003, 104). Meanwhile, a succession of weak coalition governments proved unwilling to shoulder the blame associated with fiscal retrenchment. Government debt, which had increased from 64.8 to 87.7 percent of GDP during the 1980s, reached a staggering 136.6 percent of GDP by 1987 (Mjøset 1992, 321). Rising wages, government debt, and continuing industrial unrest proved especially problematic for an economy build on cost-sensitive foreign investment. Gross domestic product, inflated by multinational transfer pricing, was flat between 1973 and 1986, while gross national product actually declined. By then, unemployment had reached 17 percent (Considine and O'Leary 1999, 120). In this dire economic context, which threatened policymakers, firms, and trade unions alike, stakeholders

---

10. Author interviews with former country manager, electronics firm (3 May 2006 Ireland); executive officer, electronics firm (1 June 2006, Ireland); government affairs manager, electronics firm (8 June 2006, Ireland); manager, electronics subsidiary (8 June 2006, Ireland); and executive officer, software firm (8 June 2006, Ireland).

11. Author interview with executive officer, software firm (8 June 2006 Ireland).

turned to a new and innovative form of neo-corporatist governance focused less on social concessions and more on wage restraint and fiscal retrenchment.

Conclusion: The Limits of Conservative Corporatism (and Liberal Capitalism)

Historical analysis of the early postwar Danish, Finnish, and Irish experiences would appear to support the traditional literature on comparative political economy. Neo-corporatism facilitated gradual upmarket movement in low- and medium-tech niches but inhibited competition in rapidly evolving high-tech industries. Finland, where neo-corporatist bargaining was most centralized and encompassing, struggled to move into new high-tech industries such as televisions and telecommunication equipment. Danish entrepreneurs, operating in a country where neo-corporatist bargaining was slightly less encompassing, found space to assume a more competitive, if modest, position in a range of specialized high-tech niches. Ireland, the most liberal economy, also occupied the most prominent position in high-tech markets, as foreign multinationals capitalized on a favorable tax regime and flexible labor market institutions.

The neo-corporatist bargains that supported postwar growth thus appeared to inhibit adaptation to new challenges. Finland's dependence on gradual upmarket movement within existing scale-intensive, resource-extractive niches rendered the country increasingly dependent on bilateral trade with the Soviet Union by the early 1980s and vulnerable to its abrupt collapse at the beginning of the 1990s. Denmark was more successful but struggled to compete as conservative labor market bargains contributed to sluggish growth and increasing unemployment. Even Ireland, a traditionally liberal economy, experienced deteriorating economic performance as it experimented with conservative corporatism in collective wage bargaining. By the 1980s, stakeholders in each country were questioning and actively withdrawing from traditional centralized collective wage bargaining.

Yet subsequent decades did not witness convergence on a liberal economic model. On the contrary, liberal institutions generate their own set of problems. Ireland struggled to attract foreign direct investment as a low-cost, low-tax location during the 1980s. Policymakers increasingly discovered that an arm's-length adversarial political and economic system actively undermined pro-market reforms, generating industrial unrest and macroeconomic instability. Liberalization proved even more costly in Denmark and Finland, not only because of its failure to secure certain public goods, but because of the considerable political costs associated with unilateral reform.

By the 1990s, stakeholders in Ireland, Denmark, and Finland were relying on neo-corporatist bargaining to manage new economic challenges. These new bargains, however, had very different implications for economic adjustment, facilitating movement into new high-tech industries. Finland emerged as a leader in mobile communications, leading the European Union in high-tech patenting. Restructuring was less dramatic in Denmark, but it revolved around an even broader range of industries, including biotechnology and software. Finally, Ireland achieved unprecedented success as a high-tech manufacturer, not only increasing its share of high-tech exports but doing so within the context of a healthy and rapidly growing economy.

The following chapters explain this puzzling turn of events by arguing that neo-corporatist institutions have been converted to perform different functions, mobilizing resources around new enterprises, activities, and industries rather than protecting existing actors. Adaptations vary in direct relation to neo-corporatist legacies. Finland and Denmark have turned to creative corporatism, using policy concertation to convert coordination to new ends. Creative corporatist bargaining has been most successful where countries could leverage a tradition of coordination, privileging private-public and interfirm cooperation in research in Finland and industry-labor cooperation in training in Denmark. Ireland also turned to neo-corporatism, constructing a system of policy concertation virtually from scratch. Absent a tradition of coordination, however, stakeholders struggled to invest in high-quality inputs. Stakeholders instead relied on competitive corporatism, using institutionalized cooperation to secure wage restraint, fiscal retrenchment, and market-based reform.

These different bargains caused these three countries to assume very different positions in new high-tech markets. Indeed, the countries effectively switched places over the course of the 1990s and 2000s. Chapter 3 demonstrates how Finland, the weakest high-tech competitor during the 1970s, leapfrogged radio-telephone producers such as Denmark to assume leadership in mobile communications. Furthermore, while Finland continues to trail Ireland in the share of high-tech manufactured exports, the historically low- and medium-tech economy now leads in more knowledge-intensive and higher value-added activity, including high-tech patents, research, and high-tech services employment. Rapid restructuring was predicated on new, creative corporatist bargains, most notably in industrial and innovation policy, in which policymakers could convert a tradition of private-public and interfirm cooperation to radically different objectives.

3

FROM PRICE-FIXING CARTELS TO RESEARCH CONSORTIA

Rapid Restructuring in Finland

In the 1970s, Finland was one of Europe's least innovative countries. By the end of the 1990s, it was a high-tech leader. What caused this transformation? Increasing dependence on the Soviet Union, an acute economic crisis, and external EU-imposed constraints discredited established stakeholders and traditional policy routines. In this environment, policymakers threatened to promote restructuring by dismantling hitherto core instruments such as the universal bank, the state-owned enterprise and credit rationing. At the same time, unilateral liberal reform was politically costly, precipitating fierce resistance by societal actors, most notably trade unions. Policymakers thus sought to promote economic adjustment by very different means, adapting neo-corporatist institutions to identify and invest in disruptive new inputs. Industry embraced these measures because they had a long history of interfirm and private-public coordination.

Policymakers experimented with a wide array of initiatives, but creative corporatism was most pronounced in R & D, where policymakers could convert a history of constructive collaboration within national projects, banking blocs, and price-fixing cartels. Here, policymakers struck a series of peak-level bipartite and tripartite deals to increase research expenditure, delegating implementation to private-public and interfirm research consortia. Research collaboration was complemented by more modest initiatives aimed at small and medium-sized enterprises, including efforts to engage new stakeholders such as pension funds in early stage risk capital. Creative corporatist bargaining was most limited in labor markets, because industry did not have a strong tradition of cooperating with organized labor in production. To the extent that it occurred, human capital investment was shaped by bipartite state-industry cooperation in higher education. Trade union participation was limited to peak-level bargaining, in which unions ratified innovative policies as an alternative to more extensive labor market reform.

Peak-level deals to invest in disruptive new inputs triggered a massive increase in public- and private-sector investment, as policymakers could use neo-corporatist institutions to build a consensus, monitor commitments, and coordinate activities. Total expenditure on R & D climbed from OECD-lagging levels during the 1970s to the second-highest in the world (after Israel) by 2009, and Finland observed significant, if slightly less dramatic, gains in early stage risk capital and human capital. Those new supply-side investments had very different implications for economic adjustment. Instead of modernizing established resource-extractive niches, these investments permitted movement into emerging industries such as biotechnology, software, and telecommunication equipment.

Restructuring was most dramatic in telecommunications. R & D, human capital investment and early stage risk capital supported experimentation during the 1980s, permitted expansion during the 1990s, and facilitated adaptation in the wake of the dot-com crash. In sharp contrast to the situation with other high-tech leaders such as Ireland, these new investments supported movement into high value-added, innovation-intensive activities. Finland was less affected by the large-scale offshoring of low-cost assembly operations in the wake of the dot-com crash, successfully shifting employment from hardware manufacturing into software development. As a result, Finland was less dependent on nontradable services than were other high-tech leaders, and it was less vulnerable to the financial crisis of 2007–9.

While knowledge-intensive competition effectively immunized Finland to the financial crisis, it has also generated new challenges. Most significant, it has exposed the country to disruptive technological innovations, such as the convergence between mobile telephony and computing. The emergence of new competitors and the resulting shift in value from hardware to services has threatened Nokia's dominant position in high-tech markets and the Finnish economy more generally. In fact, creative corporatism increased Finnish vulnerability by mobilizing resources around a handful of capital-intensive national-level research projects and by privileging formal R & D over nontechnological innovation. These challenges have precipitated a new round of institutional conversion, shifting attention to entrepreneurship and nontechnological innovation.

The Puzzle: From Paper Producer to High-Tech Leader

Conservative corporatist bargains supported incremental upmarket movement in capital-intensive low- and medium-technology industries throughout the postwar period, with pulp and paper products alone representing over one third of Finnish exports as recently as 1970 (Koski and Ylä-Anttila 2006, 18). Finland avoided cost competition and increasing commodity prices during the 1970s, but only by increasing bilateral trade with the Soviet Union (Economist 2000, 21). The ensuing collapse of the Soviet Union in 1991 underscored Finnish vulnerability as output plunged by 14 percent between 1991 and 1993, and unemployment exceeded 15 percent (Honkapohja et al. 1999, 401). The crisis devastated traditional industries, challenged established economic institutions, and provoked a broader crisis of confidence throughout the nation (Kalela et al. 2001, 10). The neo-corporatist bargains that had sustained prosperity in stable, gradually evolving low- and medium-technology niches appeared poorly positioned to adapt to abrupt changes such as the collapse of the Soviet Union or competition in a more dynamic, rapidly evolving environment (Tainio, Pohjola and Lilja 1997).

By the end of the 1990s, however, Finland had emerged as one of the fastest growing economies in Europe. Per capita GDP growth exceeded 5 percent during the second half of the 1990s, second only to Ireland in western Europe. Growth was based on new high-tech industries, as the share of manufactured high-tech exports quintupled from 4.7 percent in 1985 to 26.8 percent by 2000 (OECD 2011). For the first time in Finland's history, high-tech electronics supplanted forestry as the nation's dominant sector (Asplund 2003, 14). As a result, Finland not only leapfrogged continental peers such as Germany but rivaled traditional high-tech leaders such as Britain and Japan (OECD 2011).

Even more important, Finland specialized in knowledge-intensive, high value-added activities within this industry, leading the European Union in high-tech patenting. Finland was thus less dependent on cost-sensitive assembly operations than other high-tech leaders and less vulnerable to the dot-com crash. While the share of high-tech exports declined precipitously after 2000, Finland did not rely on nontradable services such as residential construction. On the contrary, Finland continued to lead the European Union in the share of high-tech employment, replacing traditional manufacturing jobs with new positions in software development.

Finland's largest firm, Nokia, exemplifies this unlikely transformation. Like many Finnish enterprises, its origins lay in forestry, with the foundation of Nokia

Forest and Power in 1865. The conglomerate diversified into rubber and cables during the late nineteenth and early twentieth centuries. Nokia entered the telecommunications field during the 1970s, but production remained peripheral until the 1990s. In fact, the firm was deeply dependent on bilateral trade with the Soviet Union (Steinbock 2000, 45). By the end of the 1990s, however, the firm was defined by its leading one-third share in the global market for mobile handsets. In so doing, Nokia outmaneuvered multinational incumbents such as Motorola and Nordic rivals such as Cetelco, Dancall, and Ericsson (Steinbock 2000, 146–47).

Nokia's transformation is even more impressive because it relied almost exclusively on indigenous institutions to support initial experimentation and early growth. Nokia developed technologies internally and relied on Finnish suppliers to accommodate rapidly expanding telecommunication equipment markets during the 1990s. The firm produced over half of its output in Finland as recently as 1999. Rivals such as Ericsson, by contrast, manufactured less than 5 percent of their output domestically (Steinbock 2000, xxxiii). Nokia's growth reflected more general developments within Finland, as the company was embedded within a broader information and communications technology cluster of over four thousand firms (Paija 2001, 4). While manufacturing subcontractors such as Elcoteq and Perlos outsourced most of their activity after the dot-com downturn, software contractors such as Elektrobit and Fat Hammer emerged to take their place. Their growth explains why the share of high-tech employment actually grew in the wake of the dot-com crash from 6.59 percent in 2001 to 6.67 percent in 2006 (Eurostat 2011). Indeed, Nokia's post-2008 struggles in the market for smartphones obscures the fact that the most popular gaming application on Apple's iPhone, Angry Birds, was designed by a Finnish gaming firm (Ben-Aaron 2010).

High-tech competition was thus never limited to a single firm or sector. The Finnish product-based software industry rivals other "success" stories such as the indigenous Irish software industry. The growth of the Finnish product-based software industry is particularly notable because it excludes software employees working at Nokia and its vast network of suppliers. Finland also occupies a surprisingly competitive position in other high-tech industries. For example, Finland was identified as one of the three most successful countries in biotechnology in a 2007 EU benchmarking exercise (European Commission 2007, 17) and is even more specialized than Denmark in the field of electromedical devices (Pedersen, Dahl, and Dalum 2006, 89). Finland has thus diversified from low-tech resource extractive industries to a range of knowledge-intensive activities within new high-tech industries.

In fact, we observe historically unprecedented and theoretically uncharacteristic behavior among firms in established low- and medium-technology industries such as food processing and mining. Expenditure on R & D, for example, approached 3.5 percent of turnover in food processing, one of the least research-intensive industries during the postwar period, by 1998 (Saarinen 2005, 29). Today, firms have used investments in research to introduce significant new-to-market product innovations such as Cultor's synthetic sugar, Xylitol, and Valio's line of probiotic dairy products.[1] Engineering firms such as KONE and Wärtsila have introduced similar product-based innovations, including a line of compact elevators, and they have moved into nonmanufacturing activities such as port management and energy generation.[2]

The literature on comparative political economy sheds little insight into this outburst of rapid product-based innovation, and successful high-tech competition in particular. After all, Finland is a small state and should be disadvantaged in high-tech markets (Kristensen and Levinsen 1983). Other scholars emphasize the ability to enter or defend stable niches (Casper 2007), but Finland was new to high-tech markets and specialized in disruptive segments such as mobile handsets and middleware. Some suggest that large multinational corporations can surmount these disadvantages (Dalum 1992), but this does not explain how Nokia outmaneuvered large rivals such as Ericsson, Motorola, or Siemens and did so within the confines of a neo-corporatist economy of five million people.

Several scholars resolve this puzzle by emphasizing luck, specifically Finland's participation in the Nordic Mobile Telephone (NMT) standard (Hyytinen et al. 2006, 68–69). Launched in 1981, the pan-standard created economies of scale with a joint market of over one hundred thousand people. The NMT also operated as an open standard, inducing competition between Nordic and third-party producers. Competition left Nordic players well positioned to compete in Groupe Special Mobile (GSM), the digital standard that came to be adopted by three-quarters of the countries in the world (Hyytinen et al. 2006, 69). Nokia executives themselves emphasize favorable standards, attributing the firm's success "first of all [to] the NMT technology, the NMT network. Finland became one of the leading markets in mobile services at that time."[3]

Yet explanations based on luck, and the NMT standard in particular, remain problematic. This argument does not explain how Nokia outperformed other firms with access to the same standards, including large incumbent multinationals with Nordic subsidiaries such as Motorola (Iversen 2005; Pedersen, Dahl,

---

1. Author interviews with executive officer, Finnish Funding Agency for Technology and Innovation (20 October 2005, Finland); adviser, Finnish Funding Agency for Technology and Innovation (20 November 2005, Finland); and director, food processing firm (29 November 2006, Finland).

2. Author interviews with executive officer, engineering firm (25 October 2005, Finland) and research director, engineering firm (4 November 2005, Finland).

3. Author interview with former executive officer, electronics firm (17 October 2005, Finland).

and Dalum 2006). In other words, the NMT standard does not explain Nokia's ability to exploit favorable opportunities where others failed to do so. Nor does it explain how they managed to defend their position in an increasingly competitive telecommunications market, managing rapid growth during the 1990s and diversifying into software and services during the 2000s. Finally, arguments based on luck fail to account for broader trends in the Finnish economy, as firms moved to more knowledge-intensive, innovation-based competition across a wide range of industries.

As a result, some scholars have concluded that restructuring can only reflect movement toward a liberal economic model (Andersen et al. 2007). Decentralized market competition enabled firms to capitalize on the favorable circumstances described here. Finland certainly did experience significant liberalization in late-stage financial markets, social policy, and industrial policy during the 1980s and 1990s. This period, however, witnessed *increasing*, not decreasing, cooperation in cooperation-important domains such as early stage financial markets, education, and innovation policy. Far from inhibiting restructuring, creative corporatist bargains appeared to accelerate the redistribution of resources. Finland dramatically improved its position in high-tech markets and leapfrogged over liberal economies such as Ireland. Furthermore, performance was strongest in precisely those areas where creative corporatist bargaining was most centralized and encompassing. Before illustrating how creative corporatism supported new patterns of economic competition, however, it is important to characterize and explain Finland's shift to creative corporatism.

The Argument: From Price-Fixing Cartels to Research Consortia

Finland's shift to creative corporatism began with deteriorating economic performance and the perceived failure of conservative corporatism during the 1970s. While bilateral trade with the Soviet Union insulated Finland from increasing cost competition and commodity prices during the 1970s, policymakers and industrialists alike expressed concerns about the country's political and economic dependence on a historically hostile Communist superpower. Policymakers worried about private industry's limited investment in R & D. In the words of one policymaker, "It was clear that the only way that the Finnish economy would be able to survive was to increase value-added. The Soviet trade would not provide growth opportunities. The traditional bilateral trade that we had with the Soviet Union was of that sort: the products that we were selling to Russia were not competitive [in other markets]. . . . So there was a very strong commitment both by industry and by policy circles."[4] A forest executive agreed, remarking that "during the 1980s, business, the labor unions, and government understood that we could no longer remain an exporter of more or less commodities. We needed to be an exporter of high-quality products, high value-added products.... The shift from an investment-based economy into an innovation-based economy started pretty early, and there was broad consensus for the need for this shift."[5]

These developments discredited traditional neo-corporatist institutions, which were perceived to stifle growth and innovation. Nokia, fretting about its dependence on the Soviet Union (Steinbock 2000, 28), lobbied to privatize state-owned enterprises (Lovio 1993, 199). It also unilaterally undermined credit rationing by lending surplus foreign earnings to other enterprises through non-traditional "gray" money markets (Tainio and Lilja 2003, 75). These perceived failures were bolstered by real crises in state-owned television and telecommunication companies during the late 1970s. Televa, a state-owned telecommunication equipment manufacturer established in 1975, suffered repeated budget overruns. The establishment of a state-owned champion in televisions, Valco, one year later was even more catastrophic. Hitachi's decision to divest from a proposed joint venture to manufacture television tubes not only rendered the Finnish government's investments worthless, but it also implicated Social Democratic prime minister Kalevi Sorsa and other government officials in a corruption scandal (Sabel and Saxenian 2008, 61).

The perceived failure of conservative corporatism and a very real corruption scandal led policymakers to quickly distance themselves from traditional institutions. By 1982, a Social Democratic–led coalition government (under new leadership) had abandoned the practice of state-led industrialization, privatized Televa, and forced remaining publicly owned enterprises to adhere to strict principles of profitability. Although Sorsa returned to office after 1982, his administrations adopted a similar position, loosening the state's grip on credit markets, abandoning credit rationing, relaxing capital controls, and permitting foreign direct investment over the course of 1980s (Tainio and Lilja 2003, 74).

At the same time, more extensive liberalization was politically unattractive. First and most important from the perspective of the Social Democratic policymakers governing the economy, trade unions could threaten to punish policymakers for implementing aggressive labor market reforms. This was particularly true in an environment of relatively low unemployment and greater trade union bargaining power during the 1980s. Finland in fact deepened its reliance on

---

4. Author interview with former officer, Science and Technology Policy Council (18 October 2005, Finland).
5. Author interview with former executive officer, forestry firm (31 October 2005, Finland).

conservative corporatist instruments at this time, strengthening unemployment benefits and employment protections (Kiander and Pehkonen 1999, 100; Vartiainen 1998a, 44). As in France, this move compensated workers in traditional industries that were threatened by new market-based reform (Levy, Miura, and Park 2006, 112–13; Vail 2010, 9). Policymakers struck similar, if less generous, deals in the 1990s.

Meanwhile, industrialists expressed reservations about unchecked liberalization in finance and industrial policy. Pro-market reforms threatened to reduce state aid and credit just as industries were struggling to identify new products, markets, and industries. Such concerns were particularly pronounced among traditional low- and medium-technology producers.[6] Even emerging electronics producers such as Nokia, which was even more dependent on the Soviet Union (Steinbock 2000, 28), struggled to accommodate the shift from bilateral trade to new foreign markets and restrictions on state aid. Corporate executives thus enthusiastically supported and actively promoted new public initiatives to diversify and develop industrial production.[7]

As a result, while policymakers distanced themselves from traditional neocorporatist institutions, they also avoided a purely market-based strategy. The Social Democratic–led government under Prime Minister Mauno Koivisto instead struck a deal with its Center Party coalition partners and, by extension, industry. The government abandoned nationalization and credit rationing but proposed several new initiatives to stimulate innovation and restructuring. The most successful was a proposal to convert traditional industrial policies. In the words of a former member of parliament, "The main goal was no longer to expand industrial production but to expand R & D."[8] Policymakers expanded the bipartite (and later tripartite) Science Policy Council to promote investment in research and created a new state agency, the Finnish Funding Agency for Technology and Innovation (Tekes), to implement the council's recommendations. These new initiatives sharply increased public- and private-sector expenditure on R & D.

This strategy was naturally appealing for policymakers, because they could distance themselves from the perceived failures of conservative corporatism while continuing to play an active role in the economy (and taking credit for promoting innovation). Organized labor had limited influence over industrial policy

---

6. Author interviews with former executive officer, forestry firm (31 October 2005, Finland) and former chief executive officer, electronics firm (10 November 2005, Finland).

7. Author interviews with former director, Finnish Funding Agency for Technology and Innovation (1 November 2005, Finland) and former officer, Science and Technology Policy Council (18 October 2005, Finland).

8. Author interview with former member of parliament (6 October 2005, Finland).

in the early 1980s, but it had little reason to oppose reform so long as unions were receiving generous side payments through conservative corporatist labor market bargains. The biggest puzzle is why industrialists would tolerate, and ultimately embrace, public-sector intervention, given the state's checkered record and the alternative of cost-competitive reforms such as lower corporate taxes.

Finnish industrialists, however, had a long history of constructive engagement with state agencies in national developmental projects and interfirm collaboration within banking blocs and price-fixing cartels. Early technology policies effectively converted postwar neo-corporatist structures to new ends. The bipartite Science Policy Council resembled the postwar planning committees that had organized reparation payments and industrialization, while Tekes, the state agency responsible for funding investment in research, required firms to collaborate with public-sector actors and one another to receive funding. In doing so, it effectively converted existing patterns of cooperation to new ends, capitalizing on Finnish industry's willingness to share sensitive information and commit scarce resources to collective projects. Corporate executives not only tolerated state intervention in this area but utilized formal industry networks and informal roundtables to actively lobby policymakers and fellow industrialists.[9]

If Finland's shift to creative corporatism started as early as 1980 (before Finland or Nokia were significant high-tech producers), the economic crisis of the early 1990s accelerated institutional conversion. The Conservative-Social Democratic rainbow coalition Harri Holkeri administration suffered a resounding defeat in 1991, ushering in a market-oriented, center-right coalition administration, Finland's first nonsocialist government since 1966. The Esko Aho administration's liberal stance was strengthened by several developments. First, the exceptionally severe downturn was widely interpreted as a clear failure of traditional neo-corporatist institutions (Tainio, Pohjola, and Lilja 2000). The Aho administration was not eager to associate itself with insolvent universal banks, state-owned enterprises, or restrictive labor market regulations. It also possessed a mandate to enact sweeping market-enhancing reforms. One contemporary policymaker characterized the crisis as a "game of survival. It [was] not an issue of who was going to get which benefits from society. It was about national survival."[10] The prospect of accession to the European Union further strengthened the new administration's mandate. EU membership was attractive for both

---

9. Author interviews with former director, Finnish Funding Agency for Technology and Innovation (1 November 2005, Finland) and former officer, Science and Technology Policy Council (18 October 2005, Finland).

10. Author interview with former officer, Science and Technology Policy Council (18 October 2005, Finland).

economic and geopolitical reasons because of Finland's proximity to Russia. Joining, however, would require Finland to eliminate state aid to large enterprises, break price-fixing cartels, and, beginning in 1993, limit government deficits and debt (Fellman 2008, 195–96).[11]

The Aho administration thus entered government with a strong popular and externally imposed mandate to implement comprehensive market-based reforms. The financial crisis did much of the work for them, bankrupting one banking bloc and forcing other universal banks to unravel their dense network of cross-holdings (Tainio, Huolman, and Pulkkinen 2001, 161). The Aho administration responded to the apparent failure of the universal bank by promoting equity as an alternative form of finance, weakening creditor rights, promoting greater transparency in financial markets, eliminating dividend taxation, and promoting greater product-market competition (Hyytinen, Kuosa, and Takalo 2003, 66). It simultaneously reformed Finnish industrial policy, not only renouncing nationalization, but actively privatizing state-owned enterprises over the course of the 1990s (Fellman 2008, 202). Finally, the administration advanced labor market liberalization, shortening the period during which recipients could collect social-benefits, introducing new eligibility requirements, and easing employment regulations (European Commission 1999, 28; Saari 2001, 195–99; Vartiainen 1998a, 33). All of these measures were designed to limit the inevitable increase in deficit spending and public debt, an overriding concern during the economic crisis.[12]

While the newly elected center-right government appeared ideally positioned to liberalize the Finnish economy, a purely market-based approach proved problematic for several reasons. Most notably, unilateral reform provoked fierce resistance from societal actors. If policymakers had little stomach for comprehensive liberalization during the 1980s, the 1990s illustrated why. Initiatives to lighten regulations on hiring young workers provoked mass protests by organized labor. Facing the threat of a general strike, the government withdrew its proposals on youth employment (Ornston and Rehn 2006, 89). Meanwhile, employers themselves abandoned more aggressive market-based reforms after the unilateral decentralization of collective bargaining failed to secure wage restraint (Vartiainen 1998a, 22).

In fact, market reforms also failed to address industry concerns. Just as firms struggled to diversify away from the Soviet Union during the early 1980s, Finnish industry was scrambling to identify new products and new markets in the

---

11. Author interview with former officer, Science and Technology Policy Council (18 October 2005, Finland).

12. Author interview with former member of government (6 October 2005, Finland).

wake of the economic crisis. Moreover, firms could no longer rely on traditional resources or instruments to do so. As noted, the banking crisis reduced the supply of patient capital. Small and medium-sized enterprises were even more profoundly affected as the financial crisis simultaneously weakened the nascent venture capital industry.[13] Firms also lost recourse to defensive instruments such as the producer cartel. European accession placed new constraints on interfirm collaboration (Fellman 2008, 195), and the universal banks were in no position to sponsor such action (199).

As a result, the same administration that sought to liberalize financial markets, industrial policy, and labor markets simultaneously intervened in each domain. The government prioritized R & D (Ylä-Anttila and Palmberg 2005, 5), building on the perceived success of new initiatives in this space. It also addressed capital shortages by launching several new venture capital funds (Hyytinen and Väänänen 2003, 333) and shortages of skilled labor (and youth unemployment) by increasing university enrollment (Koski et al. 2006, 61–62). In sharp contrast to competitive corporatist or liberal economies, the government did so by relying on bipartite and tripartite institutions. The tripartite Science and Technology Policy Council not only prioritized investment in R & D but helped coordinate initiatives in risk capital and education (Ylä-Anttila and Palmberg 2005, 6–7).[14] These initiatives were explicitly linked to new economic and institutional constraints. In the words of one participant, "There was a lot of debate about whether Finland would survive entry into EMU [Economic and Monetary Union], because the structure of the economy was not the same as in other EU countries. Once again, investment in R & D was the answer. . . . The good news was that this was something we could do in Finland to create a national movement to support this, for all of the stake-holders to support this."[15]

The Social Democratic–led rainbow coalition government that assumed power in 1995 was acutely aware of the perils associated with unilateral reform and adopted an even more explicitly tripartite approach to economic policy. The Paavo Lipponen administration struck a series of peak-level wage agreements with employers and trade unions that reached over 90 percent of the labor force (European Commission 1999, 33). Unions, chastened by the very real threat of unilateral reform efforts between 1991 and 1995, agreed to restrain wages in exchange for influence over fiscal retrenchment and social-benefit retrenchment

---

13. Author interviews with director, Ministry of Trade and Industry (13 October 2005, Finland).

14. Author interview with former officer, Science and Technology Policy Council (18 October 2005, Finland).

15. Author interview with former officer, Science and Technology Policy Council (18 October 2005, Finland).

(Lehtonen et al. 2001, 105). In sharp contrast to competitive corporatism, however, the social partners also agreed to *increase* expenditure on R & D.[16] Trade unions, in other words, embraced the redistribution of resources to R & D as an alternative to more comprehensive market-friendly reform.

In fact, the Social Democratic Lipponen administration launched an even broader array of reforms designed to promote innovation-based competition, drawing inspiration from Nordic Europe to the United States. For example, the government used revenue from the privatization of state-owned enterprises to establish a new venture capital foundation, Finnish Industry Investment, in 1997 (Hyytinen and Väänänen 2003, 343). It also launched a new initiative on workplace development in 1996 to promote shop-floor collaboration and lifelong learning (Schienstock and Hämäläinen 2001, 19). Policymakers thus adopted a wide range of internationally popular reforms. These initiatives, however, were most successful when they could build on and convert established patterns of coordination. In Finland, this meant that policymakers were most successful in promoting investment in R & D.

Research and Development: From Industrial Policy to Innovation Policy

Creative corporatist bargaining was most developed in innovation policy, transforming Finland from one of the least to one of the most research-intensive countries in the European Union and the world as a whole. Superficially, contemporary innovation policies bear little resemblance to the industrial policies of the early postwar period. High-profile failures in telecommunication equipment and televisions discredited traditional industrial policies during the 1970s. By 1983, both Televa and Valco were privatized, while remaining state-owned enterprises were adapted to focus exclusively on profitability. The center-right and rainbow coalition governments of the 1990s embarked on an even further-reaching program of privatization, with many shares ending up in foreign hands (Ali-Yrkkö and Ylä-Anttila 2003, 255). Policymakers also abandoned the system of credit rationing and ceded control over the exchange rate by joining the euro. European integration represented a broader shift from negotiated adjustment to "decentralized competition" as it terminated bilateral trade with the Soviet Union, reduced selective state aid, and banned traditional private-sector adjustment mechanisms such as producer cartels (Fellman 2008, 195).

---

16. Author interview with former officer, Science and Technology Policy Council (18 October 2005, Finland).

These ostensibly market-based reforms, however, did not unravel neo-corporatist bargaining. Instead, stakeholders deepened collaboration in innovation policy, and technology policy in particular. Such initiatives were not unprecedented. Firms had collaborated in sectoral and public research institutes since the interwar period, while the state had supported research by establishing research councils in the 1950s and independent foundations such as Sponsor and Sitra in the 1960s. Collaboration in research, however, was modest in size and scope until the 1980s. State-led enterprises, for example, focused on investment-driven growth in low- and medium-tech industries such as copper, steel, and forestry. Research funding was limited. Sitra funding was virtually flat following its establishment in 1968, and research expenditure as a share of GDP actually declined in subsequent years (Lemola 2004, 275). By the early 1980s, Finland ranked near the bottom of the OECD, spending less than 1.2 percent of GDP on R & D (Eurostat 2011).

Finnish policies toward R & D changed dramatically after traditional industrial policies failed to promote diversification into new high-tech industries. The parliamentary Technology Committee of 1979 represented an important point of departure, as it responded to political and economic challenges by targeting low levels of research and limited cooperation among private-sector enterprises. Officials at the Ministry of Trade and Industry embraced the proposal, launching a new body, the Finnish Funding Agency for Technology and Innovation (Tekes), to implement these recommendations. After being endorsed by the bipartite Science Policy Council and amended by parliament to incorporate employer and employee representatives, Tekes commenced operations in 1983 (Vuori and Vuorinen 1994, 21).

Tekes represented a shift from conservative to creative corporatism in three ways. First, Tekes redistributed resources from investment to innovation. The agency marked an unprecedented commitment to R & D as policymakers cut other forms of state aid. Tekes's budget increased from less than €50 million in 1984, a significant increase over Sitra's limited funds, to over €400 million twenty years later (Sabel and Saxenian 2008, 64).[17] Second, Tekes broke from reactive vertical industrial policies by relying on horizontal supports. In other words, all firms were eligible to apply for aid or participate in Tekes projects (Vuori and Vuorinen 1994, 21). Finally, this shift from vertical to horizontal aid created opportunities for new high-tech enterprises and activities. Early initiatives were disproportionately oriented toward information technologies, even though this

---

17. To illustrate the magnitude of this increase, Tekes's initial €50 million allocation in 1984 was 25% higher than Sitra's *2010* budget.

represented a relatively minor part of the Finnish economy at this time (Ylä-Anttila and Palmberg 2005, 8).[18]

Tekes was not a statist initiative but was instead organized along neo-corporatist lines. According to an early director, industry participation was critical to the success of the project: "That is normally a problem in such projects [because] the industrialists are not interested and there is no flow of information. But [firms] were positive, especially in those early days."[19] As a result, the agency was able to link firms to one another and to public-sector actors. Tekes programs from forestry to information technologies linked leading firms such as Kymmene and Repola with research institutes such as VTT and public universities such as the Helsinki University of Technology. For example, the agency engaged all of Finland's largest pulp and paper producers to develop more efficient nonchlorinated bleaching technologies during the 1980s.[20] By the end of the 1990s, large enterprises were obliged to cooperate with small and medium-sized enterprises to receive funding. As a result, Tekes has not only funded virtually all of Finland's largest firms (Castells and Himanen 2002, 52) but also extended funding to smaller firms. Together with other forms of support, government funding reached 42 percent of Finland's innovative small and medium-sized enterprises (Koski et al. 2006, 51).

Tekes was in turn embedded within peak-level neo-corporatist structures, particularly following the Science Policy Council's expansion into the tripartite Science and Technology Policy Council in 1987. In integrating the Ministry of Trade and Industry and technological innovation, the Science and Technology Policy Council sought to coordinate education, scientific research, and economic activity. The council, which had always been chaired by the prime minister, evolved to incorporate progressively greater participation by leading firms and representatives from peak-level industry and labor associations. In doing so, it mobilized political support for investing in R & D (Koski et al. 2006, 43).[21] For example, the Science and Technology Policy Council prioritized investment in R&D during the economic crisis of the early 1990s (Ylä-Anttila and Palmberg 2005, 6). One official associated with the Science and Technology Policy Council described the shift in the following terms: "We were able to make decisions that

---

18. Author interview with former director, Finnish Funding Agency for Technology and Innovation (1 November 2006, Finland).

19. Author interview with former director, Finnish Funding Agency for Technology and Innovation (1 November 2006, Finland).

20. Author interviews with former director, forestry firm (13 October 2005, Finland); executive, forestry firm (10 November 2005, Finland); and director, Finnish Funding Agency for Technology and Innovation (1 November 2006, Finland).

21. Author interview with officer, Science and Technology Policy Council (14 October 2005, Finland).

normal Western societies only dream of. [Some] public expenditures were cut by 25 percent. You can imagine what that means, if you think of any normal Western democracy. [Cutting] 25 percent of public expenditure is quite a hard thing. But at the same time the government decided to increase R & D expenditure, and still today this is the most radical reform that I have seen in any government's expenditure if you exclude war. There was a very strong shift in R & D expenditure, and these were supported by the analysis that we were very involved at the time, that Finland was ready to do anything to create jobs. . . . We were able to convince the government that the best way to create new jobs was to invest in high-tech."[22]

Interestingly, politicians confirmed this account. One government official surprisingly declined to receive any credit for what others characterized as a "brave" and "heroic" decision, noting instead that the government was acting on a broader social consensus to invest in R & D. In his words, "I have the impression that all parties—conservatives, Liberals, the Center Party, Social Democrats, and maybe even Communists—of that time were able to support that policy orientation. There was even competition to see which [party did the most] to support that."[23] Not surprisingly, the Social Democratic–Conservative Party rainbow coalition government that followed relied on a similar strategy, increasing expenditure on R & D, even as it appealed for wage restraint and reduced social spending (Hyytinen et al. 2003, 423).

The peak-level bargains previously described dramatically increased public expenditure on R & D. From 1981 to 2006, the public sector (government and university) increased from 0.56 percent of GDP to 0.97 percent of GDP. What is most remarkable about the Finnish case is that it was even more successful in increasing business investment in R & D, from 0.63 percent of GDP in 1981 to 2.48 percent of GDP. During this time period, total Finnish investment in R & D increased from 1.16 percent to 3.48 percent (Eurostat 2011). This 4.5 percent compound annualized growth rate outstripped not only that of Denmark (3.5%), Ireland (2.6%) but of the rest of the European Union. Furthermore, increasing research intensity is not limited to Nokia. Even without Finland's largest firm and the talent it attracts, investment in research is still above the EU average at 2.4 percent of GDP (Ali-Yrkkö 2010b, 30).

Peak- and lower-level neo-corporatist cooperation increased private-sector investment in three ways. First, collaboration generated a strong consensus regarding the importance of R & D. As noted, the Science and Technology Policy Council forged a tripartite and bipartisan agreement to increase expenditure on R & D. The council's recommendations were diffused within

22. Author interview with former officer, Science and Technology Policy Council (18 October 2005, Finland).

23. Author interview with former member of government (6 October 2005, Finland).

industry associations, educational courses, and informal roundtables.[24] In engaging corporate executives, neo-corporatist networks effectively strengthened research directors relative to corporate management.[25] In the words of one research director who used funding at the height of the dot-com downturn to support an ongoing project, "In all companies, these kinds of investments are so big, and they are constantly monitored by management and can even be stopped; you can only afford them here and there. . . . I think [the credibility] was quite important."[26]

Neo-corporatist networks not only pressured firms to commit resources but relied on peer monitoring to more effectively assess individual efforts. Tekes forced firms to collaborate with public-sector actors and one another. In so doing, it enabled enterprises to monitor one another's efforts and raised the costs associated with opportunistic behavior. In the words of one executive, "If you look at this Finnish system, this technology system, all key players, companies, universities know each other. So this kind of networking is key. It's quite easy to make these kinds of deals. And why is the situation like that? I believe that in ten, twenty, thirty years the Finnish system has trained the companies to work together."[27] A director responsible for attracting foreign investment concurred, noting that inward foreign direct investment was driven in part by the need to penetrate the dense, interpersonal networks that governed Finnish research.[28]

Neo-corporatist networks also enabled stakeholders to coordinate investments. For example, policymakers used neo-corporatist bargaining to link public support with private-sector priorities. For example, public funding privileged applied research rather than basic research. For example, the share of public spending dedicated to universities is only 27 percent in Finland, as opposed to 50 percent in Denmark (Gergils 2006, 35, 132). This is not to argue that universities do not play an important role in the Finnish innovation system but rather that they are more tightly integrated into corporate research consortia. Finland routinely ranks highest in measures of interfirm and industry-university cooperation (Koski et al. 2006, 50), and several industry representatives emphasized private-public cooperation as a source of technological innovation or skilled labor.[29] For example, one research director, discussing a product innovation that

---

24. Author interview with director, economics institute (10 October 2005, Finland).
25. Author interviews with former director, forestry firm (13 October 2005, Finland); executive officer, engineering firm (25 October 2005, Finland); director, forestry firm (2 November 2005, Finland); executive officer, software firm (3 November 2005, Finland); director, engineering firm (4 November 2005, Finland); and former executive officer, forestry firm (31 October 2005, Finland).
26. Author interview with director, electronics firm (19 October 2005, Finland).
27. Author interview with director, engineering firm (4 November 2005, Finland).
28. Author interview with director, Invest in Finland (23 November 2006, Finland).
29. Author interviews with director, engineering firm (4 November 2005) and manager, electronics firm (20 November 2005, Finland).

features prominently in the company's advertising, noted, "It was our R & D, one or two people who started to look at it. One of these guys was completing his PhD, studying this technology at the university. . . . [This product] was very new at that time. It was not known. The university helped these people develop these theories that were applied inside [our firm.] This theory helped us to develop a new concept, and that was a major breakthrough. . . . Without these key people on [our] side and the university side, we might not have been able to create that solution. It was not available elsewhere."[30]

Finnish innovation policies have been so successful, in fact, that policymakers and societal representatives continue to identify R & D as a strategy to promote growth and restructuring. Policymakers linked heroic public and private investments in R & D to Nokia's transformation into a telecommunication equipment leader and point to parallel developments in traditionally low-tech industries such as mining.[31] Industry association representatives made similar arguments.[32] One economist commented, "We already had the ground for this kind of recovery [because] R & D inputs in Finland were high. The state invested more and more after this recession. It was very easy for parliament to put more and more into these investments, and this helped this branch."[33] The economist continued, "In the future, for countries like Finland, we should increase our R & D inputs every year."[34] Industry executives echoed this claim.[35] Even Finnish trade unions have embraced technology policies, in part because they represent an alternative to more-polarizing social-benefit and labor market reforms.[36] As a result, public-sector and private-sector expenditure on research has climbed even *higher* since these interviews were conducted, to 1.11 percent and 3.96 percent of GDP respectively by 2009 (Eurostat 2011). Indeed, the consensus underpinning Finnish technology policies is so strong that it directly shaped bargaining in finance and the labor market.

Financial Markets: From Patient Capital to Venture Capital

Financial markets were characterized by a similar, if more modest, shift from conservative to creative corporatism. The universal banks played a less influential role

30. Author interview with director, engineering firm (4 November 2005, Finland).

31. Author interview with former officer, Science and Technology Policy Council (18 October 2005, Finland).

32. Author interviews with director, Technology Industries of Finland and former director, Confederation of Finnish Employers (19 October 2005, Finland).

33. Author interview with economist, Technology Industries of Finland (19 October 2005, Finland).

34. Author interview with economist, Technology Industries of Finland (19 October 2005, Finland).

35. Author interview with former executive officer, electronics firm (17 October 2005, Finland).

36. Author interview with director, Metal Workers' Union (28 October 2005, Finland).

in late-stage financial markets, but we observe increasing cooperation in early stage risk capital markets. Cooperation in venture capital markets was more modest owing to the abrupt collapse of traditional financial intermediaries such as the universal bank, but policymakers were nonetheless able to engage new stakeholders, most notably pension and insurance funds. Collectively, public- and private-sector investments facilitated a significant increase in venture capital fund-raising and investments over the course of the 1990s. While the aforementioned emphasis on technological innovation over commercialization contributed to a sharp contraction in the venture capital industry at the turn of the century, stakeholders have refocused attention to "soft" skills and exercised a stabilizing influence in early stage risk capital markets.

As with Finnish industrial policy, financial markets were characterized by dramatic movement away from the conservative corporatist institutions that characterized the 1960s and 1970s. Following high-profile failures in industrial policy, policymakers relaxed restrictions on lending during the late 1970s, permitted foreign competition in 1982, and abandoned credit rationing by 1986 (Hyytinen, Kuosa, and Takalo 2003, 66; Tainio and Lilja 2003, 74). Because banks had developed few tools to screen for risky projects during an era of credit rationing, however, the resulting credit boom and bust bankrupted traditional financial actors (Hyytinen and Pajarinen 2003a, 23). The cooperative banking bloc survived, but the public banking bloc was privatized, and the landmark Finnish- and Swedish-speaking banking blocs merged into a single entity. In a bid to reduce risk and raise equity, universal banks shed their industrial holdings and interlocking directorates (Tainio and Lilja 2003, 76). Whereas twenty of Finland's largest thirty enterprises had a supervisory board in 1989, only six did by the end of the decade (Hyytinen, Kuosa, and Takalo 2003, 93).

Policymakers responded to the crisis by promoting decentralized equity markets as an alternative source of finance. Regulators introduced disclosure requirements and greater regulatory oversight (Ali-Yrkkö 2003, 187), dismantled the creditor rights that underpinned bank-based finance (Hyytinen, Kuosa, and Takalo 2003, 73), and eliminated restrictions on foreign direct investment (Tainio, Huolman, and Pulkkinen 2001, 154). Nominal stock market capitalization rose from 23 percent of GDP in the early 1990s to 150 percent of GDP by the end of the decade (Hyytinen and Pajarinen 2003a, 27). The transformation from neo-corporatism to liberal capitalism appeared complete.

The shift from neo-corporatist banking blocs to liberal equity markets, however, failed to address concerns among Finland's small and medium-sized enterprises. The financial crisis thus encouraged experimentation in early stage risk capital markets. Like the innovation policies I have described, these efforts were not unprecedented. The Bank of Finland negotiated with the major banks to channel capital to small and medium-sized enterprises as early as 1954, introducing the dedicated venture capital firm Sponsor in 1967 and establishing the regional development fund Kehitysaluerahasto (Kera) to provide soft grants and consulting services in 1971 (Hyytinen and Väänänen 2003, 332). As with innovation policy, however, these efforts were modest in scale and scope. Kera focused on regional development rather than growth-oriented enterprises. Indeed, risk capital funding was virtually nonexistent in the dynamic Helsinki metropolitan area. In the words of one entrepreneur, "Kera was not allowed to give soft loans to the company that I owned. We didn't have Tekes or Start Fund of Kera then. There were no sources for soft loans in 1985 or 1986."[37]

Finnish venture capital markets only started to change during the 1980s. The research foundation Sitra shifted to early stage risk capital markets as Tekes assumed responsibility for research funding.[38] By converting its grants and soft loans into equity stakes, Sitra was able to expand its funding operations considerably and contributed to a miniboom in venture capital funding during the 1980s. The credit boom and bust at the end of the decade, however, reflected the industry's vulnerability. The number of venture capital firms declined from forty-eight in 1988 to thirty, mostly public-sector funds, by 1990. Teollistamis-rahasto, established in 1954, was one of the casualties as its new private-sector parent, SKOP bank, filed for bankruptcy. By the end of the 1980s, Finnish investment in venture capital was a modest 0.111 percent of GDP, trailing not only liberal leaders such as Britain but also Finland's Nordic neighbors (Hyytinen and Pajarinen 2003a, 37).

As the economic crisis choked off the supply of venture capital and related financing to small and medium-sized enterprises policymakers intervened aggressively (Hyytinen and Pajarinen 2003a, 62). Kera, the regional development agency, launched the Start Fund of Kera (SFK) at the height of the crisis in 1990. The fund deviated from traditional practice in that it was a national-level fund and adopted equity stakes in its clients. Like Sitra, SFK aspired to lure domestic and foreign coinvestors and raise awareness about venture capital funding more generally. In 1995, the government used revenues from the privatization of state-owned enterprises to launch Finnish Industry Investment.[39] FII channeled €40 million a year into domestic venture capital funds and individual enterprises. By then Sitra was investing €50 million a year in two hundred firms, focusing specifically on start-ups or recently established enterprises (Hyytinen and Väänänen 2003, 342).

---

37. Author interview with former owner, electronics firm (20 November 2006, Finland).
38. Author interview with director, venture capital firm (22 November 2006, Finland).
39. Author interview with director, Finnish Industry Investment (23 November 2006, Finland).

Collectively, these new initiatives transformed the Finnish financial system. Early stage venture capital investment, directed at new growth-oriented enterprises, swelled from €9.5 million (0.009% of GDP) in 1991 to €135.4 million (0.103% of GDP) by 2000, placing Finland first in the European Union in early stage venture capital investment as a share of GDP (Eurostat 2011). By then, the Finnish venture capital industry was growing so rapidly that Sitra systematically exited its biotechnology, information technology, and management buyout funds.[40] Its management teams eventually colonized private-sector venture capital funds.[41] Finland's largest and most successful funds such as Eqvitec, BioFund, and Fenno were spun off from Sitra, while Capman and 3i are staffed by Sitra veterans.

As with research, public-sector interventions are particularly striking in their capacity to mobilize private-sector investment. Like the innovation policies I have described, policymakers relied on neo-corporatist networks to build consensus, commit resources, and coordinate investments. Sitra, SFK, and FII each cofunded investment by private-sector venture capital firms and pension funds. More important, Sitra literally "organized" the venture capital industry, founding the Finnish Venture Capital Association in 1990. In the words of a former chairman, "We created awareness and a lobbying organization. . . . In Finland, the governmental authorities, banks, and pension funds had no concept of what venture capital was." More specifically, the Finnish Venture Capital Association lobbied the Ministry of Trade and Industry to relax restrictions on institutional investors such as pension funds. It also worked with the ministry to encourage investors to increase their allocation to unlisted equity.[42]

Together with the Science and Technology Policy Council, negotiations mobilized public- and private-sector resources. New financial stakeholders, including insurance funds and pension funds, played a disproportionately important role in the development of the Finnish venture capital industry. For example, pension funds and insurance companies were transformed from minor players in private equity markets, representing less than a quarter of funds raised between 1991 and 1994, into the largest single group of investors, accounting for over half of funds raised between 1995 and 2001 (Hyytinen and Pajarinen 2003a, 39). Finland's ability to stimulate voluntary pension fund investment represents a sharp contrast to Ireland (see chapter 5). By the end of the decade, only Sweden, which also engaged industry-labor managed pension funds, was more successful in this area (see chapter 6).

---

40. Author interview with director, venture capital firm (22 November 2006, Finland).
41. Author interview with director, venture capital firm (22 November 2005, Finland).
42. Author interview with director, venture capital fund (22 November 2006, Finland).

This is not to suggest that venture capital growth in Finland was unproblematic. The same neo-corporatist institutions, such as the Science and Technology Policy Council, that mobilized support for R & D focused attention on technological innovation. For example, virtually every recipient of Sitra venture capital funding received a Tekes grant to support technological innovation (Hyytinen and Väänänen 2003, 342). Unfortunately, technological novelty did not ensure commercial success. The venture capital boom of the 1990s masked considerable variation in quality (Hyytinen and Pajarinen 2003a), and investors were heavily affected by the dot-com crash. Fund-raising plummeted from €655 million in 1999 to €206 million by 2003 (FVCA 2004, 29).

At the same time, developments since the dot-com crash suggest that creative corporatist institutions have played a stabilizing role. Investments in early stage capital were considerably more stable than fund-raising activity, and the decline in Finnish venture capital fund-raising was less precipitous than in liberal countries such as Britain or Ireland (Eurostat 2011). At €380 million or 0.3 percent of GDP by 2000, Tekes's budget, which is now directed at small and medium-sized enterprises (to avoid violating EU rules), exceeded business-angel financing and rivaled the €500 million venture capital industry at its peak (Maula and Murray 2003, 22). Meanwhile, Sitra has adapted its operations to address deficits in marketing, management, and other soft skills. The foundation has launched a matching system to link entrepreneurs to more experienced business-angel investment and introduced a mentoring service to assist with business planning and venture capital applications (Teubal and Luukkonen 2006, 12). Unfortunately, labor market innovation has been even more limited.

Labor Markets: Technology as an Alternative to Training

Creative corporatism was least pronounced in labor markets, where coordination between industry and labor in the act of production was always limited. Stakeholders belatedly embraced collective wage bargaining, and even then they focused on peak-level negotiations over wages and social benefits rather than local-level collaboration in production. In contrast to Denmark, Finland did not fully institutionalize shop-floor cooperation until the 1980s (Kasvio 1994, 63). As a result, policymakers struggled to engage stakeholders, particularly firms, in training and continuing education. Finland did not adopt Danish-style "flexicurity" (see chapter 4) because firms did not value the collective investment in training that underpinned labor market liberalization and social-benefit restructuring. To the extent that stakeholders invested in human capital, it reflected bipartite state-industry cooperation in university education. Labor market bargaining, by contrast, advanced innovation policy as an alternative to more fundamental labor market reform.

Like the bank-based financial system and traditional industrial policies, conservative labor market bargains were pressured by the economic crisis of the early 1990s. As the economy soured, unemployment and social payments soared. An incoming center-right government sought to retrench public spending, reduce social benefits, and increase labor market flexibility, bringing it into conflict with the trade union movement. Meanwhile, Finnish employers sought to scale back collective wage bargaining in order to achieve greater flexibility in wage setting and workplace organization (Fellman 2008, 202).

However, unilateral liberalization proved problematic. Even vulnerable trade unions were able to oppose policymakers by threatening industrial action. Meanwhile, liberal and cost-competitive measures did not address industrial concerns. Wage restraint did not necessarily facilitate innovation. Market-enhancing social-benefit reforms eased fiscal pressures, but they did not ensure diversification. Labor market exit from declining industries such as construction or textiles did not automatically facilitate entry into unrelated industries such as telecommunication equipment. As a result, stakeholders devoted increasing attention to human capital formation throughout the 1990s. Policymakers expanded university and polytechnic enrollment over the course of the decade (Koski et al. 2006, 61–62). The return to centralized collective wage bargaining included a new initiative on adult retraining, introducing training guarantees for the long-term unemployed during the late 1990s and ultimately expanding coverage to fund vocational training for current employees (Lehtonen et al. 2001, 111). Active labor market expenditures as a percentage of GDP increased steadily over the course of the 1990s, even after unemployment stabilized (European Commission 1999, 74).

While policymakers thus attempted to implement international best practice in this area, investments were limited, both relative to Finnish innovation policy and to labor market policy in other countries such as Denmark. For example, in 2001 Finland devoted only 0.8 percent of GDP to active labor market measures, as opposed to 1.9 percent of GDP in Denmark (OECD 2009). The discrepancy is particularly striking since unemployment was twice as high in Finland (9.1%) as in Denmark (4.5%).[43] While Danish active labor market expenditure as a share of GDP fell with the national unemployment rate, Finland continued to spend a third less than Denmark on active labor market measures as a share of GDP as recently as 2007 (OECD 2009). Furthermore, unlike Denmark, Finnish active labor market schemes privileged wage subsidies and employment creation rather

---

43. While the increase in legally binding passive labor market measures such as unemployment insurance could have reduced Finnish active labor market expenditure, this does not explain why Denmark was able to significantly restructure those passive labor market measures during a period of elevated unemployment while Finland was not.

than training. For example, in 2002, the proportion of active labor market expenditure devoted to training (30%) was nearly half that of Denmark (54%), and the share of active labor market expenditure devoted to wage subsidies (16%) and job creation (14%) was three times higher (OECD 2004).

Organizational innovation remained limited as well. For example, the 1996 National Workplace Development Program was launched later in Finland than it was in its Nordic neighbors, resources were more modest, and cooperation was slower to develop (Alasoini 1999). Academics noticed a discrepancy between the careful attention to R & D and the comparative neglect of continuing education. One economist remarked, "I recently [researched] what we know about the economic effects of company-provided training, and I could not refer to even one Finnish study, because there are none."[44]

Limited investment reflected limited stakeholder cooperation and active distrust in this domain. Employer representatives expressed skepticism that state intervention or labor collaboration could yield significant benefits. For example, they dismissed Danish-style active labor market measures outright as expensive and inefficient, expressing doubt that training could furnish relevant resources to Finnish industry. In the words of one representative, "[Active labor market measures] are mainly concerning the low-productivity side of the economy. And if you think of the R & D in the Finnish economy, it represents the high-end of the economy.... From one euro you get more through research and development."[45] Even trade unions were relatively passive in pushing retraining as a policy priority, in part because they lacked the internal competence to advance these issues (Alasoini 2000, 15). Stakeholders' reluctance to invest in training is striking because it contradicts their enthusiasm for collective investment in R & D.

This is not to suggest that stakeholders neglected human capital formation altogether. On the contrary, some industry representatives claimed that skill acquisition was as important as R & D during the 1980s. One engineering chairman and former participant noted, "It was always a question of having enough human resources.... Of course, we were complaining about lack of capital, but it wasn't that. It was a lack of human resources."[46] To this end, policymakers nearly doubled university enrollment between 1993 and 1998 (Hyytinen et al. 2006, 60).[47] They also introduced conversation courses to target unemployed or un-

---

44. Author interview with director, Research Institute of the Finnish Economy (26 October 2005, Finland).

45. Author interview with economist, Technology Industries of Finland (18 October 2005, Finland).

46. Author interview with former executive officer, engineering firm (31 October 2005, Finland).

47. Author interview with planning officer, Science and Technology Policy Council (14 October 2005, Finland).

dereducated engineers.[48] Human capital investment, however, revolved around existing patterns of cooperation, most notably the highly centralized patterns of cooperation between state and firms that governed skill acquisition in previous decades (Kasvio 1994, 60). For example, educational investment was guided at the peak level by the Science and Technology Policy Council and negotiated with firms at the local level.[49] With fixed intake for each profession, university and polytechnic output could be adapted in consultation with industry.[50] This enabled stakeholders to tailor education to industry needs, much like they did with innovation policy. The emphasis on science and engineering, in which Finland ranked second only to South Korea in the number of engineers (OECD 2003b), reflected this link between innovation policy and education and an emphasis on technological innovation in particular.

These bipartite bargains supported massive investments in human capital. By the end of the decade, Finland led the European Union in tertiary enrollment, the number of researchers, and related measures, effectively leapfrogging European peers from Britain to Germany (European Commission 2006; Eurostat 2011). This expansion of skilled labor permitted expansion in emerging areas such as telecommunication equipment, even within a small economy of only five million people. At the same time, the emphasis on higher education as opposed to training inhibited adjustment in other respects. Finnish unemployment remained elevated, only falling below 8 percent between 2007 and 2008 (Eurostat 2011). This reflects not only a limited commitment to continuing education and organizational innovation but also the inability to successfully link training to market-based reforms. Finland has conspicuously opted not to pursue Danish-style flexicurity, whether defined in terms of social-benefit restructuring or employment protection reform.[51] Indeed, it has in large measure avoided such reforms by privileging new innovation policies and technologically driven adjustment. To the extent that industry and labor have struck neo-corporatist deals, they have privileged wage restraint in exchange for limited social-benefit restructuring or investment in training. This has had important and adverse consequences for the Finnish labor market and corporate strategy.

---

48. Author interview with former director, Finnish Funding Agency for Technology and Innovation (8 November 2005, Finland).

49. Author interview with officer, Science and Technology Policy Council (14 October 2005, Finland).

50. Author interview with director, Finnish Association of Engineers (2 October 2005, Finland).

51. Author interviews with economist, Technology Industries of Finland (18 October 2005, Finland); director, Technology Industries of Finland, (18 October 2005, Finland); and director, Finnish Forestry Industries Federation (11 October 2005, Finland).

Consequences: Creative Corporatism and Rapid Restructuring

Finland's distinctive pattern of creative corporatist adjustment had very different implications for economic adjustment than the conservative bargains that characterized the 1970s. Research funding enabled firms to enter rapidly evolving new industries such as mobile communications during the 1980s. Investments in risk capital, human capital, and research also enabled firms such as Nokia to rapidly scale their operations during the 1990s. The share of high-tech manufacturing employment more than doubled from 1.2 percent to 2.6 percent between 1990 and 2000, while the share of high-tech manufactured exports tripled from 8.7 percent to 26.8 percent (OECD 2011). While the high-tech manufactured exports plummeted after 2000 as firms outsourced their manufacturing operations, creative corporatist bargains enabled Nokia and other enterprises to diversify their activities, shifting from hardware to software and services.

1980–1990: Experimentation

One the most striking puzzles associated with high-tech competition is the country's capacity to enter expensive capital-intensive markets such as telecommunication equipment, where it had traditionally occupied a marginal role. Creative corporatist bargains played a central role in furnishing risk capital, human capital, and knowledge. In fact, the Finnish telecommunications industry can be traced back to private-public cooperation during the 1960s, as the Finnish army ordered radiophone prototypes from domestic electronics firms (Steinbock 2000). This public order stimulated radiotelephone production, albeit long after it had begun in other countries, including Denmark, Germany, Sweden, and the United States. Meanwhile, the army's own research laboratory emerged as one of Finland's leading radiotelephone producers alongside Nokia. In the 1970s, the post and telecommunication operator pushed the state-owned company Televa into telephone switches and network equipment (Palmberg 2002). As noted, Televa suffered persistent budgetary overruns and failed to achieve profitability. Yet these failed policies created an opportunity for Nokia. The firm collaborated with Televa in switchboard construction as early as 1978, acquired Televa's mobile phone and network equipment divisions in 1981, and launched its first digital telephone exchange shortly afterward (Lovio 1993, 197).

Creative corporatist bargains played an integral role in supporting experimentation in telecommunication equipment during the 1980s, even following Televa's privatization and the post and telephone operator's declining influence within an increasing international market. Tekes launched new projects in electronics and information technology, some aimed specifically at the emerging Groupe Special Mobile, or GSM, standard. One former executive responsible for mobile devices noted, "[Tekes] saw the opportunities over digital mobile communications. So Tekes started public programs and gave risk money, public support, for research and development.... Tekes is always important."[52] Tekes funded expensive and uncertain research in GSM technologies when Nokia was moving into completely unrelated industries such as televisions during the 1980s. These peripheral experiments proved vital. In the words of one executive responsible for mobile phones, "It was a strength of Nokia in the mid-1980s that Nokia was active in telecoms, computers and so on.... It was involved in such a wide range of high-tech industries, and that gave it in a chance to see in which sector the opportunities were best."[53]

Finnish institutions thus bankrolled a range of new technologies from digital exchanges to supporting software. For example, Tekes linked Nokia and the Public Technical Research Center, Valtion Teknillinen Tutkimuskeskus, in a collaborative project that created a foundation for Nokia's GSM technology.[54] Perhaps even more important, such projects enabled Nokia to identify and recruit talent from public institutes and private-sector firms.[55] One executive noted, "That's the reason why I started to work with Nokia in the end.... I was participating in the GSM standards competition, and I was subcontracted by Nokia. We didn't win that game, but we learned a lot. It created a network and that is the benefit."[56] Technology policies, in other words, not only helped firms develop novel products but also enabled them to cultivate and accumulate skilled labor.[57]

1990–2000: Expansion

Creative corporatism also facilitated Nokia's rapid expansion during the 1990s. As international markets grew, Nokia's challenge during the 1990s was no longer sustaining long-term research but managing its unprecedented expansion into international markets. Risk capital became less important at this time. Although Finnish innovation policies continued to protect long-term research, they did not make a significant contribution to Nokia's budget (Ali-Yrkkö 2010b, 26).

---

52. Author interview with former executive officer, electronics firm (17 October 2005, Finland).
53. Author interview with former executive officer, electronics firm (17 October 2005, Finland).
54. Author interview with former executive officer, electronics firm (17 October 2005, Finland).
55. Author interview with manager, electronics firm (25 October 2005, Finland) and executive officer, electronics firm (24 November, 2006, Finland).
56. Author interview with executive officer, electronics firm (24 November, 2006, Finland).
57. Author interview with manager, electronics firm (25 October 2005, Finland).

On the contrary, liberal accounts link Nokia's rapid growth to its ability to detach itself from traditional neo-corporatist institutions such as the universal bank and credit rationing (Steinbock 2000, 63). Nokia promoted financial liberalization during the 1980s and used its increasing independence from the universal bank to diversify into electronics. During the 1990s, it relied on domestic equity and foreign capital markets to finance rapid growth and successful internationalization (Tainio and Lilja 2003, 77–78). Creative corporatist bargaining, however, remained integral in Nokia's ability to manage challenges, and rapid expansion in particular, during the 1990s.

Human capital, for example, was central even as financial constraints faded. Financial liberalization, by itself, did not automatically create skilled labor. On the contrary, Nokia relied on neo-corporatist bargaining between state and industry to acquire relevant labor and expertise. The expansion of the Finnish university system was critical, particularly as it related to dedicated curricula and degree programs in engineering and information technology. Nokia's ability to rely on public education as a complement or alternative to in-house training permitted rapid expansion during the 1990s and explains why it retained such a large share of its activities within Finland. Indeed, Nokia representatives emphasize Finland's unusually responsive educational system as one of the most important aspects of the Finnish innovation system.[58]

Neo-corporatist bargaining also mobilized private-sector resources around Nokia. If public research support and early stage risk capital did not matter for Nokia during the 1990s, they mattered for the small and medium-sized enterprises that supplied it. Tekes was an important source of risk financing for small and medium-sized enterprises (Hyytinen and Väänänen 2003, 350; Hyytinen and Pajarinen 2003b, 228). Tekes thus oriented research in small and medium-sized enterprises toward the emerging telecommunication equipment cluster. Nokia's subcontractors, for example, routinely participated in Tekes programs on electronics and telecommunications (Ylä-Anttila and Palmberg 2005, 14). For Nokia representatives, these Tekes-brokered networks were essential to the firm's success, as they freed it from focusing on the independent construction of individual components, relying instead on flexible interfirm networks to scale production.[59]

Early stage risk capital markets were equally significant, particularly to the extent that they were linked with R & D. Risk capital markets channeled finance

---

58. Author interviews with former executive officer, electronics firm (17 October 2005, Finland); manager, electronics firm (25 October 2005, Finland); and executive officer, electronics firm (24 November, 2006, Finland).

59. Author interview with executive officer, electronics firm (24 November, 2006, Finland).

to firms that were too small to list on domestic stock exchanges or to mobilize foreign capital. Elcoteq, the sewing machine manufacturer that became one of Nokia's most prominent component suppliers during the 1990s, is a prominent example. FII channeled risk capital to Elcoteq to facilitate growth and internationalization. The firm became listed on the Helsinki Stock Exchange at the end of the decade, but it relied on a combination of private- and public-sector investment to finance its initial growth.[60] Neo-corporatist bargaining thus played an important supporting role in Nokia's growth during the late 1990s. Business analysts argue that Nokia's growth was predicated on the company's capacity to more competently manage a dense network to suppliers and subcontractors during the 1990s (Steinbock 2000). Nokia's ability to do so, however, was based in part on neo-corporatist networks, which generated a supporting cluster of over four thousands firms (Paija 2001, 4).

2000–2010: Adaptation

The breakneck growth of the 1990s ended quite abruptly with the dot-com crash at the end of the decade. Nokia and other firms responded to increasing cost pressure by relocating their manufacturing operations to lower-cost locations in eastern Europe and China. After the dot-com crash, less than half of Nokia's employees (Ali-Yrkkö 2010a, 3) and less than a fifth of its supplier network (Seppelä 2010, 42) was based in Finland. The share of high-tech exports in Finland shrank from 23.5 percent in 2000 to 17.3 percent by 2008 (Eurostat 2011). At the same time, employment remained remarkably stable despite factory closures and domestic layoffs. And, while high-tech manufactured exports dwindled to insignificance, Finnish software exports ($8 billion) rivaled those of much larger, more liberal countries such as the Netherlands ($10 billion), Britain ($15 billion), and the United States ($18 billion). Only Ireland, with $36 billion in exports (concentrated in multinational subsidiaries) was more specialized in the export of software products and services in 2008 (Rönkkö, Peltonen, and Pärnänen 2011, 14–15).

This stability reflected Nokia and Finland's ability to use risk capital, skills, and research to create new products, activities, and industries. For example, managers consistently emphasize the role that networking, or the ability to identify new partners, plays in developing new product lines or activities.[61] One research director commented on the innovation system by noting, "We know very easily

---

60. Author interviews with executive officer, electronics firm (8 November 2005) and director, Finnish Industry Investment (23 November 2006).

61. Author interviews with former executive officer, electronics firm (17 October 2005, Finland); executive officer, engineering firm (25 October 2005, Finland); executive officer, software firm (3 November 2005, Finland); and director, electronics firm (10 November 2005, Finland).

where is the know-how, who are the right contractors, how to work together. Also we have been able to work with the different authorities. In the 1990s, we changed the safety codes. There was a member from the authorities, there were some customers, there were suppliers, and there were universities. It was a whole chain of innovation, and all actors from the chain were participating."[62]

Nokia relied on similar resources to diversify from hardware manufacturing into software development, as the share of value-added mobile handset goods plummeted (Ali-Yrkkö 2010a, 7). As recently as 2006, 60 percent of Nokia's research personnel were based in Finland (Ali-Yrkkö 2010b, 33).[63] Furthermore, this figure does not include the sizeable network of subcontractors developing software for Nokia. Nokia thus continues to rely on Finland to identify and develop new technologies. While commentators suggest that Nokia's attention is focused elsewhere because its ventures organization targeted foreign firms, Nokia's ability to acquire knowledge and skilled labor through publicly brokered educational networks and research partnerships suggests that such institutions may be less essential within Finland. Nokia representatives suggest that Nokia used publicly backed research consortia to identify and partner with Finnish suppliers in software.[64] And foreign investment in the information and communication technology sector reflects the strength of these ties. One observer noted, "Everybody knows everybody in this industry. . . . That is great if you have the access and not so great if you do not have the access. . . . This is what [foreign] companies have in mind. By buying the personnel, they get immediate access. Word of mouth is still very important."[65]

Meanwhile, Nokia's efforts to expand and diversity created opportunities for small and medium-sized enterprises. During the 1990s, manufacturing suppliers such as Elcoteq and Perlos used the company's rapid growth during the late 1990s to expand and diversify their operations. Elcoteq acquired an independent customer base and emerged as Europe's largest electronics manufacturing contractor by the end of the 1990s. Perlos, another component supplier, diversified from plastic telephone covers into health-care equipment and related businesses. Slower growth and increasing cost competition led both companies to reduce or even eliminate manufacturing activity in Finland, although they retained research operations there.[66]

---

62. Author interview with director, engineering firm (4 November 2005, Finland).
63. While the share of Finnish R & D employees dropped dramatically after 2007, this was related to Nokia's acquisition activity rather than domestic layoffs. Nokia continued to conduct over a third of its R & D in Finland (Ali-Yrkkö 2010b, 31).
64. Author interview with executive officer, electronics firm (24 November 2006, Finland).
65. Author interview with director, Invest in Finland (23 November 2006, Finland).
66. Author interviews with executive officer, electronics firm (8 November 2005) and director, electronics firm (10 November 2005).

Nokia's shift away from manufacturing has in turn supported subcontractors in software development and related services. In fact, software has emerged as one of the most rapidly growing areas in the Finnish economy since the dot-com bubble burst.[67] With an estimated 13,000 employees in 2006, the Finnish software product industry overtook the indigenous Irish software industry (11,545 employees) in employment (Expert Group on Future Skills Needs 2008, 24; Rönkkö et al. 2007, 13).[68] As noted, the industry's growth is particularly notable because it does not include employees at Nokia (Finland's largest software developer) or its suppliers.

In fact, many of these enterprises have thrived by collaborating with Nokia's largest competitors. For example, the award-winning game designer Rovio Mobile has achieved international success with Angry Birds, one of the most popular applications on Apple's iPhone (Ben-Aaron 2010). Nor is Rovio Mobile's relationship with Apple unique. Apple's iOS, *not* Nokia's Symbian, was the most popular mobile operating platform for software designers in 2010 (Rönkkö, Peltonen, and Pärnänen 2011, 38).[69] And while Rovio Mobile's popularity reflects accumulated expertise in mobile communications, Finland achieved similar successes in data communications (SSH Communications) and electronic payment (APE Payment). By 2009, seven of the top one hundred software firms in Europe were based in Finland (14).

Those new firms can draw on many of the same resources, including risk capital, skilled labor, and knowledge that supported Nokia's initial movement into telecommunication equipment. Indeed, innovation policies have played an even more central role in this area, as knowledge-intensive producers lack the physical equipment to collateralize debt financing (Toivonen 2000, 5). Interviews support this point, as software producers relied on a range of institutions to support experimentation. One CEO, whose firm was transitioning from hardware production to software, noted, "Data security is an interesting area where Tekes has been involved, and we have continued small participation in those programs. We couldn't do things very well without it. It's not only [the money], but we are connected to certain things in certain programs, we get certain good people. . . . We always had this portion of the business in the research area, and we can play in that area better when we are connected to Tekes funding."[70]

---

67. Author interview with director, Invest in Finland (23 November 2006, Finland).
68. This is so, although the Finnish software industry remains smaller when measured in terms of turnover and exports (Expert Group on Future Skills Needs 2008, 46; Rönkkö et al. 2007, 6).
69. This may explain why in 2010 less than 5% of Finnish firms expected Nokia's difficulties to decrease their revenues (Rönkkö, Peltonen, and Pärnänen 2011, 47).
70. Author interview with executive officer, software firm (3 November 2005, Finland).

Diversification is not limited to information technologies. Finland is actually more specialized in electromagnetic instruments than Denmark (Pedersen, Dahl, and Dalum 2006, 89), a traditional leader in this field. The Finnish biotechnology industry is even more impressive, if less prominent, because the country had no significant pharmaceutical firms and conducted virtually no pharmaceutical research before the 1980s (Beuzekom and Arundel 2006; Blankenfeld-Enkvist et al. 2004; Brännback et al. 2005). Restructuring is based in large measure on the creative corporatist institutions I have described. Sitra used its venture capital facilities to invest in biotechnology firms as early as the 1980s.[71] Tekes soon followed suit, with over half of firms in the industry receiving some form of Tekes-based financing (Hermans and Luukkonen 2002, 25). By the twenty-first century, Finnish support for the biotechnology industry had exceeded €100 million a year (European Commission 2007, 54) and Finland ranked third in the European Union in the share of public R & D funding (9%) devoted to biotechnology (101).

Creative corporatist bargaining in turn facilitated industrial restructuring. The number of biotechnology firms established in Finland increased dramatically, however, from 16 in 1983 to 134 by 2001 (Hermans and Luukkonen 2002, 2).[72] By then, Finland ranked second to Sweden in the European Union in the population-adjusted number of biotechnology firms (European Commission 2007, 84). It also ranked sixth in per capita biotechnology patent applications, exceeding liberal market economies such as Britain and Ireland (83). As a result, the Finnish biotechnology industry was ranked third in the European Union (17). By other measures, however, the Finnish biotechnology industry has struggled. Finland has not capitalized on its leadership in firm creation, publishing, or patenting, and the industry as a whole only ranks eighth in the European Union in employment and turnover (Beuzekom and Arundel 2006). The biotechnology industry thus not only confirms the transformative potential of Finnish creative corporatism but also exposes several important limitations.

Political Compromises and Economic Constraints

Relative to other high-tech leaders such as Britain, Ireland, and the United States, the Finnish economy proved much more resilient after the dot-com crash and the financial crisis of 2007–9. Finland's ability to diversify from hardware

---

71. Author interview with director, venture capital firm (22 November 2006, Finland).
72. Fifteen of these firms ceased operations, leaving 119 active biotechnology firms in 2001.

manufacturing to software development reduced its exposure to cost competition and stabilized employment throughout the 2000s. Despite high-profile factory closures and the widespread offshoring of manufacturing jobs (exacerbated by a strengthening euro), the share of employment in high-tech industry actually increased from 6.59 percent in 2001 to 6.67 percent in 2006 (Eurostat 2011).[73] In contrast to Britain, Ireland, and the United States, Finland was thus able to increase growth and employment between 2001 and 2006 without relying on nontradable services such as residential construction.

As a result, Finland proved less vulnerable to the devastating financial crisis that hit between 2007 and 2009. The 2007–9 financial crisis posed a much less severe threat to the Finnish financial system, despite a much steeper decline in global economic output. For example, bankruptcies were 45 percent lower in 2009 than they were in 1991 (Gylfason et al. 2010, 249). Finland's relatively healthy financial position was based on residential investment only declining by a minute 0.4 percent of GDP (Gylfason et al. 2010, 247). With a healthy financial sector and no particularly significant labor shedding in nontradable services, Finland entered and exited the crisis in a much healthier fiscal position than Ireland and other counties. Debt as a share of GDP was 48.4 percent, exceeding only Luxembourg among the original eurozone members (Eurostat 2011). In fact, Finland's position is so advantageous that the country made headlines for obstructing an EU-organized bailout of Portugal in 2011 (A. Moen 2011a).

At the same time, the financial crisis revealed significant risks. Like many small states, Finland's reliance on international exports rendered the economy more susceptible to the global downturn. Exports plummeted by 14.4 percent in 2009 (Gylfason et al. 2010, 247). The resulting 8.2 percent decline in GDP in 2009 was much sharper than in larger countries such as Germany (4.7%), the United Kingdom (4.9%), or the United States (2.6%). This economic contraction weighed on the labor market, ending a brief two-year spell in which unemployment fell below 8 percent. While the economy is expected to grow more rapidly than its British, German, or U.S. counterparts in 2010 and 2011, it will take several years to recoup the losses of 2009 (Eurostat 2011). The Finnish experience suggests that even internationally competitive countries are not fully immune to a global economic crisis.

In the Finnish case, the steep decline in exports was exacerbated by Nokia's struggles in the market for high-end mobile phones. Nokia's loss of leadership in this critical market segment (Parker 2011) caused the share of high-tech exports to plummet from 17.3 percent in 2008 to 13.9 percent in 2009 alone (Eurostat

---

73. By contrast, it fell from 7.64% to 6.34% in Ireland.

2011). Nokia's decision to abandon its own Symbian operating system for Microsoft Windows Phone 7 poses significant risks for Nokia and Finland. The switch to Windows-based phones undermined demand for Symbian phones, delayed the release of new handsets, and endangered thousands of jobs in software development. Officials have characterized the loss of 1,400 jobs as the most significant structural upheaval in the history of the Finnish high-tech sector and a significant threat to the Finnish economy as a whole (A. Moen 2011b).

The same movement into new high-tech industries that sustained Finnish growth over the past two decades has thus created formidable challenges. Finland's position in knowledge-intensive activities insulated the country from the cost competition that plagued Ireland and that country's subsequent reliance on nontradable services (see chapter 5). Knowledge-intensive competition, however, also rendered Finland more vulnerable to disruptive technological innovations. The convergence between competing and telephony transformed the terms of competition in telephony. Nokia faced larger competitors such as Google and Microsoft, which were willing to heavily subsidize their operating software, and disruptive new entrants such as Apple, whose user- and developer-friendly operating system greatly expanded the number of services available to individual consumers. Within four years of the introduction Apple's iPhone and Google's Android software platform, Nokia had conceded leadership in the market for smartphones (Parker 2011).

Although the source of Nokia's difficulties is complex, the firm's struggles illuminate several problems with the creative corporatist bargains that stakeholders have struck over the last three decades. First, the same tradition of engaging firms in large national-level research projects that enabled Finland to enter and rapidly scale capital-intensive industries simultaneously increases vulnerability to disruptive technological innovations and the risk of failure. I do not mean to suggest, as some analysts do, that Finland continues to privilege established firms and industries (Sabel and Saxenian 2008; Steinbock 2004). As noted, Finland invested heavily in telecommunications while Nokia was a minor player, and it has allocated significant resources to biotechnology despite the absence of any large enterprises in this space. Effective coordination at the national level, however, has yielded a strikingly concentrated economic and technology portfolio (Nikulainen and Pajarinen 2010, 87).

Additionally, peak-level deals have increased attention to innovation policy at the expense of other policy domains. For example, Finnish firms (and trade unions) have exhibited little interest in labor market reform, whether defined in terms of social-benefit restructuring or retraining. While Finland exceeds Denmark in public and private expenditure on R & D, it spends less on active labor market measures (Eurostat 2011). Indeed, during the 1990s the ratio of passive to active labor market expenditure was one of the highest in the European Union (European Commission 2004, 63, 98). Meanwhile, while reforms on codetermination and efforts to strengthen the position of the shop steward have encouraged collaboration at the firm level (Alasoini 2004; Lilja 1998), observers suggest that collaboration and teamwork remain limited in relation to other Nordic countries.[74] Finnish reliance on R & D has obvious adverse implications for the country's labor market performance and redistributive outcomes (Ornston and Rehn 2006, 96). It also limits input from employees who are most familiar with market developments and user demands (Lundvall 2009).

In fact, Finnish innovation policies have privileged formal scientific research over nontechnological innovation. The consensus-building institutions I have described have enabled Finland to increase R & D, but they have not led to comparable investments in management, marketing, or other soft skills. As noted, Finnish higher education generates more engineers than any country outside of South Korea (OECD 2003b). Collaboration among innovation policy actors has ensured that risk capital goes to technologically innovative firms. For example, virtually all of Sitra's venture capital recipients during the 1990s received R & D support from Tekes (Hyytinen and Väänänen 2003, 342). Partly as a result of these developments, Finnish support for emerging industries is heavily skewed toward R & D support rather than firm creation or commercialization (European Commission 2007, 63).[75] This emphasis on technological innovation is even more pronounced and more problematic because limited progress in the labor market has prevented firms from engaging the employees who are closest to end users.

As a result, Finland's formidable track record in technological innovation has not always generated employment or economic growth. Breakthrough innovations from Linux in software to the synthetic sugar Xylitol in the food processing industries have not generated significant profits. The discrepancy is most striking in biotechnology, in which impressive patenting activity masks low employment and profitability. Indeed, Finland's most successful biotechnology firms, including what one fund manager claimed was the most valuable privately held pharmaceutical company in the world, succeeded *overseas*, in closer proximity to foreign investors and under foreign management.[76] Indeed, participants criticize

---

74. Author interview with managing director, engineering subsidiaries in Denmark and Finland (14 February 2006, Denmark).

75. Only Belgium devoted a higher share of public biotechnology support to R & D.

76. Author interview with director, venture capital firm (23 November 2006, Finland).

the entire Finnish approach to biotechnology for focusing on research-intensive drug development instead of areas such as food processing and forestry, where firms and employees might have greater expertise.[77]

This emphasis on technological innovation also explains some of Nokia's recent difficulties. The firm, which boasts the largest R & D budget in the telecommunications industry (Orlowski 2011), has not struggled because of its lack of engineering prowess. On the contrary, revenue from its strong patent portfolio was one of the few bright spots in an otherwise dismal 2011 (Ben-Aaron and Pohjanpalo 2011). Rather, the firm has been criticized for its inattention to design (Bilton 2011). Its weak user interface and failure to meet consumer demands more generally in turn reflect notoriously poor relations with mobile phone operators in the largest and most sophisticated consumer market in the world and its failure to attract the same sort of cadre of committed developers that surround Apple and Google (Boutin 2010). Nokia proved very effective at leveraging domestic research networks to construct Symbian, in competition with far larger rivals such as Apple, Google, and Microsoft. The firm, however, has not exhibited comparable skill in its relations with foreign customers, mobile phone operators, and software developers. Indeed, it did not establish an R & D outpost in Silicon Valley until 2006 (Sabel and Saxenian 2008, 80).

If Nokia and, by extension, Finland have exhibited significant vulnerability, however, there is little evidence that these challenges will provoke convergence on a liberal economic model. Finland has responded to new challenges by adapting rather than dismantling creative corporatist bargains. For example, policymakers have devoted even greater attention to small and medium-sized enterprises, as Tekes has increased funding for early stage enterprises in 2008 to address the gap in early stage financing that emerged after the dot-com crash (Ben-Aaron 2010). Deteriorating performance at Nokia may provide an additional stimulus to entrepreneurship, as the firm releases thousands of experienced and trained software developers. Analysts have documented similar developments in excellent regional studies of Varkaus, Finland, (Lilja, Laurila, and Lovio 2011) and Aalborg, Denmark, (Stoerring and Dalum 2007) as layoffs stimulated firm creation and industrial diversification. This may be one reason why more Finnish software firms (35.1%) viewed Nokia's difficulties as a positive development for the Finnish software industry rather than a danger (26.4%) (Rönkkö, Peltonen, and Pärnänen 2011). In fact, Nokia appears to be actively contributing to this process by complementing traditional severance pay with a ventures fund that subsidizes the creation of new firms (A. Moen 2011b).

---

77. Author interview with adviser, Finnish Funding Agency for Technology and Innovation (20 November 2005, Finland).

Stakeholders have adapted neo-corporatist institutions to support prospective entrepreneurs in other ways, particularly as it relates to both nontechnological and demand-side innovation (Breznitz, Ketokivi, and Rouvinen 2009, 72). For example, Sitra has shifted its role from venture capitalist to providing business services and other soft skills, most notably through a new angel-networking service (Teubal and Luukkonen 2006, 12), and Tekes has targeted demand-side innovation through the introduction of SHOKs, or Strategic Centers for Science, Technology and Innovation (Edquist, Luukkonen, and Sotarauta 2009, 31). Policymakers have been particularly keen in addressing perceived deficiencies in the internationalization of the Finnish innovation system (Aiginger, Okka, and Ylä-Anttila 2009, 103), most prominently through the introduction of a peak-level "re-branding" committee. The initiative not only aspires to generate publicity about the importance of marketing but also strives to attract more international business to Finland (Rantanen and Raeste 2010). Private-sector actors have organized similar initiatives using traditional neo-corporatist channels. For example, the Confederation of Finnish Industry has launched a program to facilitate internationalization among small and medium-sized suppliers.[78]

Finally, and perhaps most promisingly, increasing attention to nontechnological innovation has generated greater interest in labor market reform. Policymakers have targeted training and shop-floor cooperation as a vehicle for promoting innovation and restructuring, charging Tekes with implementing a workplace development program in 2008 (Lovio and Välikangas 2010). Meanwhile, the share of active labor market expenditure to total labor market expenditure has increased gradually, from 29 percent in 2001 to 37 percent in 2011 (Eurostat 2011). These labor market initiatives represent a positive development, not only through the incorporation of worker knowledge into enterprise innovation, but also because greater investment in training could facilitate the types of creative social-benefit tradeoffs that characterize Denmark.

At the same time, one is unlikely to observe the same dramatic leaps that characterized Finnish innovation policy. Finland is building industry-labor cooperation from scratch (or, at best, a relatively weak foundation), rather than converting established interfirm and private-public networks. As a result, debates over training have proceeded at a glacial pace over the past three decades and are still overshadowed by technology policy.[79] Indeed, it is revealing that workplace

---

78. Author interview with director, Technology Industries of Finland (9 November 2006).

79. For example, the increasing ratio of active to passive labor market expenditure between 2001 and 2008 had more to with the falling long-term unemployment rate than any policy reform, and Finland continued to spend 33% less than Denmark, despite a significantly higher unemployment rate (Eurostat 2011).

development programs have been assigned to an established actor in innovation policy, Tekes. While Tekes's new mandate promises to draw attention to continuing education, relying on established actors and networks may subordinate workplace cooperation to technological innovation and further concentrate an already centralized innovation system. The same is true for Tekes's increasingly important role in early stage risk capital markets.

To understand the circumstances under which countries might successfully implement sweeping creative corporatist reforms in the labor market, we now shift our attention from Finland to Denmark. Like Finland, Denmark also relied on creative corporatism to facilitate movement into new high-tech industries. In converting a very different tradition of coordination, based on industry-labor and local interfirm collaboration, however, Denmark targeted different inputs, investing less in research but dramatically expanding continuing education and early stage risk capital. These different investments led Denmark to assume a very different position in the high-tech market. Denmark struggled to compete in capital-intensive industries such as mobile handsets and in fact lost ground to Finland in this area. The country, however, simultaneously cultivated a much broader and more diversified array of activities in telecommunication equipment and beyond.

4

FROM SOCIAL PROTECTION TO SKILL FORMATION: DIVERSIFIED HIGH-TECH PRODUCTION IN DENMARK

Finland was not the only neo-corporatist country to enter new high-tech markets during the 1990s. Denmark defied its common characterization as a low- and medium-tech economy by entering a diverse array of industries including telecommunication equipment, software, and biotechnology. The Danish case is in some respects even more impressive than the Finnish one, because the country could not rely on large multinational corporations such as Nokia. Performance in each of the high-tech industries was based mainly on new growth-oriented enterprises established after 1975. The Danish and Finnish stories are similar, however, in that these firms relied on risk capital, new skills, and research to enter new industries. Those resources were, in turn, shaped by new neo-corporatist bargains.

Denmark, like Finland, experienced an acute economic crisis during the 1980s. Massive fiscal deficits provoked far-reaching reforms, including social-benefit restructuring and reductions in state aid. Unilateral liberalization proved politically costly, however, as societal actors, most notably trade unions, resisted reform. Stakeholder resistance encouraged policymakers to strike creative deals, converting conservative corporatist institutions to redistribute resources to new actors and industries. As in Finland, policymakers experimented with a wide range of initiatives. Creative corporatism was most pronounced in labor markets, however, where policymakers could convert a long history of peak- and local-level industry-labor cooperation to invest in training. Policymakers also engaged industry-labor managed social insurance funds in early stage risk capital markets. Innovation policies were more modest, as policymakers could not leverage a history of interfirm cooperation at the national level, although they did promote local coordination in research.

As in Finland, these creative corporatist bargains had very different implications for economic adjustment. Active labor market measures accelerated the redistribution of labor from declining industries such as shipbuilding into emerging information technologies. Meanwhile, early stage risk capital markets funded a new wave of start-ups in information technology and unrelated industries after the dot-com crash. Although the absence of national-level research consortia hindered competition in capital-intensive industries such as mobile telephony, retraining, early stage risk capital, and local interfirm collaboration supported experimentation in a much broader range of activities, including fixed-line communications, software, and biotechnology. As a result, the Danish economy has proven surprisingly resilient to technological and economic shocks.

The Puzzle: Denmark as a Diversified High-Tech Producer

Like Finland, Denmark relied on low- and medium-technology industries throughout most of the postwar period. Although Denmark enjoyed a modest position in high-tech niches such as radios and pharmaceuticals, growth revolved in large measure around agriculture, agricultural equipment, food processing, and textiles (Porter 1990, 149–50). Denmark's relatively low- and medium-technology profile, however, rendered producers vulnerable to new low-cost competitors as early as the 1960s (Mjøset 1992, 162; Porter 1990, 567–68). Policymakers successfully compensated vulnerable actors by increasing state aid and introducing new social benefits, but new measures exacerbated the problem by increasing nonwage costs and crowding out industrial investment. As a result, outside observers characterized Denmark as "a small state in big trouble" (Schwartz 1994).

By the turn of the century, however, the same authors categorized Denmark as an economic "miracle" (Schwartz 2001). Denmark enjoyed slow but steady growth while its continental peers stagnated. Per capita GDP surpassed that of France, Germany, and Italy and exceeded successful liberal economies like the United Kingdom. Employment growth was even more impressive, as unemployment fell from 9 percent in 1989 to 5 percent by the end of the 1990s and 3.3 percent by 2008 (Eurostat 2011). Analysts hailed Denmark as a model economy, emphasizing its economic competitiveness (World Economic Forum 2012), dynamic labor market (Auer 2000), innovative firms (Lorenz and Valeyre 2005), and flexible industrial structure (Campbell and Pedersen 2007).

To date, most literature has focused on Denmark's ability to modernize traditional low- and medium-technology niches such as pork, pumps, heating and cooling equipment, and machine tools (Edquist and Lundvall 1993; Kristensen 1999). Such developments played an important role in Denmark's economic recovery. Denmark's remarkable economic performance, however, also reflected surprising competence in high-tech industries such as telecommunication equipment, software, and biotechnology. Here, Denmark not only defended established positions in high-end audio equipment (Bang and Olufsen), hearing aids (Radiometer), and insulin (Novo Nordisk) but also entered fundamentally new industries such as cordless telephony (RTX), enterprise software (Navision), and biotechnology (Neurosearch).

These examples reflect a more profound, if largely neglected, transformation as the Danish share of high-tech manufactured exports increased by 81 percent between 1985 and 2000, outpacing traditional high-tech leaders such as the United States (25%) and Japan (19%) (OECD 2011). While the share of high-tech exports shrank with the widespread outsourcing of manufacturing activity, from 13.9 percent in 2001 to 11.71 percent by 2008, Denmark continues to occupy a formidable position in high-tech markets. As Europe's leading producer of biotechnology patents on a per capita basis, Denmark filed over twice as many high-tech patents per million inhabitants (40.1) to the European Patent Office than Britain (18.9) or Ireland (17.7) in 2007 (Eurostat 2011). As a result of this knowledge-intensive activity, Denmark's share of employment in high-tech services (3.6%) rivaled that of Britain (3.65%). By 2009, Denmark ranked fourth in the European Union in high-tech services employment, trailing only Finland, Ireland, and Sweden (Eurostat 2011). This data, and the evidence in this chapter more generally, challenge Denmark's enduring classification as a high-end low-tech producer (Dalum, Fagerberg, and Jørgensen 1988; Edquist and Lundvall 1993; Kristensen 1999).

Furthermore, Denmark's achievement is particularly impressive because it revolved around new firms rather than established enterprises. Denmark did not rely on the radiotelephone producers of the 1960s to compete in analogue and digital wireless networks. Denmark's leading Copenhagen-based radiotelephone producer failed to grapple with the challenges of the 1970s and languished under foreign leadership throughout the 1980s and 1990s (Iversen 2005, 180). Telecommunications growth was instead based on a new generation of firms, most notably spin-offs from the maritime communications industry in northern Denmark (Dahl, Pedersen, and Dalum 2003, 13). These firms acquired a competitive position in analogue networks and launched the first GSM-compatible mobile handsets in the world at the beginning of the 1990s (14). Although the firms were acquired by foreign multinationals, production expanded relentlessly during the

1990s. Aalborg was transformed from a sleepy regional capital and economic backwater into a hotbed for telecommunications. By the 1990s, Denmark as a whole trailed only a handful of countries in mobile telephony (Pedersen, Dahl, and Dalum 2006, 90).

One such country was Finland. Finland's own northern outpost, Oulu, proved even more dynamic than Aalborg, while the country as a whole surpassed Denmark in mobile communications. If Finland leapfrogged Denmark in mobile communications, however, Denmark entered a much wider range of activities. In wireless communications, Aalborg-based firms acquired a competitive position in a range of devices, including optical communications and cordless telephony and standards such as TD-SCDMA and Bluetooth (Palmberg and Bohlin 2006). Developments outside of Aalborg revealed even greater diversity. Copenhagen-based firms occupied a more competitive position in a range of alternative telecommunication technologies, including radio frequency identification, routers, semiconductors, and fiber optics (Pedersen, Dahl, and Dalum 2006, 96). While each of these initiatives remained modest in scope, Denmark's ability to cultivate such a broad range of internationally competitive companies speaks to the dynamism and diversity of its high-tech industry.

Indeed, Danish firms are competing in a wider range of high-tech industries outside of telecommunications, such as pharmaceuticals and software. The pharmaceutical industry not only reflects century-old niches such as insulin (Novo Nordisk) and enzymes (Novozymes) but also rapid movement into new areas, particularly biotechnology. Denmark's first and most prominent biotechnology firm, Neurosearch, was established in 1989. The industry as a whole now consistently leads the European Union, and Europe more generally, in per capita adjusted biotechnology patent applications (Eurostat 2011). And, while the biotechnology industry is not mature enough to significantly impact national export and employment statistics, the Danish biotechnology industry is the largest in the European Union in population-adjusted measures of firm creation, employment, and sales (Beuzekom and Arundel 2006; Bloch 2004). Nor is restructuring limited to biotechnology as Denmark hosts a heterogeneous cluster of software producers. Denmark's position in business software is particularly notable, with Navision dominating the market in enterprise resource planning during the 1990s and 2000s. Navision's acquisition by Microsoft has spawned a wave of greenfield investment and domestic start-ups that aspire to capitalize on their connections with Microsoft's new development center for business software.[1]

---

1. Author interview with manager, Copenhagen Capacity (9 November 2006, Denmark).

As with Finland, the literature on comparative political economy sheds little light on these developments. Denmark is a small state, with a small and medium-sized industrial structure, and it should operate at a disadvantage in high-tech markets (Kristensen and Levinsen 1983). Some scholars suggest that small states can rely on established niches or large multinationals (Dalum 1992). Yet Danish growth was in many cases based on spin-offs, such as RTX, or start-ups, such as Neurosearch, rather than large incumbent firms, such as Great Northern or Novo Nordisk. Furthermore, these firms have moved into fundamentally new activities such as cordless telephony, biotechnology, or enterprise software. Other scholars emphasize luck, and the Nordic Mobile Telephone standard in particular (Dahl, Pedersen, and Dalum 2003; Pedersen, Dahl, and Dalum 2006), but this does not explain analogous developments in fixed-line communications, enterprise software, biotechnology, or other unrelated markets.

As a result, many scholars emphasize liberalization or movement away from traditional neo-corporatist bargaining. Indeed, we observe an array of new pro-market reforms during the 1980s and 1990s. In labor markets, policymakers shortened social benefits, tightened eligibility, and introduced new requirements (Madsen 2003, 76). The decentralization of collective bargaining limited peak-level union influence over wage determination and related public policies (Iversen 1996). In industrial policy, policymakers sharply reduced expenditure on state aid, deliberately excluding neo-corporatist stakeholders from the decision-making process (Morris 2005, 92–95). Even financial markets, while never particularly neo-corporatist (see chapter 2), witnessed increasing dependency on decentralized equity financing and foreign direct investment (Hyytinen and Pajarinen 2003a, 27). Collectively, these measures subjected capital and labor to greater levels of market competition and facilitated the rapid redistribution of resources from troubled firms to new industries. In other words, these reforms created space for new actors to enter emerging industries, including high-tech markets such as biotechnology, software, and telecommunications.

Yet this liberal narrative remains problematic. Most obviously, it presents an incomplete picture of institutional change. Although Denmark benefited from market-enhancing social-benefit and industrial-policy reforms, we observe increasing cooperation in these same domains. The social partners dramatically expanded cooperation in training at the same time that they restructured traditional social benefits (Martin 2005, 55). Policymakers engaged banks and pension funds in a bid to increase venture capital investment (Gergils 2006, 61). While initiatives were more modest in innovation policy, the government subsidized local interfirm networks (Morris 2005, 97–98) and introduced new programs designed to promote industry-university collaboration in research (Gergils 2006, 79). Furthermore, these neo-corporatist bargains had very different implications for economic adjustment, accelerating rather than inhibiting restructuring. Denmark developed an unprecedented position in high-tech markets, facilitated in part by collective investments in disruptive new inputs such as risk and human capital. Finally, the liberal narrative does not explain cross-national variation, as Denmark ceded leadership to Finland in telecommunication equipment yet surpassed Ireland in knowledge-intensive high-tech industries. As in Finland, successful high-tech competition can be traced back to an acute economic crisis and the reform of traditional conservative corporatist institutions.

The Argument: Recasting Industry-Labor Cooperation

The Danish economy had suffered declining economic performance since the 1960s, as low-, medium-, and high-tech producers alike struggled to grapple with new cost-competitive rivals (Mjøset 1992, 162). Unable to rely on the Soviet Union to insulate producers from the oil crisis of the mid-1970s, Denmark relied on traditional conservative corporatist measures such as state aid, unemployment insurance, and early retirement to manage adjustment. Such strategies compensated vulnerable stakeholders but did little to facilitate restructuring. Instead, they generated dangerous imbalances within the Danish economy. By 1982, government deficits had reached 9.2 percent of GDP (Schwartz 1994, 533–34). Interest rates approached 20 percent as policymakers struggled to maintain confidence in the currency, choking off credit to domestic enterprises. An economist within the Ministry of Finance described a state of emergency in which Denmark could no longer afford to meet its international obligations. As in Finland, national sovereignty was threatened, not necessarily by a larger, hostile neighbor such as the Soviet Union, but rather by the prospect of an International Monetary Fund bailout. The economic crisis discredited the Social Democrat party that had dominated Danish politics since World War II and, by extension, the conservative corporatist institutions that they had helped construct. When a parliamentary committee chairman proposed defaulting on Denmark's debt to avoid deeper cuts in spending, the minister of finance resigned. The minority Social Democrat government collapsed two months later.[2]

The Conservative People's Party–led coalition government that replaced it was committed to market-based reform, and not only for ideological reasons. The dramatic expansion of the Danish public sector threatened the country's

---

economic performance and its national sovereignty. Indeed, the Social Democrat government's failure to address fiscal and trade imbalances directly contributed to its collapse in 1982. In fact, the Social Democrat party, and the institutions that they defended, were so thoroughly discredited that the Conservative-led coalition government enjoyed a formidable mandate. In the words of one official at the Ministry of Finance, "The incoming center-right government took over without an election and they could do anything. There was support for any necessary policies because of the crisis."[3]

As a result, the incoming government adopted a radically different approach to economic governance, breaking with the social partners to cut spending and restructure labor market relations (Mjøset 1992, 337–38). One former official at the Ministry of Finance placed these developments in perspective by noting, "They started off with an enormous budget cut. Then they suspended the price clause in the collective bargaining system for two years, and it could only come back if both the trade unions and the employers accepted it. So they destroyed the system. This was the most dramatic period in Denmark."[4] In slashing fiscal expenditure, the government sharply reduced state aid and agricultural subsidies (Mjøset 1992, 451). The government simultaneously cut social expenditure, reducing unemployment, housing, and health benefits (451). Meanwhile, the implementation of a hard-currency regime reduced the scope for competitive devaluations (Fromlet 2004, 8). Policymakers thus dismantled the compensatory institutions, from social protections for labor to state aid for firms, that underpinned postwar Danish neo-corporatism.

Denmark, however, did not witness convergence on a liberal economic model, as societal actors fiercely opposed unilateral pro-market reform. Trade unions, not surprisingly, were the most vocal in their opposition. The same Ministry of Finance representative, commenting on the decision to suspend indexation, remarked, "When the prime minister presented this legislation in parliament in the morning, the prime minister couldn't enter the building. I was asked to write the speech ... but I couldn't enter. I met my permanent secretary, and we found a place where we could send it, by fax. At 11, he had his speech, and there were 100,000 people in the streets."[5] The government was forced to back down over several of its more ambitious proposals, so that retirement benefits were temporarily frozen rather than reduced. The largest strike since World War II paralyzed the economy in 1985, and industrial unrest continued into 1986 (Jochem 2003, 131).

---

3. Author interview with former economist, Ministry of Finance (21 November 2005, Denmark).
4. Author interview with former economist, Ministry of Finance (21 November 2005, Denmark).
5. Author interview with former economist, Ministry of Finance (21 November 2005, Denmark).

Nor were trade unions the only ones opposed to liberal reform. While more supportive of liberalization, Danish firms faced their own challenges. Firms struggled to compete in traditional markets and activities, and the Single European Act of 1986 and the expansion of the Common Market were perceived to place additional pressure on struggling Danish enterprises. Pro-market reform did not, by itself, address concerns about Danish industry, most notably the country's small and medium-sized industrial structure and relatively limited investment in capital equipment, new technologies, and research (Morris 2005, 89).[6]

Industry concerns, open trade union resistance, and political competition with the Social Democrats led the Conservative government to reconsider its initial reform program (Jochem 2003, 136). Instead of unilateral liberalization, the government sought to strike creative deals with industry and with labor, converting traditional conservative corporatist institutions so that they could perform new functions. As in Finland, the Conservative government experimented with a wide range of initiatives, drawing on international best practice in industrial and social policy. For example, the same government that reduced expenditure on state aid launched the massive national-level Technology Development Program (TDP) to promote investment and innovation (Jamison 1991). The government also enlisted banks, pension funds, and other institutional investors to invest in early stage risk capital markets (Baygan 2003, 15). Finally, and most remarkably for a center-right administration, the government also struck some innovative bargains in the labor market. Denmark's fiscal crisis (and the administration's conservative orientation) committed the government to reduce social benefits. At the same time, however, policymakers sought to minimize labor unrest by subsidizing firm investments in worker training (Jochem 2003, 134).

Of course, not all of these creative corporatist initiatives were equally successful. In contrast to Finland's technology programs during the early 1980s, the Danish Technology Development Program was deeply unpopular. Danish firms had little history of collaborating with the government or one another at the national level, and as result even major beneficiaries exhibited little enthusiasm for the program. The most successful innovation policies were some of the most modest, such as a network-based initiative known as Strategy 92 that was designed to boost local innovation (Amin and Thomas 1996, 267). Creative corporatism was most pronounced in labor markets. Although training was never a centerpiece for the center-right coalition government, successful initiatives in this space would inspire a Social Democrat–led coalition government during the 1990s.

---

6. Author interview with former director, Danish Technological Institute (6 December 2005, United States).

As in Finland, this center-left coalition government deepened and broadened creative corporatist reforms during the 1990s. While Denmark did not experience a severe economic crisis as Finland did during the early 1990s, unemployment remained elevated at 9.6 percent in 1993. The political situation was also strikingly similar. The Social Democrat–led government that assumed power in 1993 was in a precarious position, requiring the support of the Moderate Liberal Party to establish a governing coalition. The Moderate Liberals in turn conditioned their participation on extending the market-based social-benefit reforms initiated under the previous government. Social Democrat politicians took these concerns seriously, as they faced the very real threat of a Liberal Party–led coalition government. Social Democrat dominance was by no means assured as the party had relied on an unrelated scandal to assume power in 1993.[7]

Meanwhile, the prospect of a Liberal-led government was particularly threatening, as it promised to adopt an even more aggressive position than its Conservative-led predecessor. One official summarized the position of the Social Democrats in stark terms, noting that "if [the Social Democrats] hadn't found a compromise, [the Liberal Party] would have entered government with the support of the [Moderate] Liberals, and the Danish model would not have survived. They would have destroyed the trade unions like Thatcher."[8] The Social Democrats thus reached a deal with the Moderate Liberals to restructure social benefits in exchange for greater investment in training and labor market services.

The government had a relatively easy time reaching a deal with organized labor, which was aware of the political situation and keen to avoid even deeper cuts to social benefits. More specifically, trade unions accepted reductions in social-benefit rates, duration, and eligibility in exchange for a more active training policy.[9] The government thus increased expenditure on education, extending training to the long-term unemployed in 1994 while limiting social-benefit eligibility to seven years and mandating participation in active labor market measures after four (Björkland 2000, 154). Social-benefit duration was reduced to five years by 1996 and four years by 2000 (Madsen 2003, 76), while new opportunities were created for educational and sabbatical leaves (Jochem 2003, 132). Such policies were particularly attractive for organized labor, not only as an alternative to Thatcherite reform but also because they played an active role in policy implementation.[10]

---

7. Author interview with former economist, Ministry of Finance (21 November 2005, Denmark).

8. Author interview with former economist, Ministry of Finance (21 November 2005, Denmark).

9. Author interviews with former director, Danish Employer's Confederation (15 November 2005, Denmark) and former economist, Ministry of Finance (21 November 2005, Denmark).

10. Author interviews with secretary, Danish Confederation of Trade Unions (17 November 2005, Denmark) and consultant, Danish Confederation of Trade Unions (18 November 2005, Denmark).

Meanwhile, employers embraced the measure because they had a long history of cooperating with trade unions in production at the shop-floor level (see chapter 2). Indeed, employers had relied on the Danish training system to retain skilled workers during the economic downturn of the 1980s (Kristensen and Zeitlin 2005, 74) and welcomed the emphasis on (state-subsidized) training (Martin 2005, 41). "Flexicurity" thus represented a politically and economically attractive way to promote restructuring. The center-right coalition government that replaced the Social Democrat–led administration protected these investments in training, while industry and labor agreed to deepen collaboration on their own in separate bipartite collective agreements (EIRO 2004).

Social policy was not the only area where the Social Democrat–led government experimented with creative corporatism. The administration drew on the success of Strategy 92 to replace remaining industrial policies with network-oriented industrial policies that underwrote local cooperation among small and medium-sized enterprises and broadening the scope to include universities by the end of the decade (Gergils 2006, 79). Policymakers were even more successful in financial markets, engaging social insurance funds in industrial restructuring during the early 1990s (Pedersen, Andersen, and Kjær 1992, 1129–31) and converting a public-sector fund, Vaekstfonden, to engage private-sector investors in early stage venture capital markets (Baygan 2003, 16–17).

These creative corporatist deals continue to structure policy, even after the center-left government lost power. The Liberal-led coalition government that followed protected popular investments in training. It also proposed to tackle perceived deficiencies by strengthening rather than dismantling neo-corporatist institutions. For example, the government increased funding for center contracts, technological incubators, and other forms of early stage risk capital (Gergils 2006, 79), launched the High Technology Fund, which was oriented toward emerging industries and activities (29–30), and sought to coordinate all initiatives within an encompassing peak-level Globalization Council (31). While the success of these new initiatives remains unclear, neo-corporatist networks continued to be used to facilitate investment in human capital, risk capital, and research. These initiatives have been most pronounced and most successful in labor markets, where policymakers could draw on a well-established pattern of industry-labor cooperation.

Labor Markets: From Social Protection to Skill Formation

Danish success in social-policy reform reflects a century-long tradition of cooperation between labor and industry from peak-level forums down to the shop floor. Policymakers actively exploited neo-corporatist networks, engaging peak-level actors within the tripartite Zeuthen Commission (Morris 2005, 256) and delegating implementation to local trade unions and employer associations (Martin 2005, 55). Collectively, these initiatives increased public- and private-sector investment in human capital, increasing university enrollment, boosting expenditure on active labor market policies, and placing Denmark first in the European Union in multiple measures of training and continuing education (Eurostat 2011).

Creative corporatist bargaining reflected a significant break from traditional compensatory deals. Employment protection was always limited in Denmark as a result of the 1899 September agreement, but the Conservative-led government of the 1980s went even further in dismantling traditional social protections. For example, the government adopted a hard-currency regime (Fromlet 2004, 8) and sharply reduced public spending.[11] In doing so, the government not only reduced the scope for public-sector job creation but also limited the generous unemployment-benefit system that had characterized postwar adjustment (Mjøset 1992, 451). Employers, emboldened by the new government, took advantage of the opportunity to decentralize collective wage bargaining (Björkland 2000, 158).

The subsequent Social Democrat–led government extended reforms, outsourcing public-sector positions and decentralizing the Danish vocational-training system (Campbell and Pedersen 2007, 319). The government was even more aggressive in social policy, limiting replacement rates, reducing benefit periods, and restricting eligibility. By 2001, unemployment benefits were limited to four years, with mandatory participation in a training and activation program after one year (Madsen 2003, 76). In contrast to Finland, the Danish government thus succeeded in significantly retrenching traditional social protections and dismantling conservative corporatist labor market institutions.

By other measures, however, neo-corporatist bargaining was more encompassing than ever. Firms relied on vocational-training networks to recruit, retain, and adapt skilled labor throughout the 1980s (Kristensen and Zeitlin 2005, 74). The Conservative-led government supported these efforts by increasing educational expenditure as early as the 1980s. Such efforts were not limited to postsecondary education but included adult education and vocational training as well (Jochem 2003, 134). Meanwhile, the decentralization of collective wage bargaining coincided with organizational centralization, as employer associations merged into a single employer association in 1991. Stakeholder consolidation not only provided a mechanism for steering and monitoring decentralized collective wage bargaining (Lubanski et al. 2001) but also provided a framework for expanding investment in training and education during the 1990s.

---

11. Author interview with former economist, Ministry of Finance (21 November 2005, Denmark).

One peak-level tripartite body, the Zeuthen Commission, had a decisive impact on Danish labor market bargaining. Formally organized by the Ministry of Finance, the 1992 commission engaged all relevant stakeholders, including employer and trade union representatives (Morris 2005, 256). Stakeholders proposed to limit unemployment-benefit duration in a context of rising unemployment and fiscal deficits. But this was not an example of negotiated liberalization or "competitive corporatism." On the contrary, the commission linked social-benefit reform to active labor market expenditure and greater collaboration in training. The 1992 commission thus formulated the link between social-benefit reform and training that underpinned post-1993 Social Democrat policy. In proposing to replace passive labor market measures with training, the commission created a focal point and consensus for subsequent bargaining. The Social Democrat–led government adopted the Zeuthen Commission's recommendations with minimal changes (280). Although it was never institutionalized like the Finnish Science and Technology Policy Council, the Zeuthen Commission performed a similar function in mobilizing a broad consensus for investments in human capital.

At the same time, policymakers could rely on local bodies to monitor commitments and coordinate investments. Danish trade unions and local producers had collaborated in training since the nineteenth century and developed a comparatively robust system of shop-floor representation decades earlier (Amin and Thomas 1996, 261). The Zeuthen Commission leveraged these local institutions. While the commission abolished the national market boards that governed labor market policy, it did so in a bid to promote regional and local cooperation in training (Morris 2005, 264). Local industry participation linked public investment to private-sector needs, with the result that jointly administered training proved more effective than comparable public-sector programs. For example, Danish employers proved more willing to utilize active labor market policies than their counterparts in liberal market economies (Martin 2005, 41).

Although analysts have focused on the shift from passive to active labor market policy (Madsen 2003; Martin 2005; Torfing 1999), neo-corporatist negotiations facilitated a broader increase in privately furnished training. For example, employers guaranteed employees two weeks of training as part of their collective wage agreements during the early 1990s (Kristensen and Zeitlin 2005, 74). Framework agreements between peak-level associations expanded training even further, in the context of full employment, during the 2000s. Though the government reduced spending on vocational training as unemployment decreased in the early 2000s, unions struck a bilateral agreement with employers to exchange wage restraint for greater access to training (EIRO 2004). This wage deal contrasts sharply with the situation in competitive corporatist countries such as Ireland where wage restraint was based on tax concessions. These collective agreements are significant because they demonstrate a broad-based societal consensus regarding the importance of training and their effective implementation by local-level organized actors. In fact, comparative studies suggest that Danish employers relied on active labor market recipients more extensively than their liberal peers (Martin 2005, 41), a point echoed by employers who identified workers, rather than their products or patent portfolio, as their greatest asset.[12]

Collectively, these tripartite and bipartite deals facilitated a massive increase in training and education. Active labor market expenditures increased from 1.1 percent of GDP in 1989 to 1.9 percent of GDP, making Denmark first in the OECD, by 2001. The increase is particularly dramatic as unemployment fell from 6.8 to 4.5 percent over that time frame. As recently as 2008, Denmark continued to lead the OECD in active labor market expenditure at 1.4 percent of GDP, despite an average unemployment rate of 3.3 percent (OECD 2009). Furthermore, active labor market expenditure was concentrated on training rather than on the public-employment schemes or job subsidies that characterized Finland and Ireland. For example, the share of active labor market expenditure devoted to training increased from 24 percent in 1990 to 54 percent by 2002. By contrast, the share of Finnish and Irish active labor market expenditure devoted to training was 30 percent and 13 percent, respectively, in 2002 (OECD 2004).

This shift was not limited to publicly sponsored active labor market programs. At 40.2 percent in 2007, the proportion of the Danish population participating in "lifelong learning" is the highest in Europe (Eurostat 2011). Furthermore, and in sharp contrast to other countries that rank highly on measures of lifelong learning, training is extended to noncore employees rather than established workers (Kristensen, Lotz, and Rocha 2011, 95). As a result, institutionalized cooperation among trade unions, employer associations, and state agencies in skill acquisition has had very different implications for economic adjustment, not only modernizing established industries, but also accelerating the redistribution of labor into emerging industries such as telecommunications. Policymakers adapted industry-labor cooperation to redistribute financial capital as well.

Financial Markets: From Social Insurance to Risk Capital

Denmark also witnessed significant cooperation in venture capital markets. While Finnish-style universal banks never assumed a prominent role in the Dan-

---

12. Author interviews with former executive officer, electronics firm (16 February 2006, Denmark); executive officer, engineering firm (20 March 2006, Denmark); and executive officer, electronics firm (24 March 2006, Denmark).

ish political economy, postwar labor market bargains permitted new forms of cooperation in venture capital. More specifically, pension funds that were established to moderate wage demands and increase worker security during the 1960s, 1970s, and 1980s were converted to invest in growth-oriented enterprises and to expand the supply of venture capital more generally. Consistent with the tradition of decentralized cooperation described in chapter 2, new initiatives privileged local implementation and focused on early rather than late-stage venture capital markets. Collectively, they propelled Denmark to the top of the European Union in the supply of early stage risk capital, surpassing traditional liberal leaders such as Britain (Vaekstfonden 2005, 7). Only Sweden, which was even more aggressive in mobilizing pension fund capital, exceeded Denmark in this area (see chapter 6).

Like the Danish financial system more generally, the Danish venture capital market was the initiative of individual entrepreneurs rather than state intervention. Private-sector entrepreneurs more or less "created" the industry in 1983, independent of any major public-sector initiative (Baygan 2003, 7). Neocorporatist bargaining, however, played an indirect role even at this early stage. Pension funds were reconceptualized as an instrument for promoting economic restructuring without violating EU restrictions on state aid (Pedersen, Andersen, and Kjær 1992, 1129–31). Supplementary pension funds, established during the early 1980s to induce wage restraint, thus emerged as important actors in Danish risk capital markets by the end of the decade (Rose and Mejer 2003, 337).

Pension fund activism was most closely associated with the "locomotive movement," merging small and medium-sized enterprises to generate economies of scale in mature low-tech industries such as food processing (Amin and Thomas 1996, 264; Pedersen, Andersen, and Kjær 1992, 1129–31). Yet pension funds supported early stage risk capital markets in other ways. Pension funds directly financed growth-oriented firms such as Dancall in the field of telecommunications, enabling it to experiment with expensive GSM technologies (Stoerring and Dalum 2007, 133). These investments in publicly listed companies also created exit opportunities for private-sector venture capital investors, particularly when coupled with a second-tier stock market for smaller enterprises (Baygan 2003, 17).[13]

The economic downturn of the late 1980s prompted even greater collaboration in risk capital. The weakly institutionalized venture capital industry was heavily affected by the crisis, with only five active firms by the end of the decade (Hyytinen and Pajarinen 2003a, 37). The Conservative-led government

---

13. Author interview with executive officer, Pension Fund (10 March 2006, Denmark).

responded by coupling pro-market reform with unprecedented intervention in early stage financial markets. More specifically, the government established the Danish Development Finance Corporation or DUF. DUF represented the first effort to institutionalize pension fund investments in Danish risk capital (Baygan 2003, 15). The Bank of Denmark contributed only 12 percent of the funding, attracting 44 percent from pension funds and an additional 44 percent from traditional financial intermediaries such as banks (16).

Although DUF was privatized in 1994, the Social Democrat–led coalition government continued to invest in venture capital through similar channels. Some measures involved unilateral intervention, such as the 1992 Business Development Fund, Vaekstfonden, which provided soft loans to high-tech start-ups. Other initiatives emphasized market signals, such as the 1994 Equity Guarantee Program, which covered 50 percent of an investor's losses from private-equity investments (Baygan 2003, 16). Institutional investors such as pension funds, however, retained a central role. Policymakers lifted the ceiling on unlisted investments to 10 percent by 1994 and 20 percent by 1998 (13). More important, they negotiated with pension fund companies behind closed doors.[14] As one former venture capital manager noted, "There's a lot of attention to what [the pension funds] are doing, and it's expected that they go into most venture funds, and some of them they do and some they don't, but they are extremely criticized if they don't. The government has been extremely pushy toward ATP [Arbejdsmarkedets Tillægspension] and LD [Lønmodtagernes Dyrtidsfond] to get them to invest in funds. Sometimes they've done it because they got their arm wrestled, but it is not legislating."[15] This combination of regulation and indirect support more than doubled early stage venture capital investments from €5.2 million (0.005% of GDP) in 1991 to €13.1 million (0.001% of GDP) by 1998 (Eurostat 2011).

Even more significant gains followed Vaekstfonden's 1998 conversion from a loan guarantor to an equity investor. For the first time, Vaekstfonden could invest its entire 200 billion crown capital base (rather than its revenue) in individual firms and venture capital funds (Baygan 2003, 16). Vaekstfonden support increased from 1 percent of venture capital investments in 2000 to approximately 6 percent by 2001 and 10 percent in 2002 (8). Vaekstfonden not only invested directly in individual firms but used a fund of funds to support venture capi-

---

14. Author interviews with professor, Copenhagen Business School (21 November 2005, Denmark) and executive officer, Pension Fund (10 March 2006, Denmark).

15. Author interview with executive officer, venture capital firm (7 November 2006, Denmark).

tal firms such as Northzone Ventures, SEED Capital, and Symbion Capital.[16] By 2002, the fund was directly or indirectly involved in one-third of the small and medium-sized enterprises that received venture capital funding (Andersson and Napier 2005, 77). In doing so, Vaekstfonden pressured pension fund managers to coinvest. Some pension fund managers resisted these efforts, but they were compelled to justify nonparticipation in Vaekstfonden-led investment efforts by launching their own independent venture capital funds.[17]

Meanwhile, the government complemented activity in formal venture capital markets with a range of initiatives designed to connect individual entrepreneurs, universities, private investors, and the public sector in the earliest financing stages. The 1 million crown innovation environment program of 1998 allowed private-sector centers to distribute public grants of 750,000 crowns (€100,000) to seed projects. The program was extended in 2001 by a Liberal-led government and the number of incubators was increased from six to eight (Baygan 2003, 16). The innovation environments were an effort to engage local-level stakeholders and link investment in early stage risk capital with Danish industrial policy.[18] Vaekstfonden has cosponsored local-level collaboration, using its fund of funds activity to attract pension funds and other private-sector venture capital firms to innovative environments.[19]

Collectively, this process of consensus building, commitment making, and coordination facilitated a dramatic expansion in Danish venture capital, particularly after 1998. By 2002, early stage venture capital investments reached €137.6 million, and Denmark ranked first in the share of GDP invested in early stage venture capital (Eurostat 2011). Although early stage venture capital investments subsequently declined, from 0.07 percent of GDP in 2002 to 0.05 percent by 2007, Denmark continues to rank third in the European Union in this category, trailing only Luxembourg and Sweden (Eurostat 2011). Interestingly, Denmark's rapid gains in this area are not merely a product of financial liberalization, given that Denmark trails countries such as Britain and Ireland in measures of stock market capitalization and financial liberalization (Hyytinen and Pajarinen 2003a, 27; Hyytinen, Kuosa, and Takalo 2003, 73). On the contrary, they followed progressively more extensive and institutionalized efforts to engage core stakeholders, most notably pension funds. These activities were complemented by similar, if more modest, innovation policies.

---

16. Author interviews with executive officer, venture capital firm (7 November 2006, Denmark); director, venture capital firm (10 November 2006, Denmark); and director, venture capital fund (16 November 2006, Denmark).

17. Author interview with executive officer, venture capital firm (7 November 2006, Denmark).

18. Author interview with director, venture capital fund (16 November 2006, Denmark).

19. Author interviews with executive officer, venture capital firm (7 November 2006, Denmark) and director, venture capital fund (16 November 2006, Denmark).

Research and Development: From Technological Modernization to Local Innovation

Creative corporatism was least pronounced in innovation policy because stakeholders could not exploit the same pattern of cooperation that existed in the Danish labor market.[20] As described in chapter 2, interfirm and labor-industry cooperation had originally emerged as a bulwark against centralized corporate and political control. Reluctant to cooperate outside of their region or sector, firms largely resisted ambitious technology policies during the 1980s, and efforts to replicate Finnish-style strategies during the mid-2000s generated considerable skepticism. At the same time, innovation policies succeeded on a more modest scale by leveraging local networks, personal connections, or established intermediaries such as the approved technological service (GTS) institutes. These small-scale initiatives failed to spark the same dramatic increase in research activity that we observe in Finland, but they did increase research intensity and technological innovation over the course of the 1990s and 2000s.

Initial responses to deteriorating economic performance during the 1980s closely resembled Finnish policies. The incoming Conservative-led coalition government sharply reduced government expenditure, including state aid, in 1982 and 1983. At the same time, the Conservative government introduced a massive and unprecedented technology program to address Denmark's ostensibly anachronistic industrial structure. The Technology Development Program made a massive commitment of public resources to new information technologies and was an apparent breakthrough in Danish industrial policy (Jamison 1991, 325). Yet Danish policymakers could not exploit the same tradition of peak-level private-public or interfirm cooperation as their Finnish counterparts. As described in chapter 2, mainland Danish firms had a history of resisting centralized political and economic power (Andersen and Kristensen 1999, 321).

The TDP was no exception and differed from Finnish technology policies in several ways. First, the TDP failed to engage organized economic actors. At the national level, technology programs were launched outside of traditional neo-corporatist channels (Morris 2005, 87). Partly as a result, the program was not particularly successful at engaging firms at the local level. While the TDP subsidized consulting activities, it did not promote cooperation among large or smaller-sized enterprises (114–16).[21] This was partly because stakeholders

---

20. Indeed, one could argue that Danish innovation policy was composed chiefly of initiatives in early stage risk capital.

21. Its capacity to sponsor interfirm collaboration in Aalborg was based on personal connections at the local level. It did not succeed in engaging foreign firms or even domestic companies in other parts of the country. Author interview with former executive officer, electronics firms (23 March 2006, Denmark).

fiercely opposed what they perceived as an excessively hierarchical and interventionist initiative. Even beneficiaries such as the steel industry opposed state intervention in the private economy (87), while smaller enterprises were intimidated by the bureaucratic procedures necessary to obtain funding (Andersen and Kristensen 1999, 323). The TDP was itself fragmented across sectors, which generated separate initiatives in information technology, materials, agriculture, and biotechnology instead of creating a broad cross-sectoral framework for promoting technological innovation.

Absent a broader cross-sectoral consensus to develop new activities of the sort that characterized Finnish technology policy or Danish labor market measures, the TDP was oriented toward existing industries. The information technology program subsidized investments in communication devices, data processing, control systems and related equipment (Morris 2005, 114). In the words of one policymaker, it "paid firms to go out and buy computers."[22] There were exceptions, including biotechnology, and the mobile communications cluster. Yet the largest share of funding was allocated to the troubled shipbuilding industry (Morris 2005, 118). While the Conservative politicians who launched the TDP had resolved to revolutionize Danish industry (Jamison 1991, 325), the program ended up defending large incumbent firms in existing industries and the consultants who worked with them (Christiansen 1988, 235). The information technology program, never popular, fell victim to fiscal consolidation at the end of the decade. Initiatives in materials, biotechnology, and agriculture were shuttered several years later (Morris 2005, 126).

At the same time, Denmark did experience some success (relative to Ireland, for example) by leveraging local interfirm networks. Strategy 92, launched in 1989 in response to the Single European Act and the prospect of a common market, adopted a very different approach than that of the TDP (Amin and Thomas 1996, 267). The program was more much modest in scope than the TDP, or Tekes in Finland, with a smaller budget and smaller grants. It also promoted interfirm cooperation by focusing on local networks where producers, suppliers, and subcontractors were personally familiar with one another.[23] To the extent that it could construct a broader network of firms, it relied on the locally administered "approved technological service" institutes that had been providing educational services and technical support for over a century (Bengtsson and Soren 2000). Within this more modest framework, the program was highly successful. The GTS institutes could rely on their position within local industrial networks to

---

22. Author interview with former head of section, Ministry of Business (13 March 2006, Denmark).

23. Author interviews with former director, Danish Technological Institute (6 December 2005, United States) and director, Danish Ministry of Science, Technology and Innovation (14 March 2006, Denmark).

attract firms, while established networks facilitated monitoring, raising the reputational costs associated with shirking and other forms of opportunistic behavior.[24] Enrollment exceeded expectations, with over 3,500 networks in the first six months, and firms and 90 percent of participants intended to maintain the network once funding expired (Shukla 1997). Most important, Strategy 92 was institutionalized in subsequent Danish innovation policies.

While Strategy 92 was not renewed following its expiration in 1992, the incoming Social Democrat government introduced a similar array of modestly financed small-scale programs designed to link local firms and technological institutes (Morris 2005, 195). For example, the government launched a series of "center contracts" to cofund cooperation among two or more firms, universities, and GTS institutes. Firms matched the modest €2 million public grants to participate in the network (Gergils 2006, 80). Each initiative targeted the experimental developments of new enterprises and activities, in sharp contrast to the technology programs of the 1980s. Meanwhile, the center contracts reflected a broader pattern of nonfinancial cooperation designed to tackle nontechnical challenges. For example, the Social Democrat–led coalition government created a forum for collaboration within industrial clusters or "resource areas" to coordinate public research, product market regulation, taxation, procurement, and other policies. The program leveraged interfirm networks, while respecting local aversion to expensive national-level programs (Morris 2005, 277).

The Liberal-led coalition government that assumed power in 2001 continued these innovation policies. The administration renewed the center contracts in 2003 as "innovation consortia" and complemented them with "regional clusters" from 2002 (Gergils 2006, 77). Indeed, it has addressed weaknesses in the Danish economy by convening in 2005 the tripartite Globalization Council that is modeled on the Finnish Science and Technology Policy Council (31). The Globalization Council, in turn, is perceived as a vehicle for increasing investment in R & D. The government has underscored its commitment to technological innovation by redirecting revenues from natural gas to the 16 billion crown High Technology Fund, which is oriented toward biotechnology and information technology (64). That said, it remains to be seen whether these efforts to scale local interfirm collaboration to the national level will succeed or even survive. Stakeholders have already criticized initiatives as a pet project of the prime minister.[25]

---

24. Author interviews with director, Danish Technological Institute (24 November 2005, Denmark); former director, Danish Technological Institute (6 December 2005, United States); and director, Danish Ministry of Science, Technology and Innovation (14 March 2006, Denmark).

25. Author interviews with secretary, Danish Confederation of Trade Unions (17 November 2005, Denmark); consultant, Danish Confederation of Trade Unions (18 November 2005, Denmark); and consultant, Confederation of Danish Industry (9 March 2006, Denmark).

Danish experiments with creative corporatism at the local level have had been modestly successful. On the one hand, policymakers have not yet engaged firms in national or even industrywide networks, and efforts to promote research have fallen short of expectations. Expenditure on R & D as a share of GDP remained below average within the OECD until the financial crisis of 2008–9 (and the resulting drop in national income), and the Danish government has failed to meet its own self-imposed targets (Gergils 2006, 20). In this respect, Denmark trails Finland in the level of creative corporatism and corresponding investment in disruptive new inputs.

On the other hand, local experimentation has yielded some successes, pointing to the potentially transformative impact of engaging interfirm networks to invest in disruptive new inputs. The TDP, while it failed to restructure Danish manufacturing, created opportunities for IT-based consulting firms. Strategy 92 and center contracts proved even more successful in revitalizing the GTS institutes and interfirm collaboration. Denmark now ranks near the top of the European Union (but behind Finland) in the share of firms collaborating with other firms and universities in innovation (Koski et al. 2006, 50). While industry-university cooperation is more modest, ranking ninth in the OECD (Gergils 2006, 66), survey data suggests that the share of firms collaborating with universities has increased, from 15 percent of firms in 1997 to 27 percent by 2004 (Christensen, Goldstein, and Bertrand 2004, 21). Firms, particularly small and medium-sized enterprises, are demonstrating greater competence in scientific-based research. If expenditure on R & D as a share of GDP remains below the OECD average, it has increased steadily over the course of the 1990s, growing more rapidly than in larger economies such as Britain, Germany, or the United States (Eurostat 2011). Together with more significant investments in human capital and early stage risk capital, these creative corporatist bargains have had very different implications for economic adjustment.

Consequences: Creative Corporatism and High-Tech Competition

In fact, Danish economic adjustment is noteworthy in three ways. First, Denmark has broken with its traditional reliance on incremental innovation in low- and medium-tech niches (Dalum, Fagerberg, and Jørgensen 1988; Edquist and Lundvall 1993) and has entered a range of dynamic new high-tech markets. Between 1985 and 2000, the share of high-tech manufactured exports increased by over 80 percent, reflecting gains in biotechnology, software, and telecommunication equipment. While these gains were impressive relative to large economies such as

Germany, Japan, and the United States, Denmark simultaneously lagged behind Finland in high-tech markets, and mobile communications in particular (OECD 2011). The discrepancy is striking, because Denmark enjoyed a head start in radiotelephone production, participated in the NMT standard, and developed the first GSM-compatible handset. Finally, while Denmark failed to capitalize on its head start in several markets, it specialized in a much broader range of high-tech activities, from fiber optics and cordless telephony in telecommunications to unrelated industries such as biotechnology and software. A unique pattern of creative corporatism, based on decentralized industry-labor cooperation, enabled Denmark to assume a unique position in high-tech markets as a diversified, niche-based producer.

1980–1990: Experimentation

Denmark's competitive position in telecommunications rests less on the incumbent Copenhagen-based radiotelephone giants of the 1960s than on a collection of small and medium-sized spin-offs at the northern tip of the Danish mainland. By the end of the 1990s, new entrants like Dancall, Cetelco, RTX, and ATL had transformed Aalborg, a diminutive regional capital, into a locus for research into mobile handsets, fourth-generation wireless networks, and Bluetooth technology. The origins of the Aalborg telecommunications cluster lie with the Jutland-based radio and television producers of the early postwar period. Simon Petersen established SP Radio in 1948, joining a broad cluster of Danish consumer-electronics firms. As colleagues and competitors flirted with bankruptcy during the 1960s and 1970s, SP Radio moved into maritime communications, constructing closed-end communication networks for local fishing boats and yachts (Dahl, Pedersen, and Dalum 2003, 13). SP Radio broke up into two firms in maritime communications, as employees established Dancom in 1973 and Shipmate in 1977. Both enterprises entered mobile communications by establishing Dancall in 1980 and Cetelco shortly thereafter. By the end of the decade, each firm had assumed a competitive position in mobile handsets for the NMT system (16–17).

Dancall and Cetelco's success was closely linked to the establishment of Aalborg University in 1974. While the university reform was a product of regional politics rather than creative corporatist bargaining and was not designed to facilitate economic restructuring, it nonetheless illustrates the potentially transformative role that industry-university cooperation can play in economic adjustment. Aalborg University introduced electrical engineering to graduate students in 1979, a year before the first firms moved into mobile telephones. Consistent with Danish creative corporatism, the university's primary contribution thus revolved around human capital formation.[26] In the words of one executive, "We do have the university in the area, and without that I don't think we'd have the cluster of companies that we do have. That indirectly meant that especially in the beginning of the life of [our firm]. It was fairly easy to attract a lot of good and experienced engineers. . . . And also lately a lot of newly graduated engineers have been hired coming directly from the university. Of course that's very important. If we had to attract people from Copenhagen it would be very tough. Without the background of the university and the whole community up here it wouldn't have been possible to grow the way we did."[27] The university also emerged as a forum for research collaboration in GSM and DECT (Digital European Cordless Telecommunications) technologies at the end of the 1980s and supported the creation of a formal industry association by the end of the 1990s (Dahl, Pedersen, and Dalum 2003, 16–17; Dalum and Villumsen 2005).

During the 1980s, Aalborg-based start-ups relied on the creative corporatist institutions described here to support technological experimentation in two ways. Creative corporatist bargains channeled risk capital to emerging actors. While the TDP program did not target emerging industries like IT as explicitly as did its Finnish counterpart, the program did underwrite interfirm cooperation in Aalborg, financing 20 percent of the research into digital communication technologies.[28] Pension funds represented an even more important source of capital, targeting firms such as Dancall, as a high-tech, growth-oriented enterprise (Stoerring and Dalum 2007, 133). Dancall also relied on risk capital from DUF to finance long-term research as it expanded from a small firm with a handful of engineers to a medium-sized, growth-oriented enterprise with eight hundred employees.[29] Dancall was thus directly connected to early initiatives in venture capital. While modest by international standards, they played an important role for Aalborg's small and medium-sized enterprises and laid a foundation for rapid growth and diversification during the 1990s.

Cooperation was not limited to risk capital. Danish firms also relied on creative corporatist bargains to finance and conduct research into expensive new digital communication technologies. The digital GSM standard represented a particularly formidable challenge for small and medium-sized Danish producers. The two leading suppliers, Dancall and Cetelco, pooled their efforts in a TDP-sponsored development project, DC Development, in 1988 (Dahl, Pedersen, and Dalum 2003, 16). DC Development linked engineers from both firms in pre-

---

26. Author interview with former executive officer, electronics firm (23 March 2006, Denmark).
27. Author interview with executive officer, electronics firm (24 March 2006, Denmark).
28. Author interview with former executive officer and TDP board member (23 February 2006, Denmark).
29. Author interview with former executive officer, electronics firm (23 March 2006, Denmark).

competitive research into the GSM mobile standard. Although it was a success, the experience underscores the challenges associated with constructing broad research consortia in Denmark. One participant explicitly attributed the program's success to personal ties between the two firms. In his words, "One of the [owners] was my old colleague. . . . So what we did was we met and [we agreed that] we can't do that ourselves and you can't, so why don't we join [together]. . . . There were five companies discussing whether to develop the technology together at NOVI, and we ended up being the only two that did that at NOVI. That was possible because we knew each other and trusted each other."[30]

Nationally sponsored local cooperation was in turn perceived as a necessary condition for Danish firms to be able to enter next-generation telecommunication equipment markets.[31] Indeed, Dancall and Cetelco not only maintained their position within next-generation wireless networks, but they assumed leadership within these segments. Cetelco and Dancall launched the first two GSM-compatible mobile handsets at the turn of the decade, beating rivals such as Ericsson, Motorola, and even Nokia. Aalborg thus emerged as a leading center for R & D in mobile handset production throughout the 1990s (Dahl, Pedersen, and Dalum 2003; Stoerring and Dalum 2007).

1990–2000: Expansion

The same neo-corporatist bargains that facilitated experimentation in GSM technologies supported rapid growth throughout the 1990s. The University of Aalborg assumed a more conscious and deliberate position within the Aalborg telecommunications cluster over the course of the decade. First, the university promoted interfirm cooperation by sponsoring NOVI and related initiatives in IT. The university also encouraged networking among its engineering students and participated in the formation of NorCOM, a regional industry association to coordinate private- and public-sector activity (Dalum and Villumsen 2005).[32] Cooperation became more extensively institutionalized, even though core firms were acquired by multinational enterprises and ultimately shut down by their new owners.

The University of Aalborg and related institutions facilitated growth even more directly in the area of human capital. As in Finland, the university dramati-

---

30. Author interview with former executive officer, electronics firm (23 March 2006, Denmark).

31. Author interviews with professor, Department of Economics, University of Aalborg (23 November 2005, Denmark); former secretary, Ministry of Business Affairs (6 March 2006, Denmark); and former executive officer, electronics firm (23 March 2006, Denmark).

32. Author interview with professor, Department of Economics, University of Aalborg (23 November 2005, Denmark) and executive officer, electronics firm (23 March 2006, Denmark).

cally expanded the output of master's graduates in electrical engineering. By the end of the 1990s, the University of Aalborg accounted for half of Denmark's master's students in electrical engineering, despite the university's modest position within the Danish educational system (Pedersen and Dalum 2004, 6). Indeed, the University of Aalborg's central role in human capital formation reflected a broader pattern of cooperation linking local employers, vocational institutions, and trade unions. Public training programs enabled firms to expand production facilities continuously throughout the 1990s despite the region's peripheral location, diminutive population, and high labor costs.[33]

The Aalborg telecommunications cluster grew rapidly during the 1990s. Dancall, for example, employed 600 workers at the beginning of the 1990s (Dahl, Pedersen, and Dalum 2003, 17). By 2000, when it was acquired by Flextronics, the unit employed 350 employees in R & D and an additional 1,300 in manufacturing (Stoerring and Dalum 2007, 134). By 2002, at its peak, Flextronics had expanded employment at its manufacturing facility to 1,700 (135). Dancall's dramatic expansion reflected rapid growth in other enterprises, as indigenous firms and multinational parents alike struggled to meet the demand for mobile devices. Meanwhile, prominent multinationals such as Ericsson and Nokia generated additional increases in employment by making greenfield investments around Aalborg (Dahl, Pedersen, and Dalum 2003, 19).

While the rapid growth of this new high-tech industry was impressive and unprecedented, Danish producers nonetheless failed to match the pace of their Finnish rivals. As described, early stage risk capital investments and research support paled in comparison to risk capital furnished by Tekes, Sitra, and related actors in Finland (Gergils 2006). While the TDP financed up to 20 percent of the research into new GSM technology, it was discontinued after several years (Morris 2005, 128). Nor were private-sector actors able to generate economies of scale by cooperating at the national level. Local producers never engaged multinational subsidiaries such as Philips or Motorola, despite their experience in radiotelephony and interest in NMT and GSM-based technologies. Indeed, cooperation within Aalborg was incomplete, as only two of five producers made serious commitments to DC Development. Danish innovation policies appeared to be most successful at engaging firms that were already personally familiar with one another but struggling to promote collaboration at the cross-regional or inter-sectoral level.[34]

Partly as a result of this, domestic firms were already struggling in the early 1990s. Cetelco was drained by investments in DC Development and was acquired

---

33. Author interview with former director, Danish Labor Market Authority (14 March 2006, Denmark).

34. Author interview with former executive officer, electronics firm (23 March 2006, Denmark).

by the German firm Hagenuk in 1992 and sold to the Italian company Telital in 1998. Dancall, meanwhile, struggled to service rapidly expanded markets and was itself acquired by the British firm Amstrad in 1993 and sold to the German producer Bosch in 1997. Both subsidiaries were hard hit by the dot-com downturn. Bosch sold its production facilities to Flextronics and its research unit to Siemens in 2000. By 2006, Flextronics had closed all production facilities and the troubled research unit had been sold again, to BenQ. Cetelco fared little better. The subsidiary was closed by Telital in 2002 after a tumultuous period with Hagenuk (Dalum and Villumsen 2005, 7).[35]

2000–2010: Adaptation

The Aalborg mobile communications cluster, however, did not disappear following foreign acquisition and the dot-com crash. On the contrary, firms turned to the same institutions to support diversification and adaptation. The ease of firing and retraining facilitated the rapid redistribution of labor. A director at one electronics firm noted, "A lot of the early people we employed were previous employees from other companies, typically Dancall. . . . You see that with other companies—they grow because they can attract people from other companies or the universities." He conceded that "of course we have lost a few people lately, because other [companies] have been growing more rapidly than we have."[36]

Those same firms relied on interfirm cooperation outside of the labor market. RTX Telecom, established shortly after Dancall's acquisition by Amstrad, relied on a strikingly similar precompetitive joint venture at NOVI to enter cordless telephony between 1993 and 1995. Danish firms assumed a leading position in the industry by creating a shared DECT standard (Dahl, Pedersen, and Dalum 2003, 18). While mobile telephony supplanted the cordless standard, RTX Telecom emerged as one of Aalborg's most successful and fastest growing domestically owned firms. One industry representative attributes RTX's success to its ability to identify and enter new product markets and emerging technologies.[37] Whereas Dancall staked its future almost exclusively on mobile handsets in the early 1990s and was overtaken by technological developments in other fields, RTX Telecom has moved from cordless telephony into other wireless technologies such as Blutooth, CDMA, and the Chinese TD-SCDMA standard (Stoerring and Dalum 2007, 135).[38] The firm relied heavily on the University of Aalborg,

---

35. Author interviews with former employee, software firm (13 December 2006, Denmark) and former executive officer, software firm (13 December 2006, Denmark).
36. Author interview with executive officer, electronics firm (24 March 2006, Denmark).
37. Author interview with executive officer, electronics firm (24 March 2006, Denmark).
38. Author interview with former executive officer, electronics firm (23 March 2006, Denmark).

not only utilizing NOVI to establish shared standards, but engaging its Center for Personal Communications to diversify beyond cordless telephony.[39]

The industry association NorCOM, founded in 1997 and formalized in 2000, has emerged as an important vehicle for creating and implementing such initiatives (Dalum and Villumsen 2005). In addition to promoting informal cooperation among engineers and firms, the industry lobbied for the creation of the €75 million "Digital Lighthouse" to invest in telecommunication technologies in 1999 (Dalum, Pedersen, and Villumsen 2002, 22). In 2004, industry and the university have jointly established the Center for Teleinfrastructure to research fourth-generation networks. The initiative has expanded cooperation to the national level for the first time, engaging Copenhagen-based actors such as Nokia Denmark and Danish Technological University (Pedersen, Dahl, and Dalum 2006).

These new collaborative ventures have facilitated diversification into a range of new activities. As noted, RTX Telecom relied on the Center for Personal Communications to identify new DECT-based applications and to shift from cordless telephony to other technologies such as Bluetooth.[40] Indeed, most spin-offs and start-ups in the Aalborg mobile communications cluster can be traced to research on Bluetooth (Dahl, Pedersen, and Dalum 2003, 18). The Digital Lighthouse project shifted attention from wireless to optics at the peak of the mobile communications bubble (Dalum, Pedersen, and Villumsen 2002, 22–23). Meanwhile, expanding risk capital markets enable firms to capitalize on new opportunities. There were more start-ups than closings after the dot-com crash, as start-ups like Blip-Systems, Wirtek, TTPCom, M-Tec, Top Link, Futarque, EB Denmark, PI Engineering, and Mobintech replaced stalwarts like Nokia, Lucent, Flextronics, and Telital (Dahl, Pedersen, and Dalum 2003, 19). One executive of a start-up attributes his company's existence to the expansion of early stage risk capital at the turn of the century. While he relied on a local business angel to fund product development, he could not have started without early stage risk capital from Vaekstfonden.[41]

As a result, employment has held relatively steady since peaking at the height of the bubble. Excluding Flextronics, whose closure affected 1,700 workers, employment in the information technology cluster has actually increased by 250 employees (Stoerring and Dalum 2007, 135). Moreover, it is distributed across a broader range of enterprises and activities than ever before. If Danish neo-corporatism leaves little room for coordinating across firms and regions or

---

39. Author interview with executive officer, electronics firm (24 March 2006, Denmark).
40. Author interview with executive officer, electronics firm (24 March 2006, Denmark).
41. Author interview with executive officer, electronics firm (15 November 2006, Denmark).

constructing large national-level experiments in emerging technologies, this distinctive pattern of decentralized cooperation has created space for smaller local-level experiments in Bluetooth or optics and encouraged start-ups to experiment in a range of unrelated applications and technologies. Although smaller than its Finnish counterpart, the Aalborg mobile communications cluster is in some respects more diverse, with a strong position in a much broader range of technologies such as optics and chipsets as well as alternative wireless standards like DECT, Bluetooth, CDMA, and TD-SCDMA (Palmberg and Bohlin 2006).

The heterogeneous cluster of firms in Aalborg reflects developments at the national level. Copenhagen was equally dynamic during the 1990s. Nokia acquired Philips's small Copenhagen-based research unit in the early 1990s and converted it into Denmark's largest information technology subsidiary.[42] The unit attracted a range of supporting firms, most notably prototype and original equipment manufacturers, including Foxconn, Nicro, and Nolex, as it designs mobile handsets around technology platforms developed in Helsinki.[43] While this wireless ecosystem is likely to change following Nokia's decision to close its 1,200-employee Danish R & D unit, Copenhagen hosts a range of other information technologies as well, including radio frequency identification technology, satellite communications, optics, semiconductors, and routers. As in Aalborg, participants have emphasized close cooperation with the local research university, public funding for risky long-term research into the 1990s, a significant expansion of skilled labor with the creation of an IT university during the late 1990s, and the increasing availability of early stage risk capital.[44]

Nor is high-tech competition limited to information technologies. In fact, Denmark occupies an even more impressive position in biotechnology. Here, Denmark ranks third in the European Union in population-adjusted measures of biotechnology publications (European Commission 2007, 80) and firms (84), second in patent applications (83), and first in various measures of industry employment and turnover (Beuzekom and Arundel 2006). Interestingly, Denmark has not only assumed a leading position in the biotechnology industry but entered radically innovative fields such as therapeutic technologies, where neo-corporatist economies should be most disadvantaged (Okamoto 2010, 147). Growth is based in large measure on new growth-oriented enterprises, with virtually all drug-based biotechnology firms having been established during the 1990s or 2000s (142).[45]

---

42. Author interview with executive officer, electronics firm (24 November 2006, Finland).

43. Author interview with manager, Copenhagen Capacity (9 November 2006, Denmark).

44. Author interviews with manager, Copenhagen Capacity (9 November 2006, Denmark); executive officer, electronics firm (8 November 2006, Denmark); and executive officer, electronics firm (14 November 2006, Denmark).

45. Author interview with professor, Copenhagen Business School, (13 March 2006, Denmark).

These actors have relied on a similar combination of institutions in facilitating adjustment and restructuring. Biotechnology was one of the only areas in which the technology programs of the 1980s focused on creating human capital rather than investing in technologies or capital equipment. Ironically, the 1989–1993 program's distinctive focus was shaped by the backlash against ambitious national-level industrial policies. Policymakers responded to these concerns by focusing on training.[46] These efforts, if anything, proved even more transformative, expanding university and graduate student output at a time of acute labor shortages and contributing to the industry's subsequent development during the 1990s.[47]

Cooperation in providing early stage risk capital proved even more critical, as the Danish biotechnology industry did not take off until the late 1990s. The oldest dedicated biotechnology firm (Neurosearch) was established in 1989, and industry representatives estimate that three-quarters of the firms were established after 1998. Vaekstfonden and related initiatives supported growth by facilitating the development of a viable venture capital industry and supplying direct funding. Indeed, Denmark's oldest biotechnology firms, Neurosearch and Pharmexa, relied on a combination of pension fund capital and the DUF funding to support initial experimentation in biotechnology during the 1990s.[48] Copenhagen-based producers in communications and other high-tech industries like biotechnology thus relied on a very similar pattern of cooperation in human capital formation and early stage risk capital to stimulate and sustain high-tech growth.

Political Compromises and Economic Constraints

Like Finland, Denmark's relatively robust position as a high-end producer in high-tech markets insulated it from the 2007–9 financial crisis. For example, while Aalborg lost 1,700 manufacturing jobs after the dot-com crash, high-tech employment as a whole actually increased (Stoerring and Dalum 2007, 135). Employment gains were concentrated in knowledge-intensive activities such as research, development, and design, as evidenced by the increasing number of multinational research subsidiaries in Aalborg and Denmark's leading position

---

46. Author interviews with professor, Copenhagen Business School (27 February 2006, Denmark) and former executive officer, pharmaceutical firm (13 November 2006, Denmark).

47. Author interview with former executive officer, pharmaceutical firm (13 November 2006, Denmark).

48. Author interview with professor, Copenhagen Business School, (13 March 2006, Denmark) and executive officer, venture capital firm (7 November 2006, Denmark).

in high-tech services more generally. Consequently, the Danish economy was less dependent on residential investment than other former high-tech leaders, such as Ireland, and less affected by the subsequent contraction of credit. For example, the decline in residential investment in 2009 represented only 1.1 percent of GDP, as opposed to a staggering 2.9 percent of national output in Ireland (Gylfason et al. 2010, 247). As a result, Danish GDP only declined by 5.2 percent in 2009, as opposed to 7.6 percent in Ireland. By 2011, Denmark was positioned to over-take Ireland as the fourth-wealthiest economy in the European Union (Eurostat 2011).[49]

At the same time, Denmark was not immune to the financial crisis. While the 5.2 percent decline in national output in 2009 was not as steep as that in Finland (8.2%), the Danish economy was more heavily affected by the crisis in other ways. For example, Denmark witnessed a significant increase in housing prices between 2001 and 2006, and relied more heavily on residential construction for job growth than did Finland (Gylfason et al, 2010: 247). When real estate prices collapsed, Denmark experienced a banking crisis, albeit one that was significantly less severe than that in Ireland. It also witnessed a much sharper increase in un-employment than Finland did, from a low of 3.3 percent in 2008 to 7.7 percent by 2010 (Eurostat 2011).

While many factors, from housing policy to financial regulations, contributed to the Danish construction boom and banking crisis, Denmark's difficulties also illuminate the limitations of the creative corporatist pacts that stakeholders have struck over the last three decades. As in Finland, creative corporatist bargains that facilitated restructuring simultaneously contributed to the country's subse-quent economic difficulties. In the Danish case, policymakers and societal actors privileged industry-labor cooperation in social policy over private-public and interfirm collaboration in R & D. Denmark dramatically increased investment in training and continuing education over the course of the 1990s, but public- and private-sector commitment to R & D was considerably more modest.

When Denmark did launch new innovation policies, they tended to favor de-centralized, early stage, local-level cooperation. Denmark used pension funds that were jointly managed by industry and labor and local technological insti-tutes to dramatically increase the supply of early stage risk capital, but national-level research initiatives foundered over industry skepticism and resistance. The landmark TDP was fragmented across multiple domains and never effectively promoted investment in research, and it was eliminated after five years (Mjøset 1987, 444). Although subsequent programs were more successful in their efforts

---

49. It is important to note that Irish GDP has always been inflated by transfer pricing.

to engage firms and promote innovation at the local level, they were significantly smaller in scale and scope. As a result, the government has consistently failed to meet its own targets to increase public expenditure on R & D, and Denmark continues to trail Finland in measures of industry-university cooperation (Gergils 2006, 66) and formal technological innovation (Eurostat 2011).

In fact, one observes similar trends even in the area where Denmark has been most successful–in skill formation. For example, Danish gains in tertiary education, as opposed to training, are more modest. Denmark (33.5%) actually trails Finland (34.6%) in the share of the population with a tertiary degree (European Commission 2006). Shortcomings in science and technology are even more acute. These differences not only reflect a weaker commitment to formal R & D but also limited national-level coordination. Finland and Ireland rely on a system of quotas to influence university output, in consultation with industry representatives and national-level bodies such as the Science and Technology Policy Council in Finland. Denmark lacks such instruments and, partly as a result, trails both Finland and Ireland in the proportion of university-educated engineers (Eurostat 2011; Pedersen, Dahl, and Dalum 2006, 93).

As a result of these distinctive bargains, Denmark has struggled to scale more technologically and capital-intensive industries. For example, policymakers bemoaned the relatively modest and inconsistent support for local-level research and discontinued funding for digital mobile communication technologies after five years.[50] In finance, managers could draw on one of the most robust early stage markets in Europe yet complained about the limited supply of later-stage venture capital and the disproportionate emphasis on early stage financing.[51] Indeed, Danish politics continues to constrain innovation, with the national government initially resisting and only reluctantly agreeing to underwrite the Center for Teleinfrastructure. Nor could firms replicate the national-level consortia that pooled private-sector resources or lobbied the government in Finland. Absent meaningful national-level collaboration, Aalborg telecommunication equipment producers struggled to compete against larger rivals and eventually succumbed to bankruptcy or acquisition by foreign corporations.

Some scholars suggest that Aalborg-based firms could never have succeeded in mobile communications because they were so small relative to Nokia (Pedersen, Dahl, and Dalum 2006, 96). Of course, Denmark's small and medium-sized industrial structure is shaped by national-level political bargaining. Furthermore, even Denmark's largest conglomerates have experienced similar difficulties. Great

---

50. Author interview with former secretary, Ministry of Business Affairs (6 March 2006, Denmark) and director, Danish Investment Fund (20 March 2006, Denmark).
51. Author interview with former director, electronics firm (23 March 2006, Denmark).

Northern, the "Danish Nokia," sold Storno, despite the division's leading position in radio telephones in Europe. At the time, consultants argued that the unit could become very profitable, but management viewed investments in research and capital equipment as too risky (Iversen 2005, 120). Similar developments prevailed at the NKT Group, a diversified conglomerate whose cable interests and eastern European exposure even more closely resembles that of Nokia. The NKT Group also developed new high-tech activities, most notably in the case of the semiconductor designer GiGA. The division was successful, but it was sold to Cisco in 2000. Industry participants suggest that NKT was unable to expand rapidly enough and unprepared to assume the risk of doing so.[52]

Similar dynamics prevail in other industries. Despite the presence of several medium-sized international pharmaceutical companies, the Danish biotechnology industry is dominated by small and medium-sized firms (Bloch 2004). Furthermore, most of these firms are positioning themselves for acquisition rather than long-term growth.[53] Even low- and medium-technology industries such as windmills have encountered difficulty, as they require progressively larger and riskier investments in capital equipment and scale. Like the telecommunications, semiconductor, and biotechnology fields, the Danish windmill industry has been characterized by several foreign acquisitions as it struggles to manage large-scale competition.[54] Those foreign investors can mobilize more capital than their Danish counterparts, but there is also the danger that they will acquire new technologies without investing in their subsidiaries, or that they may even move production offshore altogether.

In inhibiting competition in more capital-intensive, high-tech industries, creative corporatist bargains contributed to the 2007–9 financial crisis. Denmark did not scale emerging high-tech industries as rapidly as did Finland (or Ireland) during the 1990s, despite an advantageous position in telecommunication equipment and continued leadership in biotechnology. The country instead relied more heavily on the expansion of nontradable, low-productivity services during the 1990s and 2000s (OECD 2009). When global credit tightened, Denmark experienced a significantly sharper decline in residential investment (1.1% of GDP) than Finland did (0.4%) in 2009. As a result, Denmark experienced a banking crisis in 2008. Peaking at 7.7 percent in November of 2010, the Danish unemployment rate rivaled that of Finland (8.1%), a longtime laggard.

---

52. Author interview with director, electronics firm (14 November 2006, Denmark).
53. Author interviews with professor, Copenhagen Business School (27 February 2006, Denmark); director, venture capital firm (7 March 2006, Denmark); executive, biotechnology firm (15 March 2006, Denmark); and executive officer, venture capital firm (7 November 2006, Denmark).
54. Author interview with director of engineering subsidiaries in both Denmark and Finland (14 February 2006, Denmark).

The banking crisis and higher unemployment in turn threaten established policy routines. For example, government-orchestrated financial bailouts and expensive labor market policies increased public debt from 27.5 percent of GDP in 2007 to 43.6 percent of GDP by 2010 (Eurostat 2011). While public deficits and debt remain well within the EU's Maastricht criteria, domestic and outside observers argue that Denmark has less room to maneuver outside of the eurozone (Kjær and Pedersen 2011; OECD 2009). Consequently, the government faced pressure to retrench public expenditure, threatening the supply-side inputs I have described (Alderman 2010). In 2010, parliament restructured Denmark's social safety net, reducing the period during which an individual can collect unemployment benefits from four years to two (European Commission 2011, 93).

The financial crisis, however, appears unlikely to undermine creative corporatism. On the contrary, Denmark continues to rely on a similar process of institutionalized cooperation among organized actors and similar policies to manage economic adjustment. Although Denmark reduced investment in continuing education as employment increased during the early 2000s, the economic downturn since then has renewed interest in training (Kristensen, Lotz, and Rocha 2011, 133). Postcrisis proposals to trim fiscal deficits have focused on further tightening unemployment-benefit eligibility rather than targeting training (Alderman 2010). Furthermore, in 2007, labor market actors again reached an agreement to restrain wages, with the understanding that employees would utilize savings to invest in further education. A similar agreement to promote upskilling in the public sector suggests that the crisis has reinforced rather than undermined creative corporatist labor market bargaining (EIRO 2007).

In fact, stakeholders have responded to perceived deficiencies by adapting rather than dismantling neo-corporatist institutions. As noted, the center-right administration addressed Denmark's inability to compete in capital-intensive high-tech industries and its low-productivity, more generally, by redoubling its commitment to "center contracts" and launching the 16 billion crown High Technology Fund (Gergils 2006, 64–77). While the government has since moved to retrench public expenditure, it has maintained its commitment to new initiatives in innovation policy. The High Technology Fund, particularly when integrated into peak-level forums such as the Globalization Council and local-level initiatives such as the innovation consortia, has the potential to increase interest in and the resources devoted to formal R & D by addressing perceived deficiencies in formal technological innovation.

As in Finland, such changes are unlikely to occur overnight, as industry has little tradition of cooperating with policymakers or among themselves in large national-level research projects. Partly because this, these measures have been criticized as modest in their size and scope (Gergils 2006), ineffective in their capacity to promote collaboration (Kristensen, Lotz, and Rocha 2011), and inappropriate for a country that has relied on nonscientific innovation (Andersen and Kristensen 1999). At the same time, one does observe promising if gradual shifts in terms of how Danish firms compete in the international economy. Denmark has witnessed significant improvement in industry-university cooperation (Christensen, Goldstein, and Bertrand 2004, 21) and research expenditure. On the latter front, the 3.02 percent of GDP devoted to R & D in 2009 placed Denmark third in the European Union, trailing only Finland and Sweden (Eurostat 2011). Although increasing research intensity was amplified by a sharp decline in GDP, it nonetheless provides additional evidence of movement away from a historically low- and medium-tech innovation system.

Meanwhile, the disadvantages associated with Danish creative corporatism may prove less problematic over a longer period of time. After all, the lack of national interfirm coordination that inhibited large-scale investment in R & D and delayed the redistribution of resources to emerging industries simultaneously limited Danish dependence on a single firm or industry. In Aalborg, for example, local producers were less likely to be locked into a single standard like GSM or CDMA because they were not united within one or several overarching technology programs. This was even more evident at the national level, as the Aalborg-based and Copenhagen-based IT industries had relatively little interaction. Their independent development supported differing emphasis on optics, semiconductors, and mobile communications and a different cluster of firms within the wireless space. Partly as a result of this greater diversity within and outside of the IT industry, Denmark suffered a significantly smaller decline in exports (−5.5%) than Finland (−14.4%) in 2009 (Gylfason et al. 2010, 247). And while Danish reliance on foreign direct investment increased vulnerability to offshoring during the 1990s and 2000s, layoffs also encouraged the creation of new firms, particularly when coupled with the easy and increasing availability of early stage risk capital. In this respect, Denmark is in an even stronger position than Finland, notwithstanding the former's weakness in more capital-intensive, high-tech industries.

Denmark's advantages are even more pronounced when it is compared to Ireland, which struggled to maintain leadership in high-tech industries after the dotcom crash and was deeply affected by the 2007–9 financial crisis. While Ireland was more specialized than Denmark in high-tech industries during the 1990s, it relied on activities that were less knowledge intensive. As a result, it was more sensitive to cost competition and more dependent on nontradable services after 2001. In the following chapter, I explain why. While Irish policymakers sought to replicate Danish and Finnish initiatives in labor market and innovation policy, they struggled to engage private-sector actors in this space. In contrast to Denmark (and Finland), Irish firms operated at arm's length at *both* the national and local level, and relations with trade unions were even more contentious. In this comparatively low-trust environment, firms were reluctant to commit significant resources or to share sensitive information with policymakers, trade unions, and even other firms. Neo-corporatist bargaining, to the extent that it occurred, revolved around "competitive" and largely redistributive measures related to fiscal retrenchment, wage restraint, and tax concessions. These competitive corporatist bargains facilitated rapid movement into new high-tech industries, but they privileged assembly and related services rather than research, design, or other knowledge-intensive activities.

5

A LOW-END PRODUCER IN HIGH-TECH MARKETS: ECONOMIC ADJUSTMENT IN IRELAND

Ireland also relied on neo-corporatist bargaining to facilitate entry into new high-tech industries. Like Denmark and Finland, policymakers struck bargains with vulnerable stakeholders to facilitate restructuring, in some cases actively replicating creative corporatist strategies. In contrast to Denmark and Finland, however, Ireland was a historically liberal economy with little tradition of industry-labor or interfirm coordination in production. Policymakers thus struggled to engage stakeholders, most notably firms, in the construction of supply-side resources. Neo-corporatist bargaining, to the extent that it occurred, linked wage restraint to fiscal retrenchment and tax cuts.

These competitive corporatist bargains had distinctive implications for economic adjustment. Ireland attracted foreign investment by converting industrial subsidies into tax concessions. Centralized collective wage bargaining supported this internationally oriented, cost-competitive strategy by securing fiscal retrenchment, macroeconomic stability, and wage moderation throughout the 1990s. This stable, low-cost, English-speaking environment attracted U.S. investment in new high-tech industries such as pharmaceuticals, biotechnology, software, computers, and telecommunication equipment. As a result, Ireland rivaled Finland in its shift from low- and medium-technology manufacturing to high-tech exports and Denmark in the breadth of its high-tech activity.

At the same time, limited investment in disruptive new inputs inhibited movement into more knowledge-intensive activities. High-tech production instead revolved around basic assembly operations until the late 1990s and related services after the dot-com crash. As a result, Ireland was much more sensitive to cost competition than either Denmark or Finland. Ireland's inability to construct a more durable comparative advantage in high-tech industries rendered the country more dependent on nontradable services to support income and employment growth after the dot-com crash. The subsequent housing crash and banking crisis led to the steepest economic downturn of any country in western Europe, with gross domestic product declining 12.1 percent between 2008 and 2010 and unemployment reaching 14.6 percent (Eurostat 2011). Although Ireland successfully retrenched public spending at the height of the crisis, disinvestment threatens to exacerbate its status as a low-end producer in high-tech markets.

The Puzzle: A Low-End Producer in High-Tech Markets

Ireland has come a long way over the past twenty years, although obviously not as far as boosters of the Celtic Tiger initially suggested. Ireland was one of the poorest countries in western Europe until the 1980s. While Ireland rivaled Italy in per capita GDP in 1950, it largely missed out on the postwar economic boom (Ó Grada 1997, 3). The country continued to lag behind its western European peers, even following its shift from import-substituting industrialization to free trade and foreign direct investment in 1959 (36). Ireland was relegated to low-tech manufacturing industries such as food processing, footwear, and textiles, while efforts to recruit high-tech U.S. multinationals to locate in Ireland were compromised by wage inflation, industrial unrest, and macroeconomic uncertainty. Government efforts to stimulate growth using fiscal policy exacerbated the problem, causing public debt to reach 136.6 percent of GDP by 1986. Emigration, one of the most visible symbols of Ireland's deteriorating economic situation, reached 1 percent of the population per annum by this time, rivaling the postwar peak of the dismal 1950s. Even with substantial emigration, unemployment approached 17 percent by 1987 (Considine and O'Leary 1999, 120; Mjøset 1992, 321).

A little over a decade later, however, Ireland was perceived as an economic star (Clinch Convery, and Walsh 2002; MacSharry and White 2000). Economic growth averaged 6.4 percent between 1988 and 1998 (Fink 2004, 32), accelerating to 10.4 percent between 1997 and 2000 (34). By 2001, per capita GDP was higher than in Denmark or Finland (Eurostat 2011). Gross national income, which does not include income generated by foreign corporations, was 16 percent lower than GDP (Department of Finance 2005, 22), leading some observers to argue that income growth merely reflected the tendency of foreign multinationals to overstate profits and capitalize on Ireland's low corporate tax rate (O'Hearn 1998).

Per capita GNP growth, however, was almost as impressive, averaging 8.9 percent between 1997 and 2000 (Fink 2004, 34). Irish performance was also strong along dimensions that are not proportional to GDP, with unemployment dropping to 4.3 percent by 2000 and remaining below 5 percent until 2008 (Eurostat 2011).

Irish growth was based on rapid movement into new high-tech industries such as electronics, software, and pharmaceuticals. The share of high-tech manufactured employment more than doubled, and the share of high-tech manufactured exports more than trebled between 1985 and 2000 (OECD 2011). Although high-tech exports declined sharply after 2000, Ireland still leads western Europe and the United States in the share of high-tech exports (Eurostat 2011) and ranks as the largest software exporter in the world (Breznitz 2007, 166). Ireland's status as a high-tech leader revolved in large measure around foreign direct investment. Foreign multinationals, and U.S. information technology firms in particular, relocated to Ireland or expanded existing operations. The 1980s witnessed greenfield investment by hardware producers such as Apple, Wang, and Zenith and software firms such as Corel, Lotus, and Oracle. These firms expanded their operations during the 1990s and were joined by prominent U.S. firms such as HP, IBM, Dell, Gateway, and Intel (Barry and Egeraat 2008; Sterne 2004). Indigenous enterprises also enjoyed robust growth, with software employment quadrupling and exports increasing tenfold over the course of the 1990s (Breznitz 2007; Ó Riain 2004; Sands 2005; Sterne 2004).

If Ireland emerged as a high-tech competitor, however, it relied on relatively low-end activities within high-tech markets. The foreign direct investment of the 1990s was concentrated in manufacturing rather than research (O'Sullivan 1995, 387), and the post-2000 movement into services has focused on customer support rather than product development (Barry and Egeraat 2008, 39). Interestingly, this characterization extends to indigenous industry, which is dominated by relatively low-tech industries such as food processing (O'Malley, Kennedy, and O'Donnell 2008, 164). In food processing, for example, indigenous firms have relied heavily on undifferentiated commodities such as butter (O'Connell, Egeraat, and Enright 1997, 1). Even in high-tech niches, Irish firms are characterized by a comparatively modest position in more capital-intensive industries such as hardware or dynamic and technologically demanding market niches such as middleware (Breznitz 2007, 179).

Aggregate-level statistics confirm these weaknesses. While the share of high-tech exports in Ireland (25.7%) was almost 50% higher than in Finland (17.5%) and over twice as high as Denmark (11.7%) in 2007, measures of high-tech employment were significantly less impressive. The share of the labor force employed in high-tech industries in Ireland (6.20%) was only 17 percent higher than in Denmark (5.27%) and 8 percent *lower* than in Finland (6.71%). Furthermore,

Irish employment was concentrated in manufacturing, with a smaller share of the population employed in high-tech services (3.80%) than in either Finland (4.85%) or Denmark (4.30%) (Eurostat 2011). These statistics are troubling because they suggest that Irish leadership in high-tech markets is to a large degree shaped by the decision of foreign multinationals to overstate their Irish revenues (O'Hearn 1998).

In fact, Ireland occupies an even weaker position in other measures of high-tech competition. For example, the country devotes a significantly smaller share of GDP into R & D (1.25%) than either Denmark (2.48%) or Finland (3.47%) (Eurostat 2011). While R & D as a share of GNP might be up to 20 percent higher, this does not come close to closing the gap with Denmark or Finland. In fact, Ireland trails on measures that are not denominated in national income. With 17.7 high-tech patent applications to the European Patent Office per million individuals in 2007, Ireland trailed both Denmark (40.1) and Finland (86.3). Ireland also trailed Denmark and Finland in the number of high-tech patent applications to the United States Patent Office in 2005 (Eurostat 2011). In the same year, Ireland not only demonstrated a lower propensity to patent but was less specialized in high-tech patents (20.5%) than either Denmark (22.7%) or Finland (49.1%) (Eurostat 2011).

Developments after the dot-com crash underscore Ireland's reliance on relatively low-end activities within high-tech markets. The country has struggled to compete with cost-competitive eastern European rivals such as Estonia and Hungary, which also benefit from EU membership, low corporate taxation, and a well-educated labor force (OECD 2001). In the wake of the dot-com crash, high-profile companies such as Alcatel, Gateway, Ericsson, and Motorola outsourced their manufacturing activity (Barry and Egeraat 2008).[1] The share of high-tech exports fell from 40.8 percent in 2001 to 29.9 percent by 2003 and 22.1 percent by 2009. The 27 percent contraction in the share of high-tech exports between 2001 and 2003 was significantly sharper than the 5 percent decline in Denmark or the 12 percent decline in Finland (Eurostat 2011).

Nor, in contrast to Denmark and Finland, did Ireland appear to move upmarket into more knowledge-intensive activities during this time period. For example, expenditure on R & D as a share of GDP was roughly constant at 1.3 percent between 1997 and 2007 (Eurostat 2011). The share of employment in high-tech services actually declined in the wake of the dot-com crash, from 4.09 percent of the labor force in 2001 to 3.70 percent of the labor force in 2007 (Eurostat 2011). High-tech service activity not only failed to offset an even steeper decline in high-tech manufacturing (from 3.5% of the labor force in 2001 to 2.5% by 2007), but it

---

1. Author interview with manager, Industrial Development Authority (5 May 2006, Ireland).

was concentrated in less knowledge-intensive customer service operations rather than research or design (Barry and Egeraat 2008, 39). Ireland thus had a more difficult time defending and diversifying its high-tech activities than both Denmark and Finland. While the economy continued to grow at a rapid clip between 2001 and 2006, increasing national income and employment growth was based on nontradable services such as construction. The Irish economy was thus far more vulnerable to decreasing credit availability beginning in 2007.

The housing crash and banking crisis triggered a significantly steeper decline in GDP. The decline in residential investment reached 2.9 percent of GDP in 2009, as opposed to 1.1 percent in Denmark and 0.4 percent in Finland (Gylfason et al. 2010, 247). As a result, Irish gross domestic product contracted by 12.1 percent between 2008 and 2010, as opposed to a 4.6 percent decrease in Denmark and a 3.6 percent decline in Finland (Eurostat 2011). In fact, these figures *understate* the magnitude of the Irish recession, as the income of Irish nationals fell more rapidly than the income generated by foreign multinationals. In fact, unemployment was almost twice as high in Ireland at the end of the 2010 (14.6%) than it was in either Denmark (7.6%) or Finland (8.0%) (Eurostat 2011).

Existing literature sheds little insight into Ireland's emergence as a low-end producer in high-tech markets. Explanations based on comparative advantage fail to explain why Ireland improved its performance so dramatically, effectively leapfrogging incumbent high-tech producers such as Japan or the United States. In 1985, Ireland (12.9%) lagged behind both Japan (26.6%) and the United States (28.3%) in the share of high-tech exports. At the same time, Ireland's advantageous position relative to Denmark (9.7%) and Finland (4.7%) did not translate into more research- or knowledge-intensive activities two decades later (OECD 2011). On the contrary, Ireland failed to capitalize on its comparatively strong position within these markets, despite its more liberal economic institutions.

Some other scholars emphasize the role of large firms, specifically U.S. multinationals, in facilitating entry into low value-added industries (Fink 2004; Jacobsen 1994; O'Hearn 1998). Multinational corporations play a central role in Irish adjustment, but this does not explain why Ireland was so strikingly successful in attracting high-tech foreign direct investment after decades of poor performance (Haughton 1995; Ó Grada and O'Rourke 1996; Ó Grada 1997). Nor does it explain why multinational corporations such as Microsoft and Tellabs focused on lower-value activities in Ireland than their counterparts in Denmark and Finland.[2] Critiques based on multinational ownership also fail to explain

---

2. Observation based on author interviews with research director, electronics firm (19 October 2005, Finland); head of corporate affairs, software firm (1 June 2006, Ireland); and representative, Danish Information Technology Industry Association (8 March 2006, Denmark).

why indigenous firms, in low- and high-tech industries alike, have also struggled to move into more knowledge-intensive activities (Breznitz 2007, 179). Poor indigenous performance cannot be attributed to insufficient state intervention. Policymakers have repeatedly attempted to engage domestic firms with innovative industrial policies, to such a degree that Ireland has been characterized as a paradigmatic "flexible developmental state" (Ó Riain 2000, 2004).

Explanations based on luck, including Ireland's having an English-language workforce (Dunning 1992), its attractiveness as a European export platform (Barry 2004), and its having access to EU structural funds (Sexton et al. 1997) similarly fail to explain Ireland's newfound success in attracting foreign direct investment as well as its inability to move upmarket. EU support, ranging from 2–3 percent of GDP (Fink 2004, 39) and representing up to 10 percent of public investment in supply-side resources such as education and research during the 1980s and 1990s are particularly puzzling as they should have given Ireland a considerable advantage relative to Denmark and Finland (Sexton et al. 1997, 216).

A final approach, emphasizing liberalization, appears to explain rapid movement into new high-tech industries by linking Ireland's newfound ability to attract foreign direct investment to its light regulatory environment, low taxes, decentralized equity-based financial system, and liberal labor markets (O'Malley, Hewitt-Dundas, and Roper 2008, 176). Stated concisely, Ireland became even more liberal over time, decentralizing collective wage bargaining at the beginning of the 1980s (Durkan 1992; Hardiman 1988) and slashing fiscal expenditure later in the decade and tax rates in the 1990s (Clinch, Convery, and Walsh 2002, 91). In reducing government expenditure from 50 percent to 37 percent of GDP between 1986 and 1988, Taoiseach Charles Haughey's administration exceeded the budget cutting of neoliberal icons like Margaret Thatcher and Ronald Reagan (Haughton 1995, 45). Fiscal retrenchment extended from massive cuts in public housing (McCarthy 2001, 14) to reductions in state aid (O'Malley, Kennedy, and O'Donnell 1992, 26). This combination of market-based policy reforms, together with EU-subsidized investments in basic education, enabled Ireland to capitalize on the favorable circumstances described here (Clinch, Convery, and Walsh 2002; Considine and O'Leary 1999; Sexton et al. 1997).

Yet there are two problems with this liberal narrative. The first and most glaring problem is that Ireland relied on very nonliberal institutions to achieve neoliberal objectives. Macroeconomic stabilization, for example, was shaped by the active recentralization of collective wage bargaining in 1987 (Taylor 2002; Thomas 2003). And Ireland was characterized by increasing, not decreasing, cooperation under the auspices of social partnership over the course of the 1990s (O'Donnell 1998, 17). Second, the liberal narrative fails comparatively. Ireland should have outperformed more extensively corporatist economies such as Denmark and Finland. In fact, the opposite has occurred. Ireland has excelled in manufacturing and assembly activity, but it continues to lag behind its more corporatist peers in high-tech employment, high-tech services employment, and per capita patenting (Eurostat 2011).

I resolve this apparent contradiction between Ireland's rapid entry into new high-tech markets and its relatively low-end status in those markets by arguing that Irish policymakers turned to neo-corporatist bargaining to manage Ireland's deteriorating economic performance in the late 1980s. Policymakers in Ireland, however, could not leverage the same tradition of coordination as they could in Denmark or Finland. As a result, they constructed a distributional coalition favoring fiscal retrenchment, wage restraint, and lower taxation. This pattern of "competitive" corporatism simultaneously explains Ireland's ability to attract foreign direct investment after 1987 as well as its difficulty in moving into higher value-added activities.

The Argument: From Liberal Capitalism to Competitive Corporatism

As in Denmark and Finland, Irish experimentation with neo-corporatist bargaining was a response to the economic failures of the 1970s and 1980s. Ireland suffered deteriorating economic performance throughout this period. Real per capita GNP declined between 1973 and 1986 and unemployment approached 16 percent (Considine and O'Leary 1999, 120). As in Denmark and Finland, declining economic performance was perceived as a structural challenge. Traditional low- and medium-technology industries such as food processing and textiles shed jobs as Ireland struggled to compete with new cost-competitive rivals (O'Sullivan 1995, 367). Brief experiments with conservative neo-corporatist bargaining, which traded industrial peace for social benefits and countercyclical fiscal policies, appeared to exacerbate these problems (see chapter 2). The agreements secured industrial peace at the cost of wage inflation and fiscal profligacy (Sexton et al. 1997, 354). By the early 1980s, virtually all actors rejected neo-corporatist bargaining. Employers sought a more decentralized framework to limit wage increases and wage compression (Thomas 2003, 104), trade unions in tradable sectors saw an opportunity to secure greater wage gains (88), and policymakers welcomed relief from the pressure to deliver a centralized income agreement. As a result, policymakers and unions acquiesced when employers withdrew from centralized collective wage bargaining in 1981.

Yet liberalization appeared to make the economy worse, not better. Decentralized collective wage bargaining reduced wage compression (Cradden 1999, 56), but it was only moderately successful in reducing industrial unrest. The number of worker days lost to industrial disputes declined only modestly from 434,000 in 1981 to 309,000 by 1986 (ILO 1982; 1987). Decentralized collective wage bargaining was even less effective in inducing wage restraint. Labor cost growth was the highest within the European Monetary System (EMS) between 1980 and 1986 (Sexton et al. 1997, 64). Nor did separating fiscal policy and wage formation stem the massive growth in government expenditure. A succession of weak and unstable governments proved unwilling or unable to impose fiscal discipline (Thomas 2003, 100). Public-sector debt, which reached 136.6 percent of GDP by 1987 (Mjøset 1992, 321), exacerbated capital flight (Haughton 1995).

In this environment, stakeholders returned to centralized wage bargaining under the auspices of "Irish social partnership" in 1987. The center-right Fianna Fail government, trade unions, and domestic employers signed a three-year national-level wage agreement, the Program for National Recovery. The PNR emerged as a tripartite vehicle to achieve neoliberal ends, trading wage restraint for fiscal retrenchment and modest tax cuts. The PNR was also a watershed in Irish industrial relations, as its success inspired a series of three-year national agreements that have persisted to the present day (O'Donnell 1998; Thomas 2003). The 1990 Partnership for Economic and Social Prosperity broadened the scope of the bargain to address tax policy and deepened cooperation in the form of local "area-based partnerships" (Sabel 1996). By the mid-1990s, social partnership was addressing a broad range of issues, most notably collective investments in training (Boyle 2005, 7; Sexton et al. 1997, 116).

Analysts have advanced several reasons to explain why Ireland, a traditionally liberal economy, turned to neo-corporatist bargaining, and social partnership in particular. Explanations range from there being a series of forced mergers within the trade union movement during the 1980s (Allen 2000, 115–16) to the existence of a more effective institutional architecture for governing neo-corporatist bargaining, including a new monitoring and enforcement body (Sexton et al. 1997, 83), to the role of a centralized research organization, the National Economic and Social Council, which served as a "focal point" for cooperation (Culpepper 2008, 15). Each of these institutional innovations permitted new forms of cooperation, but they do not, by themselves, illuminate shifting attitudes toward centralized collective bargaining, and social partnership more generally.

As in Denmark, Finland, and other countries, the shift to social partnership was driven by a sense of economic crisis and political vulnerability (Compston 2003). Like their Danish counterparts, Irish interviewees allude to the specter of "national bankruptcy" when describing their experiences during the 1980s.[3] By 1987, the crisis had become so acute that Ireland was considering an "emergency presidential committee" to resolve the situation (Thomas 2003, 126). In this environment, politicians viewed social partnership as an instrument to tackle Ireland's deteriorating macroeconomic position. Successive governments had proven incapable of tackling Ireland's mounting fiscal deficits for fear of being attacked by their political rivals (99). The decision by the opposition party, Fine Gael, to support the government in implementing austerity measures following an electoral defeat in 1987 created a window for fiscal retrenchment. But Taoiseach Charles Haughey recognized the fragile and conditional nature of the agreement (166). He was also sensitive to the danger of alienating Fianna Fail's blue-collar electoral base. Haughey proposed social partnership, a very personal initiative, in a bid to diffuse political responsibility across multiple stakeholders, labor in particular (167).

Trade unions supported the initiative from a position of acute weakness. While export-oriented sectors had secured considerable wage gains during the early 1980s, inflation and tax increases had eroded their purchasing power (Haughton 1995). More important, the Irish trade union movement was devastated as unionized industries such as food processing and textiles shed workers and unemployment approached 16 percent. Trade union density declined from almost 60 percent in 1980 to 51 percent by 1990 (OECD 2004). The decline was particularly alarming in the context of the 1980s. The Irish government's political vulnerability notwithstanding, contemporaries were all too aware of Margaret Thatcher, her campaign against organized labor, and the prospect of similar developments within Ireland (Allen 2000, 113). Indeed, the government demonstrated its credibility when the finance minister, Ray "Mac the Knife" MacSharry canceled a scheduled raise for senior civil servants two days into his tenure (Ó Grada 1997, 32). In the words of one trade union representative, "We were looking at Margaret Thatcher and we said, 'Holy shit, this is heavy stuff. We can't have that happen here. What if it does?' We read British papers. We watched British television. We, on the union side, said that we have a crisis. Real earnings fell by 8 percent in less than a decade; unemployment was very high; inflation had hit 24 percent in the early 1980s; and manufacturing was being decimated, particularly indigenous industry."[4] The PNR offered a vulnerable trade union movement some influence over the structure and content of fiscal retrenchment (O'Donnell 1998; 2001). More specifically, unions offset the costs of fiscal retrenchment with

---

3. Author interview with former executive, Department of the Taoiseach (14 June 2006, Ireland).
4. Author interview with adviser, Irish Congress of Trade Unions (16 May 2006, Ireland).

tax reductions totaling 225 million pounds sterling (Department of the Taoiseach 1987, 11).

Employers also embraced the turn toward tripartite concertation. Decentralized bargaining failed to induce wage restraint, as Irish wages outpaced British compensation during the 1980s (Thomas 2003, 155). Tripartite bargaining represented an instrument for stabilizing and containing wage increases. Just as important, employers viewed the PNR as an instrument to tackle Ireland's deteriorating economic situation. The Irish Business Employers Confederation were eager to reach a national-level policy agreement to tackle the national debt and increasing tax burden (Thomas 2003, 154). This was particularly true for IBEC members that did not benefit from Ireland's low corporate tax rate on manufacturing corporations. The National Economic and Social Council and the Taoiseach both made the case that the only way to rein in government spending was by linking spending to a collective wage agreement (157–58). Employers were willing to extend social partnership after the PNR stabilized government expenditure, secured industrial peace, and reduced labor-cost growth to the second lowest in the EMS. More specifically, IBEC embraced efforts to tackle labor shortages and invest in infrastructure during the late 1990s and early 2000s.[5]

Unlike Denmark and Finland, however, policymakers could not exploit a tradition of cooperation with labor or industry. Policymakers faced three obstacles related to the state, labor, and industry. First, state agencies such as the Industrial Development Authority and, to a lesser extent, Enterprise Ireland were staffed by generally trained career civil servants with few ties to traditional stakeholders such as industry, banks, or trade unions (Breznitz 2007, 188). While tripartite forums served as a focal point for collective wage bargaining, they exercised limited influence over educational, industrial, and financial policy (Ó Riain 2000, 182; Ó Riain and O'Connell 2000, 338). One participant, commenting on the tripartite National Competitiveness Council remarked, "The developments which took place in finance, education, and R & D were not hugely influenced by the partnership process. . . . [The National Competitiveness Council] has just one trade unionist on it, and it is a creature of IBEC to a degree. My impression is that STI [science, technology, and innovation] policy is shaped by institutions that are much less tripartite."[6] The developmental agencies themselves engaged policymakers and industry representatives, but they did so on an individual basis.[7] This hub-and-spoke structure discouraged bilateral cooperation between or within

---

5. Author interviews with former director, Irish Business and Employers Confederation (24 May 2006, Ireland) and director, Training and Employment Authority (2 June 2006).

6. Author interview with director, National Economic and Social Council (2 May 2006, Ireland).

7. Author interview with former director, Industrial Development Authority (6 June 2006, Ireland).

state, labor, and industrial actors. While some scholars applaud the autonomy and flexibility associated with the "flexible" developmental state (Ó Riain 2000; 2004), these weak ties limited state capacity in important respects.

In fact, societal actors were internally fragmented. As described in chapter 2, Irish labor market relations were adversarial in nature, with craft-based unions competing with one another to secure higher wages. In contrast to Denmark, the postwar Irish trade union movement did not play a central role in vocational train-ing and exercised limited influence over social policy (Mjøset 1992; White 2001). Nor did Ireland possess an infrastructure for local-level training like the Danish shop steward system (Prondzynski 1998, 56). The foreign-owned enterprises that dominated the postwar Irish economy were even less hospitable to cooperation, with only 24 percent of foreign enterprises recognizing unions in 1995 (Gunnigle 1998, 195). While multinational enterprises shadowed national pay agreements, they did so on a strictly voluntary basis. Multinational enterprises did not formally sign the national wage agreements (Ó Riain 1999, 277), rarely participated in local bargaining (Gunnigle 1998, 195), and, along with domestic counterparts, resisted any national-level agreement on union recognition (EIRO 2002). Partly because of local shop-floor management's exclusion from national policymaking, trade unions possessed limited competencies in the areas of training, skill formation, in-dustrial policy, and related issues. In other words, trade unions found themselves overstretched, even when invited to participate in such discussions.[8]

Interfirm relations were no less contentious. For example, Ireland lags be-hind both Denmark and Finland on several measures of cooperation (O'Malley, Hewitt-Dundas, and Roper 2008, 174). Where Irish firms do exhibit a propensity to collaborate, it reflects a reliance on vertical supplier relations rather than hori-zontal cooperation between firms and public-sector actors (175). Studies of Irish high-tech industry confirm that agglomeration stems from basic infrastructure and regional policy rather than a common pool of advanced skills or special-ized knowledge (Egeraat 2006). This arm's-length relationship was especially pronounced among multinational firms, as subsidiary managers expressed little interest in cooperating with other enterprises.[9]

Indigenous enterprises were also divided. Policymakers constructed the Na-tional Software Directorate, a successful example of cooperation, because the private-sector organization, the Irish Software Association, was so weak.[10] One

---

8. Author interview with adviser, Irish Congress of Trade Unions (16 May 2006, Ireland).
9. Author interviews with manager, electronics firm (7 June 2006, Ireland); director, electronics firm (8 June 2006, Ireland); and manager, electronics firm (8 June 2006, Ireland).
10. Author interview with former director, National Software Directorate (31 May 2006, Ireland) and manager, Enterprise Ireland (13 June 2006, Ireland).

participant commented, "Our association, the Irish Software Association, represented only a quarter of the firms. It was mainly a lobbying group to convince government that the taxation system is in their favor, and it failed to have much of an influence on the other things."[11] While the National Software Directorate was partially successful as a lobbying group, interfirm collaboration remained limited.[12] Some entrepreneurs acknowledged sharing labor and equipment, but they commented that this was exceptional. Collaboration in product development was even more unusual.[13] Traditional industries such as beef, pork, and dairy processing were no more organized, and interfirm relations were at times openly hostile (Enright 2001; Kennelly 2001; Mjøset 1992).

As a result, industry was reluctant to engage even those institutions where it had the strongest voice. The Irish Business and Employers Confederation was only partially engaged with its "own creature," the National Competitiveness Council. One policymaker commented, "[The Irish Business and Employers Confederation] was more a takeover by the Federated Union of Employers and the disappearance of the Confederation of Irish Industry. The Confederation of Irish Industry had the people that were into innovation policy and structural supply side and all of that. So there was almost a level at which the employer side didn't have for a long piece of the period almost an expertise in this area. You would have thought it was one which would naturally arise more from the employer side."[14]

The unwillingness and inability to engage core stakeholders inhibited Irish investments in high-quality inputs such as skill formation, research, and risk capital. Policymakers, animated by the same concerns as their Finnish and Danish counterparts, repeatedly attempted to promote upmarket movement by investing in these resources. In some cases, policymakers were directly inspired by and sought to replicate Danish and Finnish strategies.[15] While inspired by similar ideas, however, Irish policymakers were constrained in two important respects. First, they struggled to create a broad societal consensus regarding the importance of these resources. As noted, industry representatives exhibited limited

---

11. Author interview with manager, Enterprise Ireland (13 June 2006, Ireland).

12. Author interviews with executive officer, software firm (19 May 2006, Ireland); former director, software firm (25 May 2006, Ireland); former executive officer, software firm (30 May 2006, Ireland); and former director, National Software Directorate (31 May 2006, Ireland).

13. Author interviews with former executive, software firm (25 May 2006, Ireland); former director, National Software Directorate (31 May 2006, Ireland); and former executive officer, electronics firm (9 June 2006, Ireland).

14. Author interview with former executive, Department of the Taoiseach (14 June 2006, Ireland).

15. Author interviews with director, Enterprise Ireland (7 June 2006, Ireland) and manager, Enterprise Ireland (16 June 2006, Ireland).

interest in supply-side investments and tripartite collaboration more generally. Moreover, policymakers lacked the meso- and microlevel institutions to diffuse new ideas, mobilize private-sector resources, or monitor firm commitments that existed in Denmark and Finland. Second, and related, policymakers struggled to gather information about relevant industrial needs. Supply-side investments were not always closely aligned with industrial requirements. This disconnect further reduced interest in neo-corporatism and social partnership, in particular, and its capacity to deliver relevant high-quality inputs.

As a result, neo-corporatist bargaining was most successful in its efforts to secure fiscal retrenchment, wage restraint, and tax cuts. These objectives were less demanding in that they did not require stakeholders to share sensitive information regarding their skill profiles, research activity, or capital requirements. Furthermore, industry was also more confident about the social partnership's ability to deliver on these commitments, particularly following successful retrenchment in 1987.[16] The following sections develop this argument in detail, characterizing competitive corporatist content and the absence of creative corporatism in three domains: labor markets, industrial policy, and finance.

Labor Markets: Competitive Corporatism and Cost Competition

In Ireland, neo-corporatist bargaining revolved around the labor market in the form of centralized collective bargaining among state agencies, trade unions, and employer federations. "Irish social partnership" was initially founded as an austerity pact, designed to retrench runaway fiscal expenditures and to introduce wage restraint. The initial 1987 PNR was renegotiated in subsequent years, exchanging wage moderation for an increasingly ambitious program of tax cuts. As the Irish economy recovered, social partnership was adapted to address unemployment and skill shortages. The link between wage moderation and lower taxation remained central throughout the 1990s, however, and investments in human capital formation lagged behind those in Denmark and Finland throughout the 1990s and 2000s.

The PNR represented a radical departure from the decentralized labor markets of the 1970s and the conservative corporatist experiments of the 1970s. The 1987 agreement eliminated the jobs of 20,000 public workers (Haughton 1998, 45) and reduced government spending as a share of GDP from 49.0 percent in

---

16. Author interviews with former director, Irish Business and Employers Confederation (24 May 2006, Ireland) and director, Training and Employment Authority (2 June 2006).

1986 to 37.9 percent by 1989 (European Commission 2003b, 448). An average GDP growth rate of 4.1 percent contributed to the decline, but fiscal retrenchment was also achieved through a recruitment freeze, an early retirement scheme, pay cuts, and deep reductions in public housing (McCarthy 2001, 14). In signing the PNR, trade unions had some influence over its content. The government pledged to reduce taxes on wage earners and to maintain social-policy expenditures at a constant level in order to secure trade union support (14).

In exchange, trade unions agreed to restrain wages to restore economic competitiveness. Initial agreements were highly successful in this respect. Hourly labor-cost growth was the second lowest in the EMS between 1987 and 1992 (Sexton et al. 1997: 64). Real wage increases averaged 2.5 percent between 1987 and 1993 while the economy grew at 3.3 percent (Sexton et al. 1997, 60), resulting in a pronounced shift in the ratio of wages to profits (O'Hearn 1998, 125). Subsequent agreements including the 1990 Program for Economic and Social Progress, the 1993 Program for Competitiveness and Work, and the 1996 Partnership 2000 agreement also prioritized restraint. Labor unit costs continued to plummet through 1998, falling twice as fast as the European Union average (Thomas 2003, 326). In 2000, average hourly compensation for manufacturing employees ($12.50) was still among the lowest in the European Union, trailing Germany ($23.00), Denmark ($21.50), Finland ($19.50), and even liberal Britain ($16.50) (Barry 2004, 31). Even liberal economists conceded that these very nonliberal agreements supported wage restraint in the late 1990s (Clinch, Convery, and Walsh 2002, 92).

Wage restraint was based on tax relief from the very first agreement (OECD 1999, 25). Tax reductions were used as early as 1987 to secure agreement on a program of "wage freezes, wage cuts and the recruitment of new employees on lower entry pay scales" (Sexton et al. 1997, xiii).[17] Tax concessions expanded rapidly under subsequent agreements. Whereas the initial PNR cut taxes by 225 million pounds sterling, the Program for Economic and Social Partnership pledged 400 million pounds. By Partnership 2000, the government was pledging one billion pounds in tax relief (Department of the Taoiseach 1998, 9). An individual with average earnings saw her or his marginal tax rate decline from 40.0 percent at the introduction of the PNR to 24.2 percent by the end of the 1996 Partnership 2000 agreement (NESC 1999, 223). Tax reductions were less dramatic after the dot-com crash, but the marginal rate continued to decline in line with the OECD average (Gylfason et al. 2010, 222). By 2005, the gross tax burden was lower than

---

17. As the concluding section relates, the lack of fiscal leeway generated by financial bailouts and two decades of tax concessions is one reason why policymakers, industry, and labor failed to reach a wage agreement during the 2007–9 crisis.

in any other western European country except Greece (Gylfason et al. 2010, 218). Collectively, these concessions helped to maintain a broad coalition of domestic employers and unionized labor while restraining public- and sheltered-sector wages.

Proponents note that social partnership was deepened and broadened in subsequent agreements. Stakeholders placed less emphasis on wage restraint, in part because there was less room to reduce taxes. Policymakers and trade union representatives also demonstrated increasing interest in the types of active labor market policies that were pioneered in countries such as Denmark. These creative corporatist experiments started as early as 1990, as rapid growth failed to generate employment gains. The Program for Economic and Social Prosperity introduced regional area-based partnerships to tackle unemployment (Sabel 1996), and representatives were formally integrated into peak-level bargaining as part of the "third strand" in 1996. Not surprisingly, the third strand was most effective in providing tax relief for low-income workers (Clinch, Convery, and Walsh 2002, 85).

The social partners also increased expenditure on active labor market policies from 1.4 percent of GDP in 1993 to 1.5 percent by 1999 (Haughton 1998, 41). This increase is impressive when one considers that unemployment fell from 15.6 percent to 4.3 percent between 1993 and 2000. By 1999, social partnership was focusing on skill shortages (Sexton et al. 1997, xix). Stakeholders sought to promote lifelong learning by introducing the National Training Fund, financed by a 0.7 percent share of an employer's social-insurance contributions (OECD 2003a, 66). Meanwhile, university enrollment doubled between 1985 and 1995 and increased even further following the state's decision to provide free tertiary education in the mid-1990s (White 2001, 282). Collectively, these initiatives are hailed as convergence toward a deeper pattern of neo-corporatist cooperation characteristic of continental European economies such as Denmark and Finland (O'Donnell 1998; Thomas 2003).

Yet Irish social partnership never achieved the kinds of creative corporatist bargains that characterized Denmark. First, analysts criticized Irish active labor market policies as poorly coordinated (Hardiman 1998, 142). The programs themselves emphasized tax incentives (Hardiman 1998; O'Connell 1999) and public employment rather than training (Sexton et al. 1997, 162). Indeed, the share of the workforce engaged in continuing education in 2007 (10.8%) was considerably lower than either Denmark (40.2%) or Finland (33.9%), even following the introduction of the National Training Fund (Eurostat 2011). One participant in the social partnership process conceded, "The one area where there's a significant deficit in Ireland is our programs for ongoing training and education. That is, we have singularly failed to crack that area. For some reason or other we keep producing report after report which draws attention to the need for this."[18] Multinational and indigenous employers indirectly acknowledged the limitations of the Irish labor market, emphasizing their reliance on expatriate labor and skilled European immigrants in meeting human capital needs.[19]

Second, the training that was provided was less targeted to industrial needs. In contrast to Denmark, policymakers relied more heavily on state agencies such as FAS (An Foras Áiseanna Seothair) rather than societal actors to administer training. Studies criticize public training for its limited impact on labor market outcomes (Boyle 2004, 20) and its inability to take on even basic skills such as literacy (27). In other words, publicly sponsored training was only loosely connected to industry needs, and the basic skills that it supplied proved more relevant for basic assembly or construction than engineering or design.

These limitations extend to vocational, secondary, and tertiary institutions, which are not as tightly linked to the labor market as in other European economies such as Denmark or Finland (Smyth and Hannan 2000). For example, Irish investments in education and human capital formation focused on type B tertiary education, or short-term technical education at local technical colleges (White 2001, 282). Yet these investments did not support more knowledge-intensive and higher value-added forms of production. One software analyst dismissed the regional technical colleges as training grounds for "technically qualified secretaries" (Sterne 2004, 73). These colleges represented a valuable resource for multinational companies seeking to expand their manufacturing capacity or shifting into customer support call centers. Interviewees at software firms, however, argue that they relied on four-year universities for skilled labor and product development in particular.[20] Ireland lagged behind Denmark (38.8%) and Finland (40.7%) in this area, with only 29.3% of the population receiving type A degrees, or theory-based education providing sufficient qualifications for advanced research and professions with high skill requirements (O'Malley, Hewitt-Dundas, and Roper 2008, 167; OECD 2008). Neo-corporatist bargaining, in other words, was highly successful in securing wage restraint, but it was less effective in pro-

---

18. Author interview with former general secretary, Irish Council of Trade Unions (22 May 2006).

19. Author interviews with former executive officer, software firm (25 May 2006, Ireland); head of corporate affairs, software firm (1 June 2006, Ireland); and director, electronics firm (8 June 2006, Ireland).

20. Author interviews with executive officer, software firm (19 May 2006, Ireland); former director, National Software Directorate (31 May 2006, Ireland); and former executive officer, electronics firm (9 June 2006, Ireland).

moting skill formation. The following section documents similar developments in industrial policy.

Industrial Policy: Tax Competition and Foreign Direct Investment

Neo-corporatist bargaining was more limited in industrial policy, because state agencies such as the Industrial Development Authority were largely insulated from organized industry, labor, and social partnership more generally. The IDA relied on social partnership to secure a stable and cost-competitive climate for economic investment, but it relied heavily on tax competition to attract foreign direct investment. That said, the IDA and its domestic counterpart, Enterprise Ireland, have expressed greater interest in promoting interfirm collaboration and research. Cooperation and investment in resources such as research, however, remain modest relative to Denmark and Finland.

The economic crisis of the 1970s and 1980s extended to industrial policy, as the once formidable IDA struggled to combat capital flight and mounting unemployment during the 1980s. As described in chapter 2, the IDA had emerged as a powerful force in postwar Irish politics following the decision to shift from import-substituting industrialization to free trade and foreign direct investment in 1958 (Fink 2004; O'Hearn 1998). The independent agency wooed multinationals through a combination of tax concessions, employment subsidies, equipment grants, and subsidized leases (Breznitz 2007; Mjøset 1992; Ó Riain 2004). The IDA's ability to lure foreign direct investment placed it in a powerful position during the 1960s (Breznitz 2007, 153). By the 1980s, IDA subsidies represented 2 percent of GDP and 12 percent of all public investment (Ó Grada 1997, 55). The IDA's leading role in attracting multinational corporations, however, rendered the agency vulnerable when capital flows reversed, growth stagnated, and unemployment soared during the 1970s.

Interestingly, it was a neo-corporatist institution, the tripartite National Economic and Social Council, that challenged the IDA in 1982. The council commissioned the Telesis Report of 1982, which criticized the IDA's reliance on employment and equipment grants and its propensity to target highly mobile, cost-sensitive low-tech producers in industries such as food processing, footwear, and textiles (Telesis Consultancy Group 1982). The Culliton Report, one decade later, led to the division of the IDA into foreign and domestic branches in 1993 and the creation of a tripartite steering body, Forfas (Culliton Industrial Policy Review Group 1992). The agency responded by targeting new high-tech industries and linking them to local suppliers and cultivating indigenous entrepreneurship. One former executive described a deliberate shift to high-tech industry during the 1980s, because higher fixed costs made high-tech less sensitive to wage inflation and reduced corporate mobility.[21]

In attracting new investments, the IDA placed less emphasis on traditional subsidies or the generous investment and equipment grants that it had used to attract multinational investment in the past. Real expenditure on industrial policy declined by 29 percent between 1985 and 1989. Investment and equipment grants were especially hard hit, declining from 38 percent to 30.1 percent of the IDA's budget (O'Malley, Kennedy, and O'Donnell 1992, 26). Yet the IDA continued to rely heavily on cost competition throughout the 1980s and 1990s, defending its low-tax regime. The European Commission forced Ireland to raise its tax on export-generated profits from 0 percent to 10 percent in 1981, but the government extended this low rate to cover all manufacturing firms (Fink 2004, 80). This 10 percent tax, the lowest in the European Union, was broadened to export-oriented services such as software and finance in 1984. In 1998, the Irish government, again ceding to EU pressure, increased its corporate tax to 12.5 percent in 2003 but extended coverage to include all services (Barry 2004, 16). This tax regime remained the lowest in the European Union, as Irish standard and effective corporate tax rates were less than half those of competitors like Britain and Germany (17).

Initiatives were not limited to tax competition. Just as policymakers were inspired to experiment with active labor market policies, they also launched innovative industrial policies designed to stimulate investment in new inputs. They did so by targeting the same interfirm networks as their Danish and Finnish counterparts (Ó Riain 2000; 2004). In 1984, the government launched the National Linkage Program, engaging 250 foreign suppliers and 70 domestic suppliers in a bid to promote upmarket movement (O'Doherty 1998, 112; O'Malley, Kennedy, and O'Donnell 1992, 102). Efforts to promote cooperation among indigenous enterprises were even more explicit. For example, the government created the National Software Directorate in 1991 to organize the fragmented Irish software industry. The NSD was designed to increase awareness about the software industry, identify relevant industrial needs, and lobby for supporting infrastructure, including venture capital (Ó Riain 2004; Sterne 2004). Enterprise Ireland followed with the Inter-Firm Cooperation Program in 1996. Modeled after the Danish network program of the early 1990s (see chapter 4), the initiative subsidized cooperation between domestic enterprises in a bid to promote technology transfer and applied research (O'Doherty 1998). Such initiatives continue

---

21. Author interview with former executive, Industrial Development Authority (6 June 2006, Ireland).

in traditional industries such as beef, dairy, and food processing, where the government has promoted consolidation (O'Connell, Egaraat, and Enright 1997).

Collaboration was designed to facilitate investment in resources such as R & D. While reducing expenditures on state aid, the government introduced the Technology Acquisition Grant in 1986 to cover the cost of technological development and launched the university-based Programs for Applied Technology in 1987 (O'Malley, Kennedy, and O'Donnell 1992, 14). The latter were designed to promote technological diffusion within existing industries (O'Malley, Hewitt-Dundas, and Roper 2008, 162) but included programs in optics, electronics, software, and other high-tech industries.[22] The programs supported a broader increase in university R & D, from €133 million in 1993 to €294 million by 2001 (163). By then, the government had resolved to target research more explicitly, creating the Office of Science and Technology to promote and coordinate innovation policy in 1997 and a new instrument, Science Foundation Ireland, to invest in research. The latter's unprecedented €120 million budget supported basic research in a range of strategic fields including biotechnology and information technology. Like Tekes, Science Foundation Ireland requires firms to collaborate with one another and knowledge-bearing institutions (172). Such initiatives are significant in supporting unprecedented cooperation in R & D.

While Irish policymakers were influenced by similar ideas and adopted similar measures, cooperation and expenditure in this domain remained modest relative to Finland and even Denmark. "Network-oriented" industrial policies such as the Inter-Firm Cooperation Program, the National Linkage Program, and the Programs for Applied Technology have struggled. The former two were discontinued within three years (O'Doherty 1998; O'Malley, Kennedy, and O'Donnell 1992), while the latter was criticized for its mixed success in linking universities to industry (Sterne 2004, 83). Science Foundation Ireland has attempted to address these shortcomings with an even more formidable commitment of public resources, yet it remains significantly smaller than Tekes (and other investors in the Finnish innovation system), both in terms of its annual budget and the size of the research consortia that it supports. Indeed, the program's success in promoting collaboration among partners is questionable. Managers of multiple multinational subsidiaries that participated in consortia remarked that cooperation was limited to the initial construction of the project. They do not cooperate in research, even when participating within the same project.[23] Meanwhile,

---

22. Author interview with former director, Program for Applied Technology (16 June 2006, Ireland).

23. Author interviews with manager, electronics firm (7 June 2006, Ireland); director, electronics firm (8 June 2006, Ireland); and manager, electronics firm (8 June 2006, Ireland).

indigenous software enterprises have played a conspicuously minor role in early funding rounds (Breznitz 2007, 156), weakening efforts to construct a broader coalition supporting R & D.

Partly as a result of these dynamics, gains in R & D have been relatively modest. Public expenditure on R & D as a share of GDP was virtually flat between 1980 and 2005. While corporate funding fueled a significant increase in research expenditure from 0.79 percent to 1.25 percent of GDP over this period, Ireland continued to trail Denmark and Finland, even when adjusting for transfer pricing (Eurostat 2011).[24] This is remarkable, given Irish gains in per capita income and its apparent comparative advantage in high-tech industry. Ireland's inability to engage stakeholders within peak- and local-level forums sheds some light on why public- and private-sector investments remain limited. Indeed, while policymakers promote Ireland's status as a center for R & D, multinational representatives asked to comment on the advantages of Ireland continue to emphasize the country's status as a stable, low-tax location for multinational investment rather than an ideal base for R & D. Nor, unlike their Finnish counterparts, do they appeal for greater government support for research.[25]

Finance: Foreign Direct Investment as Risk Capital

Neo-corporatist bargaining was least pronounced in financial markets, where national-level organized stakeholders such as the universal bank or the cooperative movement were virtually nonexistent. Here, policymakers relied on a large and liquid pool of multinational capital to finance experimentation and restructuring. Increasing attention to indigenous entrepreneurship, however, sparked greater interest in early stage risk capital markets during the 1980s and 1990s. As in labor markets and industrial policy, early initiatives relied on tax competition. The government subsequently assumed a more active role as a direct investor and broker. Such initiatives were significant in stimulating venture capital investment. The government, however, was less effective than its Danish and Finnish counterparts in engaging domestic institutional investors such as pension funds. As a result, venture capital markets, and early stage risk capital markets in particular, remain underdeveloped relative to Denmark and Finland.

---

24. While the share of GDP devoted to R & D increased sharply from 1.29% to 1.77% between 2007 and 2009, this reflected a precipitous decline in GDP. In fact, R & D as a share of GDP jumped in Denmark and Finland as well, increasing to 3.02% and 3.96%, respectively (Eurostat 2011).

25. Author interviews with former manager, electronics firm (3 May 2006, Ireland); executive officer, software firm (8 June 2006, Ireland); and director, electronics firm (15 June 2006, Ireland).

As noted, policymakers have embraced foreign direct investment as an instrument for creating new actors, activities, and industries since 1958, and foreign direct investment continues to play a central role in the Irish economy. Indeed, many indigenous enterprises relied on foreign capital to finance their own growth and development, whether one focuses on high-tech firms concentrating in localization (Eurostat 2011; Sterne 2004, 106) or traditional enterprises like the Kerry Group, whose activities as a casein supplier bankrolled its subsequent expansion into food ingredients (Kennelly 2001, 66). The Irish financial system has thus revolved first and foremost around efforts to recruit foreign direct investment.

Domestic institutional arrangements are also consistent with the liberal emphasis on decentralized market competition and the preference for decentralized equity financing over long-term relational finance in particular. Irish banks have eschewed the long-term relationships and dense network of cross-shareholdings that characterized the Finnish financial system and continental European capitalism more generally (Brennan and McDermott 2002). Banks have instead preferred to issue short-term debt financing. Irish firms, meanwhile, can turn to a comparatively robust domestic equity market (Casey 2000, 7) and double list in Britain or the United States (Breznitz 2007, 178). Indeed, equity markets remain a more feasible and attractive fund-raising strategy in Ireland. Traditional dairy and food-processing cooperatives such as the Kerry Group and Glendale have turned to domestic equity markets (Kennelly 2001, 226, 246) in contrast to their counterparts like Finland's Valio and Denmark's MD Foods (now Arla Foods). Equity markets have grown rapidly over the course of the 1990s, fueled in part by this increase in initial public offerings.[26]

Finally, Ireland has also been characterized by a light regulatory touch that persists to the present day. As noted, Ireland liberalized international capital flows beginning in 1958. To the extent that it adapted its financial system, it embraced further deregulation during the 1980s in a bid to attract financial services (MacSharry and White 2000). Indeed, the government has played such an indirect role in shaping investment and corporate governance that the country has been popularized as "the Wild West of European finance" (Brennan 2006).[27] These highly liberal financial institutions should have supported relatively robust early stage risk capital markets, creating a large liquid pool of capital to invest in young enterprises and an array of attractive exit opportunities, including relatively ro-

---

26. Author interview with equity analyst, financial firm (30 May 2006, Ireland).
27. Light financial regulation contributed to the real estate and financial bubble of the mid-2000s and its subsequent collapse (Honohan 2009).

bust domestic equity markets and foreign acquisition (Ali-Yrkkö, Hyytinen, and Liukkonen 2003; Hyytinen and Pajarinen 2003a). In fact, Irish investments in early stage risk capital trailed not only those of large liberal economies but also small, nonliberal ones such as Denmark and Finland (Eurostat 2011).

As a result of this, policymakers launched a series of programs designed to target indigenous enterprises and early stage risk capital markets as early as the 1980s. As with efforts to attract foreign investment and increase employment, these measures emphasized tax incentives. Foremost among these was the Business Expansion Scheme. Launched in 1984, the initiative enabled individual investors to pool their capital in tax-advantaged funds and invest in unlisted companies (Casey 2000, 101). Significantly, policymakers relied on private-sector banks to administer the program and engage individual investors. The program nonetheless emerged as perhaps the most important vehicle for channeling risk capital to domestic firms, with almost all Irish IT companies drawing on the Business Expansion Scheme for seed capital (Breznitz 2007, 184).

Policymakers also intervened more directly in early stage risk capital markets, beginning with a range of services targeted toward small and medium-sized enterprises (O'Malley, Kennedy, and O'Donnell 1992, 11). This support included grant aid and loan guarantees under the Enterprise Development Program from 1978. Although the Enterprise Development Program was not initially conceptualized as a venture capital vehicle, the agency increasingly substituted equity stakes for grants and loan guarantees as a way to circumvent restrictions on state aid and to deal with mounting fiscal pressures.[28] By the mid-1990s, this shift was formalized in the first systematic venture capital program, which distributed €43 million to sixteen venture capital funds for investment in new high-tech firms and software firms in particular. The government also targeted pension fund capital (Breznitz 2007, 177). Collectively, the ability to engage private actors supposed a significant increase in venture capital over the course of the 1990s. Early stage venture capital investments increased from €4.6 million (less than 0.01% of GDP) in 1991 to €111.6 million (0.016% of GDP) in 2000 (Eurostat 2011).

Yet developments remained limited relative to Denmark and Finland. The Irish government not only made a belated and more modest commitment to venture capital financing, but it was also less successful in promoting cooperation among different financial intermediaries. In contrast to what was done in Denmark and Finland, the Irish government legislated pension fund participation, threatening to directly tax their assets.[29] Pension funds responded by limit-

---

28. Author interview with director, Enterprise Ireland (19 May 2006, Ireland).
29. Author interview with director, venture capital fund (2 June 2006, Ireland).

ing participation to a quarter of funds raised in 1999 (Ó Riain 2004, 96) and, more important, focusing on more conservative, later stage investments than their Danish and Finnish peers (Breznitz 2007; Christiansen, Goldstein, and Bertrand 2007; Hyytinen and Pajarinen 2003a). Official accounts confirm tense relations between policymakers and pension fund investors. Financial representatives blame "risk averse" Irish managers for underdeveloped venture capital markets (Casey 2000, 110), conceptualizing early stage risk capital markets as an exclusively public responsibility (114).

As a result, Irish venture capital markets are surprisingly weak, given Ireland's status as a liberal market economy. Although the industry's performance was very impressive in 2000, Ireland lagged behind Finland on a three-year rolling basis throughout the late 1990s and early 2000s. Performance after the dot-com crash was even worse. Early stage venture capital investments fell to €37.6 million (0.03% of GDP) by 2001 and shrank even further to €32.8 million (0.01% of GDP) by 2007. By contrast, Finland invested €71.9 million (0.04% of GDP) and Denmark invested €116.8 million (0.05% of GDP) in 2007. Not surprisingly, early stage risk capital investments fell even further, to €23.5 million in 2008 as a result of the financial crisis (Eurostat 2011). Nor do informal networks, like business angels, appear to compensate for this discrepancy (O'Malley, Hewitt-Dundas, and Roper 2008, 177). The limited availability of risk capital and related supply-side resources constrained high-tech competition in significant ways during the 1990s and 2000s. Before elaborating on these constraints, however, it is first important to recognize the constructive role that competitive corporatism played in facilitating early experimentation and growth.

Consequences: Competitive Corporatism and Rapid Restructuring

Collectively, fiscal retrenchment, wage restraint, tax concessions, and related pro-market reforms supported significant restructuring and rapid movement into new high-tech markets during the 1980s and 1990s. As noted, Ireland emerged as one of Europe's most dynamic economies after 1987. GDP growth increased, averaging 4.4 percent between 1987 and 1993 and accelerating to 9.3 percent between 1994 and 2000 (European Commission 2003b, 228). Meanwhile, Ireland's share of high-tech manufactured exports more than tripled between 1985 and 2000 (OECD 2011), placing it at the top of the European Union (Eurostat 2011). Neo-corporatist bargaining, and competitive corporatism in particular, facilitated initial experimentation in new high-tech industries during the 1980s and rapid growth during the 1990s. At the same time, these strategies exposed Ireland to mounting cost competition after the dot-com crash. The limited supply of high-quality inputs has constrained diversification into knowledge-intensive activities, forcing Ireland to rely on low value-added activities to sustain growth such as call centers or, even more problematically, nontradable services such as residential construction.

1980–1990: Experimentation

In contrast to Denmark and Finland, Ireland surmounted financial and techno-logical barriers to entry with recourse to foreign direct investment. Foreign mul-tinationals such as Apple, Digital Equipment, Ericsson, and Motorola enabled Ireland to enter new high-tech industries such as computers and telecommunica-tion equipment virtually overnight. Foreign direct investment increased sharply during the mid-1980s, trebling between 1985 and 1995 and quintupling between 1995 and 2000 (Barry 2004, 12). Intel, for example, arrived in 1991 and eventu-ally constructed a $7 billion production facility that employed over a thousand individuals.[30] Hardware firms including IBM, Dell, Gateway, and Logica (Barry and Egeraat 2008) and software enterprises including Microsoft, Novell, Oracle, and Symantec (Breznitz 2007, 166) followed shortly thereafter. Finally, estab-lished firms, most notably telecommunication equipment providers Ericsson and Motorola, expanded their operations (Sterne 2004, 21). Employment in for-eign multinationals increased by 50 percent between 1987 and 2000, accounting for 48 percent of the jobs in Irish manufacturing (Barry 2004, 10). Employment in high-tech industries was even more concentrated, representing 62.3 percent of all employment in electrical machinery, 85.3 percent in telecommunication equipment and 88.3 percent in office equipment (22).

Multinational corporations even dominated industries characterized as indig-enous success stories such as software (Ó Riain 2004; Sterne 2004). Multinational corporations represented half of all employment in the software industry by the end of the 1990s (Barry 2004, 21; Ó Riain 2004, 57). Other measures were even more skewed. A single subsidiary, Microsoft, not only dwarfed indigenous output but was single-handedly responsible for Ireland's status as the world's leading software exporter (Breznitz 2007). While Microsoft's impressive output may be a better example of transfer pricing than high-tech innovation, it nonetheless underscores Ireland's reliance on foreign direct investment (O'Malley, Hewitt-Dundas, and Roper 2008, 184–85).[31]

---

30. Author visit to Intel Ireland (8 June 2006, Ireland).
31. Although it is difficult to determine exactly how much of the Irish IT industry's revenue can be attributed to transfer pricing, Microsoft Ireland's annual reports highlight its significance.

Indeed, multinational capital played an important role in financing indigenous experimentation. This link was perhaps most explicit in software localization (Sterne 2004, 106), but some of Ireland's most prominent indigenous firms such as Mentec relied on their status as an original equipment manufacturer for U.S. multinationals such as Digital Equipment (Breznitz 2007, 162; Sterne 2004, 15). In addition to direct financial support, foreign multinationals trained Irish engineers on new software platforms. Kindle, one of Ireland's first exporters, exploited its familiarity with ICL's (International Computers Limited) platform to export banking software (Breznitz 2007, 158), while Aldiscon acquired familiarity with telecommunications from their time as employees at Nortel (Sterne 2004, 218). Digital Equipment made perhaps the most significant contribution to Irish high-tech industry, as the firm's decision to shutter development and production dispersed technological expertise and managerial experience throughout Ireland (Barry and Egeraat 2008, 51).

Foreign direct investment, in turn, was based on a low-tax, low-cost, stable economic climate. Tax concessions played a central role, particularly after the European Union forced Irish policymakers to abandon their preferential zero percent tax on manufactured exports in 1978 (Barry 2004, 16). As noted, Ireland retained a preferential 10 percent tax on manufacturing firms and extended this preferential rate to targeted services, including software, in 1981. The first dedicated investments in software followed shortly thereafter, with Lotus arriving in 1985 (Sterne 2004, 101), followed by Oracle, Microsoft, Symantec, Novell, and Corel (Breznitz 2007, 166). This pattern extended to other sectors. The 10 percent corporate-profit tax was broadened to include international financial services in 1987, in a deliberate effort to target U.S. multinationals (MacSharry and White 2000). Employment in this sector more than quadrupled over the course of the 1990s (Thomas 2003, 339).

Multinational representatives argued that these tax concessions were even more compelling than the employment and equipment grants that preceded them. Company representatives noted that IDA grant aid never made a significant contribution to a multinational subsidiary's bottom line, particularly for large U.S. corporations.[32] Ireland's low tax rate on corporate profits, on the other hand, was considerably more lucrative, especially when corporations could rely

---

Microsoft Ireland's 689 employees generated €11.35 billion in revenue and €1.43 billion in profits (Collins 2011). Despite representing less than 1% of Microsoft's workforce, its Irish employees generated almost a quarter of the firm's revenue and a tenth of its profits. These figures do not include a smaller separate subsidiary, Round Island One, which generates billions of Euros in licensing revenue (Simpson 2005). Collectively, these subsidiaries generate over ten times the revenue of the indigenous Irish software industry with less than a tenth of the personnel.

32. Author interview with director, electronics firm (15 June 2006, Ireland).

on transfer pricing to inflate revenue from their Irish subsidiary (O'Hearn 1998). A former executive at the National Software Directorate notes, "The fact is that the tax regime is hugely important in that. It is the single most important factor. You can talk about the people, but I have no doubt that taxes are a reason why an awful lot of these companies are here."[33] One former country manager confirms, "The whole tax structure–the corporate tax–was a big issue, and for some it still is a big issue, and corporate tax rates in Ireland are extremely low. That is almost always one of the two or three fundamental points around which an initial decision is made."[34] Other industry representatives argued that tax concessions were more reliable, or were at least perceived as such by corporate headquarters. In the words of one manager, "We will not make an investment decision as a company purely on grants, because grants are transient. . . . From the point of view of the supports, the only one that we make a lot of reference to is the tax advantages. I see that as the key support that can drive a lot of growth."[35]

Tax concessions proved particularly effective after 1987 when linked to a stable macroeconomic environment and peaceful labor market. High-tech experimentation, in other words, was predicated on political and economic stability, particularly for capital-intensive high-tech industries. Neo-corporatist bargaining, and Irish social partnership in particular, created that environment by constructing a broad coalition to support fiscal retrenchment and the adoption of a credible hard-currency regime (O'Donnell 1998; Thomas 2003). Economists argue that macroeconomic stability played a central role in explaining increasing industry investment after 1987 and throughout the 1990s (Barry 2000; Clinch, Convery, and Walsh 2002; Haughton 1995, 1998).

Industry representatives express similar sentiments, arguing that they signed on to the initial PNR to secure a more stable business environment. The relationship between political and economic stability and industry investment is less abstract when one considers the level of investment that was required for Ireland to enter new high-tech industries. Intel has invested close to $7 billion in its production facility, and policymakers argue that corporate representatives were very concerned about the political and economic climate when deciding to invest in Ireland.[36] Another multinational representative noted, "When we came here ten years ago, [social partnership] was a selling point for sure, because it gave stability. We were going to make a major investment in the country."[37]

---

33. Author interview with former executive, National Software Directorate (31 May 2006, Ireland).
34. Author interview with former manager, electronics firm (3 May 2006, Ireland).
35. Author interview with executive officer, software firm (8 June 2006, Ireland).
36. Author interview with former executive, Industrial Development Authority (6 June 2006, Ireland).
37. Author interview with director, electronics firm (8 June 2006, Ireland).

Furthermore, Irish social partnership achieved macroeconomic stabilization within a relatively peaceful labor market. The number of worker days lost to industrial disputes declined dramatically from 1,951,079 between 1982 and 1986 to 522,309 between 1992 and 1996 (Thomas 2003, 360). Foreign direct investment was contingent on labor market stability as much as it was on macroeconomic stabilization. Multinational representatives thus viewed a consensual framework for resolving industrial disputes as central to Ireland's success, even as they themselves eschewed any formal negotiations with the unions. One multinational representative noted just how disruptive traditional Irish industrial relations could be, pointing out how sensitive their corporation was to wildcat strikes, and any disruption in the supply of electricity in particular. The representative commented, "[Social partnership] doesn't matter to us directly. We would be shy in anything that would smack of negotiating with the unions. That would be considered dangerously heretical back [at headquarters]. . . . However, the industrial relations tranquility, the environment, the supporting infrastructure—we are very keen to ensure industrial peace."[38] A former executive at the Irish Development Authority added, "We marketed our record on strikes quite heavily. It was considered quite important as a marketing tool."[39]

1990–2000: Expansion

In addition to supporting initial experimentation in high-tech industries, competitive corporatist bargaining also facilitated rapid growth during the 1990s. Multinational firms noted the benefits of a relatively low-cost labor force in attracting investment and supporting competitiveness.[40] While multinational firms in particular avoided any formal engagement with Irish social partnership, they benefited from a broader low-cost environment within Ireland and often tracked the social partnership agreements on a voluntary basis. A former executive at the Irish Development Authority noted, "Although most companies were nonunion, they looked on the settlements that were reached as a key part of bargaining with their own employees. You have to remember that most [multinational corporations], because they want to maximize their profits in a low-tax environment, are very profitable and therefore vulnerable to large wage demands. So they used the settlements as a guideline in negotiating their own wage levels."[41] A multinational

---

38. Author interview with manager, electronics firm (8 June 2006, Ireland).

39. Author interviews with former executive, Industrial Development Authority (6 June 2006, Ireland) and former manager, electronics firm (3 May 2006, Ireland).

40. Author interview with director, electronics firm (8 June 2006, Ireland).

41. Author interview with former executive, Industrial Development Authority (6 June 2006, Ireland).

representative confirmed, "We wouldn't want to see social partnership agree on levels of wage increases or salary increases that would put our positioning out of kilter."[42] In securing wage restraint throughout the 1990s, Irish social partnership thus facilitated continuing investment in rapidly expanding high-tech industries.

Social partnership also created a coalition to invest in basic resources, most notably training and education. Analysts emphasize the importance of a large, well-educated labor force in driving initial investment decisions (Barry 2004; Clinch, Convery, and Walsh 2002), and a large supply of human capital was even more imperative, as multinational enterprises attempted to expand within the confines of a small, rapidly growing economy. Irish social partnership directly contributed to the supply of human capital by constructing a coalition to invest in active labor market measures and expanding university output. At the same time, the IDA engaged enterprises, adapting regional technical college curricula to meet multinational human capital needs.[43] Representatives of multinationals confirmed that training was easy to coordinate with Ireland, partly as a result of the linkages that the IDA established to local regional technical colleges.[44]

The IDA's central position in supplying human capital reflects its broader role as a mediator in the Irish economy, together with its indigenous counterpart, Enterprise Ireland. Foreign multinationals had always relied on the IDA, the largest property owner in Ireland, to lease land and office space at favorable rates (Breznitz 2007, 163). But the agency increasingly linked multinational corporations to resources beyond its direct control, including national departments and municipal governments. For example, the IDA accommodated multinationals by adapting highway construction to facilitate commuting and shipping for an electronics firm, creating radio spectrum for testing for a telecommunications firm, and laying fiber optic cable for new software firms.[45] Multinational managers described the relatively easy access to and coordination among different levels of government as one of the attractive features of investing in Ireland.[46]

This pattern of informal cooperation was frequently used to maintain Ireland's light regulatory environment, effectively lobbying against efforts to formalize union recognition at the national level (Thomas 2003, 371) and dissuading unions from organizing at the firm level. One former IDA executive,

---

42. Author interview with manager, electronics firm (8 June 2006, Ireland).

43. Author interview with former director, Institute of Technology (23 May 2006, Ireland).

44. Author interviews with manager, electronics firm (8 June 2006, Ireland); director, electronics firm (8 June 2006, Ireland); and executive officer, electronics firm (15 June 2006).

45. Author interviews with former executive, Industrial Development Authority (6 June 2006, Ireland); former executive officer, electronics subsidiary (1 June 2006, Ireland); and executive officer, software firm (8 June 2006, Ireland).

46. Author interviews with former manager, electronics subsidiary (3 May 2006); manager, electronics firm (8 June 2006, Ireland); and director, electronics firm (8 June 2006, Ireland).

commenting on the virtues of social partnership, described his success in dissuading union leaders from organizing at a U.S. multinational.[47] A multinational representative, citing the importance of this IDA-brokered cooperative network, cited proposals to tax expatriate employees. Indeed, the interviewee noted, "We're continually networking.... There's the American Chamber of Commerce, which has a very high political profile, which works on the corporate taxation rate. So, yes, we do network, and we do have access to high-level government involvement when we need to."[48] As noted, these networks also created a foundation for investing in high-quality inputs, particularly once Ireland faced competition from new low-cost rivals throughout eastern Europe.

2000–2010: Adaptation

In fact, these creative corporatist experiments were modestly successful in facilitating diversification into new and higher value-added industries. Managers at four separate subsidiaries linked their expansion into R & D to Science Foundation Ireland.[49] One subsidiary relied on Science Foundation Ireland to maintain its presence in Ireland after the multinational parent decided to close all manufacturing and software development activity.[50] Another country manager went even further, noting that corporate headquarters has looked more favorably on the subsidiary's research activities because "the ecosystem provided by the government is becoming stronger." In this particular instance, Science Foundation Ireland created a forum not only for private-public collaboration but also cooperation within the public sector. In the representative's words, "The idea to make a c-set was a logical one, so we pulled together the different players we were already funding, and they came from [one university], the physics department from [another university]. We were saying, 'You guys should get together and put together a submission here.' They had never even talked to each other. So we put together a day-and-a-half meeting. We said, 'Talk to each other, we'll facilitate.'"[51] Indeed, the process of network building in the application process has supported investments in R & D by corporate parents, even when the applications ultimately failed.[52]

---

47. Author interview with former executive, Industrial Development Authority (6 June 2006, Ireland).

48. Author interview with executive officer, software firm (8 June 2006, Ireland).

49. Author interviews with head of corporate affairs, software firm (1 June 2006); manager, electronics firm (8 June 2006, Ireland); director, electronics firm (15 June 2006); and executive officer, electronics firm (15 June 2006, Ireland).

50. Author interview with director, electronics firm (15 June 2006, Ireland).

51. Author interview with manager, electronics firm (8 June 2006, Ireland).

52. Author interview with executive officer, electronics firm (15 June 2006, Ireland).

Initiatives have played an even more central role for indigenous enterprises. The Enterprise Development Program was a central source of capital for domestic enterprises looking to diversify away from their multinational clients or strike out on their own. Indeed, its loan guarantees and grant aid were virtually the only source of capital for indigenous entrepreneurs during the 1980s (Breznitz 2007, 162). One software entrepreneur noted, "[The state] threw us some R & D funding, not a huge amount of funding. . . . If you looked at the total cost, [it would have been] a 1 percent contribution, but it was very early on the cycle when you were just looking to make payroll, and it was great to get that additional boost. We wouldn't have had as much momentum."[53] IDA intervention not only permitted firms to engage in expensive R&D but also had the affect of publicizing and encouraging entrepreneurial activity for the first time (165–66).

By the late 1990s, Irish software firms were able to draw on expanding, if modest, risk capital markets (Breznitz 2007; Ó Riain 2004). An active venture capital market continues to support diversification by encouraging Irish engineers to spin out from their multinational parents (Sterne 2004). Ericsson, for example, has supported half a dozen Irish software spinouts.[54] An entrepreneur familiar with one of those firms cites publicly backed risk capital markets and support for internationalization in permitting entrepreneurship and growth.[55] As a result, analysts emphasize diversification along a range of different dimensions, as established multinationals shift from physical manufacturing into knowledge-intensive services, substitute production with R & D, or spur the creation of new growth-oriented indigenous firms (Barry and Egeraat 2008; O'Malley, Hewitt-Dundas, and Roper 2008; Ó Riain 2004).

Diversification into higher value-added and more knowledge-intensive activities remains limited, however, particularly when compared to Denmark and Finland. Although computer equipment producers have moved from manufacturing into knowledge-intensive services, the latter are concentrated in customer-support call centers (Barry and Egeraat 2008, 39). Ireland's largest software companies have allocated increasing resources to R & D, but most R & D focuses on software localization, adapting and translating finished software products for local markets (Ó Riain 2004, 57).[56] Similar dynamics prevail outside of information technology. Irish biotechnology, for example, reflects movement into biopharmaceutical production rather than the proliferation of multinational

---

53. Author interview with cofounder, software firm (25 May 2006, Ireland).
54. Author interviews with former manager, electronics firm (3 May 2006, Ireland) and former executive officer, electronics firm (1 June 2006, Ireland).
55. Author interview with director, software firm (30 May 2006, Ireland).
56. Author interviews with head of corporate affairs, software firm (1 June 2006, Ireland) and executive officer, electronics firm (15 June 2006, Ireland).

laboratories or indigenous startups.[57] Collectively, these developments reflect up-market movement, but they perpetuate Ireland's reliance on high-tech markets. Indeed, Ireland continues to lag behind Finland and even Denmark in research intensity, high-tech services, per capita patenting, and patenting specialization, despite its status as a high-tech leader.

Ireland is behind in these activities because limited investments in experimental inputs are a real constraint, even for large multinational firms. Human capital has been the least acute, in part because it was a target for the IDA and social partnership more generally. As noted, Ireland invested heavily in education during the 1980s and 1990s (White 2001, vii). Multinationals acknowledge that the regional technical colleges played a central role as they sought to expand their manufacturing operations over the course of the decade.[58] Yet the number of university graduates that firms relied on for development work did not increase as dramatically over the course of the decade (Sterne 2004, 73; White 2001, 282). These weaknesses were perhaps most acute in IT hardware, where advanced education and specialized knowledge is even more critical.[59] As a result, employers stated that they had to rely on returning emigrants and immigration for highly skilled labor.[60]

These constraints are more evident in R & D, where Irish investments were even more limited. While country managers relied on domestic resources to expand their mandate into R & D, Irish investments in research remained modest throughout the 1980s and 1990s. Many entrepreneurs were forced to rely on European framework programs, which were not always relevant for local industry (Sterne 2004, 81–82). Others relied on a makeshift combination of procurement, employment grants, and other forms of state aid for development.[61] As a result, research activity remained limited, and the activities that firms did conduct were smaller scale and less sophisticated. Multinational corporations that successfully expanded their investments in R & D have relied on relatively inexpensive projects. This is most conspicuous at traditional software firms such as Microsoft, which have focused on software localization, adapting software to meet local linguistic and cultural requirements.

---

57. Author interview with professor, University of Maynooth (11 May 2006, Ireland).

58. Author interviews with manager, electronics firm (8 June 2006, Ireland) and manager, electronics firm (8 June 2006, Ireland).

59. Author interview with partner, venture capital firm (26 May 2006, Ireland).

60. Author interviews with former executive, software firm (25 May 2006, Ireland); head of corporate affairs, software firm (1 June 2006, Ireland); and director, electronics firm (8 June 2006, Ireland).

61. Author interviews with former manager, electronics firm (3 May 2006, Ireland); executive officer, electronics subsidiary (1 June 2006, Ireland); manager, electronics firm (8 June 2006, Ireland); managing director, electronics firm (15 June 2006, Ireland); and executive officer, electronics firm (15 June 2006, Ireland).

It also extends to leading hardware companies such as Ericsson, Intel, Motorola and HP. Here, research is based on software rather than equipment (Breznitz 2007, 187). Managers admit that the focus on software is deliberate because it requires fewer resources.[62] Absent a dense public-sector and interfirm network to support expensive research into hardware, firms have turned to relatively inexpensive software development to expand their mandate into research. This stands in sharp contrast to Finland, and even Denmark, where domestic firms such Nokia and GiGA have maintained active research in hardware as well as software. Indeed, even Danish and Finnish subsidiaries appear to maintain a more active research agenda in hardware, as evidenced by Tellabs Finland's work on routers and servers or Motorola Denmark's center for radio frequency identification. The limitations of the Irish innovation system are thus reflected in the activities of its most research-intensive firms.

These constraints are more pronounced in indigenous industry. Domestic firms are even more sensitive to limited investments in R & D because they cannot leverage the resources of their multinational parent. Indeed, industry entrepreneurs acknowledge that research and risk capital funding were sharply limited until the mid-1990s.[63] Ireland's first information technology firms relied on foreign capital, consulting, subcontracting for multinationals, or recruiting managerial and technical expertise (Breznitz 2007, 158). While venture financing for start-up enterprises has improved (Ó Riain 2004, 94), Irish firms have fewer options for supporting expensive long-term research. Enterprises cannot rely on Tekes-sponsored technology platforms as they can in Finland (Ornston and Rehn 2006, 93) nor is there a history of local collaboration in standard setting as there is in Denmark (Dahl, Pedersen, and Dalum 2003, 237) that would enable them to move into more expensive and technologically sophisticated domains.

As a result, indigenous industry exhibits similar weaknesses. Hardware firms have been particularly disadvantaged, and Ireland occupies a strikingly weak position in this space. Irish firms have proven more successful in software, because research is less expensive and firms can identify narrow niches (Breznitz 2007, 185).[64] Yet the industry is characterized by predominantly small and medium-sized enterprises specializing in consulting, application-oriented software, and other less demanding market segments. While there are a handful of exceptions,

---

62. Author interviews with former manager, electronics firm (3 May 2006, Ireland) and former executive officer, electronics firm (1 June 2006, Ireland).

63. Author interview with former executive, electronics firm (9 June 2006, Ireland).

64. This point was confirmed in author interviews with director, venture capital fund (2 June 2006, Ireland); partner, venture capital fund (25 May 2006, Ireland); and manager, Enterprise Ireland (13 June 2006, Ireland).

Irish firms are not competing in expensive, risky, or technologically sophisticated fields such as middleware. Dan Breznitz contrasts developments in Ireland and Israel (Breznitz 2007), but one can generalize the argument to Nordic European countries such as Sweden, which have cultivated a surprisingly high share of middleware firms (Casper 2007, 141).

This argument extends to traditional industries as well. Here, we observe similar difficulties in moving into higher value-added and more knowledge-intensive activities. Irish dairy-processing firms have relied heavily on commodity production, even following agricultural reforms (O'Connell, Egeraat, and Enright 1997, 47). Policymakers cite the recent success of the Kerry Group, one of the largest and most research-intensive food ingredient companies in the world, as an example of successful upmarket movement.[65] The Kerry Group, however, is the exception that proves the rule. Diversification was not based on indigenous research capacities, but reflected the Kerry Group's conversion into a publicly listed company and its subsequent acquisition of foreign brands, knowledge, and human capital.[66] Indeed, the Kerry Group is not only weakly connected to Irish research institutions but had an openly antagonistic relationship with adjacent dairy cooperatives (Kennelly 2001). Kerry's distance is conspicuous in a small state, with one interviewee noting, "We had huge difficulties accessing the Kerry Group. When I was in academe I thought it was because of that, but [it is the same] even here at the Center."[67]

Kerry's impressive performance notwithstanding, the industry has been slow to consolidate and continues to lag behind in research intensity and product development.[68] Progress, where it has occurred, has been driven in large measure by government intervention rather than bilateral cooperation (Enright 2001; O'Connell, Egeraat, and Enright 1997). Enterprise Ireland, for example, has aggressively lobbied industry and underwritten research in a bid to shift to higher value-added products.[69] Even here, these initiatives have struggled to surmount a legacy of arm's-length competition. One policymaker, characterizing industry attitudes toward collaboration, noted, "The chief executive of [one cooperative] said that to get the real benefit of research it has to be something that is done for yourself. . . . Research is only useful or maximized when it can be related to

---

65. Author interview with director, Enterprise Ireland (7 June 2006, Ireland).

66. Author interviews with equity analyst, financial firm (30 May 2006, Ireland) and professor, University of Cork (12 June 2006, Ireland).

67. Author interview with manager, National Center for Partnership and Performance (15 May 2006).

68. Author interviews with former director, Teagasc (22 May 2006); equity analyst, financial firm (30 May 2006, Ireland); professor, University of Cork (12 June 2006, Ireland) ; and former executive, Department of Agriculture (15 June 2006, Ireland).

69. Author interview with director, Enterprise Ireland (7 June 2006, Ireland).

a single manufacturer and he can get the full benefit of it. The more it becomes available to others, the more it becomes closer to a commodity and, therefore, in his view, gives you a lesser return."[70]

The dairy-processing industry and its enduring dependence on commodity products such as butter underscores Ireland's more general vulnerability to shifting patterns of competition. High-tech industry proved particularly susceptible to the dot-com crash of 2001. As noted, Ireland's share of high-tech exports contracted sharply between 2000 and 2003, with the 27 percent decline exceeding the 12 percent drop in Finland and the 5 percent decrease in Denmark (Eurostat 2011). The share of employment in high-tech manufacturing increased in 2000, but it declined from 3.55 percent to 2.50 percent between 2001 and 2003. Although policymakers argue that this reflected a shift to knowledge-intensive services, the share of employment in high-tech services also shrank from 4.09 percent of the labor force in 2001 to 3.89 percent in 2003 (Eurostat 2011). Furthermore, those services jobs that were created were based on relatively low-end activities such as call centers and other customer-support operations (Barry and Egeraat 2008). The indigenous software industry, which was not influenced by transfer pricing, was particularly hard hit, even as the global economy started to improve. Between 2001 and 2004, sales contracted by 9 percent, exports fell by 23 percent, and employment decreased by 25 percent (NID 2006). To put these developments in perspective, employment in the Finnish software product industry increased by 25 percent and revenue grew by 33 percent during the same period (Lassila et al. 2006, 17, 22).

Political Compromises, Economic Constraints, and the Uncertain Future of Irish Neo-Corporatism

While the Irish economy continued to expand rapidly after 2001, with GDP growth averaging 5.5 percent between 2001 and 2007 and unemployment falling to 4.5 percent (Eurostat 2011), the country's robust macroeconomic performance obscured more fundamental problems. More specifically, Ireland had largely failed to adapt to the dot-com crisis. Whereas Finland, and to a lesser extent Denmark, responded to the loss of uncompetitive manufacturing jobs by expanding R & D operations, Ireland exited high-tech industry, particularly in those sectors that were not based on transfer pricing and tax arbitrage. Economic and employment growth instead reflected the expansion of nontradable services,

---

70. Author interview with former executive, Department of Agriculture (15 June 2006, Ireland).

mostly in residential construction. The share of the population employed in construction nearly doubled from approximately 7 percent in 1997 to over 13 percent by 2007 (Honohan 2009, 212). The Irish real estate bubble increased national wealth and construction but proved dangerously sensitive to global credit markets.

In fact, when global credit markets tightened in 2008, Ireland found itself facing a far graver financial and economic crisis than either Denmark or Finland. Irish banks had invested far more aggressively in real estate and faced insolvency as housing prices declined and global credit tightened. Policymakers sought to prevent insolvent banks from choking off credit to the rest of the Irish economy by guaranteeing and then recapitalizing the Irish banking sector (Honohan 2009). The resulting measures, however, turned a financial crisis into a fiscal one. Government debt increased from 25 percent of GDP in 2007 to 96.2 percent of GDP by 2010. In contrast to 1987, Ireland did not have the capacity to reduce accelerating double-digit fiscal deficits domestically, and it turned to the European Union and the International Monetary Fund, which orchestrated an €85 billion bailout package in 2010 (Labanyi 2011).

Ireland's financial and fiscal crisis had devastating consequences for the real economy. Per capita gross domestic product fell by 12.1 percent between 2008 and 2010, converging with that of Denmark. The decline in gross national product, which is more sensitive to nontradable activity, was even sharper. In contrast to Finland, the economy did not rebound sharply with international markets and was projected to grow by only 0.6 percent in 2011. Unemployment, meanwhile, nearly tripled to 14.6 percent of the labor force by December 2010 (Eurostat 2011). Ireland, previously the fastest growing economy in the European Union, had thus become one of its most fragile, rivaled only by the Baltic States of Estonia, Latvia, and Lithuania (Bohle and Greskovits 2012).

Of course, many factors contributed to the Irish real estate bubble of 2001–7 and the country's subsequent financial crisis. As in other crisis-affected countries, analysts have focused on the financial sector, criticizing imprudent private-sector borrowing on international markets (Honohan 2009, 208) and inadequate government oversight (Whelan 2010, 243–45). While the financial sector may have influenced the shape and structure of the crisis, analysts note that Ireland faced more fundamental, underlying challenges relating to pay (Regling and Watson 2010, 21–22) and fiscal policy (Whelan 2010, 239). Indeed, scholars note that the construction boom started before banks began relocating resources to real estate (Honohan 2009, 212).

The Irish financial crisis thus illustrates the limitations associated with the neo-corporatist pacts that Irish policymakers and societal actors reached between the 1980s and 2000s. Neo-corporatist agreements to reduce pay in exchange for tax concessions lured foreign direct investment to Ireland, enabling the country to enter new high-tech industries, and high-tech manufacturing in particular. Institutionalized cooperation can thus play a constructive role in supporting high-tech competition. At the same time, competitive corporatist bargains focused on wage restraint and tax concessions weakened adjustment in two respects.

The narrow emphasis on wage restraint made Ireland an attractive destination for cost-sensitive multinational manufacturers. Wage agreements, however, also increased Irish vulnerability to other low-cost competitors in eastern Europe, particularly once they joined the European Union and replicated Irish tax strategies (Cowell 2003). They also attracted employers that were less interested in upgrading their operations by using the types of creative supply-side bargains that characterized practices in Denmark and Finland. Indeed, Ireland's unique tax structure actively discouraged investment in R & D. Whereas Danish trade unions restrained wages in exchange for investments in training, and Finnish workers restrained wages with the understanding that profits would be allocated to R & D, Irish social partnership traded wage moderation for tax concessions.

These tax concessions in turn exacerbated the housing bubble and subsequent crash. It is not only that Ireland failed to invest in the types of high-quality inputs that facilitated upmarket movement in Denmark and Finland. Tax concessions also had a procyclical impact on the economy, amplifying domestic consumption during the late 1990s and early 2000s (Whelan 2010, 239). They also heightened vulnerability to the subsequent collapse of the Irish economy, as the government became increasing reliant on property-related taxes to finance public-sector operations (240). While the state's double-digit fiscal deficits reflected its outsized commitment to the financial sector, they were also exacerbated by an 18 percent decline in revenue between 2007 and 2009 (241).

Policymakers were aware of the limitations associated with competitive corporatist bargaining as early as the 1990s, and they responded with experimental initiatives in risk capital, skill formation, and research. Policymakers used social partnership, for example, to mobilize a broad tripartite consensus behind active labor market measures during the 1990s. They have also attempted to engage firms more directly in the process of skill formation, introducing an employer-financed national training network, Skillnets, and promoting industry-university cooperation in graduate education through the Program for Research in Third Level Institutions. The peak-level National Competitiveness Council has targeted investment in R & D. Science Foundation Ireland represents an unprecedented commitment of public-sector resources to this area, while relying on local cooperation among universities, multinationals, and small and medium-sized enterprises to implement and monitor investments. Finally, policymakers have attempted to promote local cooperation in early stage risk capital markets by launching ten regional venture capital funds (Breznitz 2007; O'Malley, Hewitt-Dundas, and Roper 2008; Ó Riain 2004; Department of the Taoiseach 2008).

As with Finnish initiatives in the labor market and Danish research policies, these initiatives played a constructive role in promoting investment and upmarket movement. Ireland witnessed modest but significant increases in each of these resources over the course of the last two decades, particularly in human capital. Furthermore, these investments represented a valuable resource for multinational and domestic enterprises seeking to diversify into more knowledge-intensive activities. As described, indigenous entrepreneurs relied on public venture capital to experiment with new technologies, foreign firms used training programs to expand their labor force, and multinational subsidiaries relied on new research initiatives to diversify their operations. These developments confirm the broad scope and potentially transformative implications associated with new supply-side investments. The problem is not necessarily that neo-corporatist bargaining is too encompassing but that it has been so limited in its scope.

Indeed, Ireland has failed to scale experiments in the same way that their Danish and Finnish counterparts have. While policymakers and societal actors were able to construct competitive corporatist pacts virtually overnight, creative corporatism appears significantly harder to construct absent a strong pattern of private-public, industry-labor, or interfirm coordination. Societal actors have been slower to embrace and promote investment in new resources, and state initiatives have not generated corresponding commitments by private-sector actors. This is not to suggest that movement toward creative corporatism is impossible in Ireland. The proliferation of peak- and local-level bodies creates multiple opportunities for interaction, and Ireland's increasing cost structure is likely to attract firms that are more interested in and receptive to a strategy based on supply-side investment. At the same time, this process of consensus building and collective investment proceeds at an extremely slow and incremental pace. Like labor markets in the wake of the Finnish Civil War of 1918, which evolved from outright hostility to centralized collective wage bargaining, increasing coordination is measured in decades rather than years.

In the meantime, Ireland's fiscal, financial, and economic crisis makes it even more difficult to strike creative corporatist deals. The financial crisis not only reduced the resources available for collective investment but it also triggered deep cuts in fiscal expenditure. Such cuts have been concentrated in social policy, but supply-side investments are not immune. For example, policymakers proposed to cut expenditure at Science Foundation Ireland and related agencies by 5 to 15 percent (Kennedy 2009). The European Union and International Monetary Fund will require further fiscal retrenchment, not counting resources diverted from the National Pension Reserve Fund (Labanyi 2011).

The financial crisis has reinforced reliance on a low-tax, cost-competitive economic regime, if not competitive corporatism. While the government has raised taxes, Ireland successfully defended its 12.5 percent corporate tax rate in domestic and international negotiations. Meanwhile, the tripartite National and Economic Social Council's most recent report places even greater emphasis on macroeconomic stabilization and wage restraint as an instrument for restoring competitiveness (NESC 2009, 51). Fiscal retrenchment has reduced growth but also wages, most dramatically in the public sector, where the government imposed a 5 to 8 percent pay reduction on civil service employees (EIRO 2010). The government also intervened in the private sector, reducing the minimum wage by 12 percent (EIRO 2011). In this respect, policymakers have proven quite successful in restoring competitiveness. The danger, however, is that Ireland is no longer a low-cost country. Furthermore, wage competition, to the extent it succeeds, may reinforce Irish reliance on cost-competitive enterprises that have little interest in upgrading operations or coinvesting in supply-side resources.

In fact, the financial crisis appears to have undermined the foundations for *competitive* corporatism. If the aforementioned NESC strategy paper reflects a strong tripartite consensus on fiscal retrenchment and cost containment as a way to bolster competitiveness, efforts to implement these measures through collective wage bargaining have failed, hindered in part by the inability to secure agreement using tax concessions. As a result, the government failed to reach a negotiated settlement with trade unions over public-sector wage cuts, and collective wage bargaining collapsed altogether in 2009 (EIRO 2010). It remains unclear whether this represents a temporary breakdown of centralized collective wage bargaining of the variety that occurred in Finland during the early 1990s (Fellman 2008, 201–2), the "organized" decentralization of collective wage bargaining that occurred in Denmark during the 1980s (Iversen 1996, 399), or more a profound movement away from neo-corporatism.

On the one hand, the Irish government paid a heavy electoral price for reducing public-sector expenditure and wages. Fianna Fail's crushing defeat, its worst showing at the polls in the history of the political party (Lyall 2011), underscores the risks associated with unilateral liberalization when unions are relatively well organized. Like the Finnish Aho administration of the early 1990s, budgetary cutbacks may spark neo-corporatist bargaining to diffuse the costs associated with retrenchment. Employers appear willing to consider such measures, as evidenced by their 2009 commitment to standardizing bargaining processes and implement a national-level framework agreement (EIRO 2010). The "collapse" of social partnership may thus prove temporary.

At the same time, there are other factors that inhibit successful bargaining. Previous agreements have reduced the scope for the types of tax concessions that supported even the earliest collective wage bargaining agreements as well as the innovative tradeoffs in research and training that characterized Denmark and Finland. And Ireland's success in lowering wage and nonwage costs has the unfortunate side effect of increasing its dependence on cost-competitive foreign multinationals. The future of Irish corporatism thus appears highly uncertain. This is not to suggest, however, that creative corporatism is limited to Denmark and Finland. On the contrary, as the following chapter reveals, other countries with a robust history of coordination in production have successfully adopted similar creative corporatist strategies.

6

COMPARING CORPORATISMS

The Danish, Finnish, and Irish cases challenge popular narratives about the causes and consequences of rapid technological change. During the 1990s, scholars predicted convergence on a liberal economic model, as arm's-length financial arrangements, flexible labor markets, and limited state intervention facilitated the redistribution of resources to disruptive new information technologies (Friedman 1999; Ohmae 1990; Streeck 1997). This liberal economic model, most closely associated with Reaganite and Thatcherite reform in 1980s Britain and the United States (Levy, Kagan, and Zysman 1997), has been replicated by other postindustrial democracies such as New Zealand (Schwartz 1994), developing countries such as Chile (Piñera 1995), and transitional economies such as Estonia, Latvia, and Lithuania (Bohle and Greskovits 2007). The Danish, Finnish, and Irish experiences, however, suggest that liberalization is neither as universal nor as necessary as its advocates claim.

First, institutionalized cooperation among organized actors is rooted in path-dependent social interactions and political institutions that prevent or delay convergence on a liberal economic model (Kitschelt and Streeck 2004; Thelen 1991; Zysman 1994). Traditional literature on "conservative" corporatism suggests that these path-dependent interactions insulate neo-corporatist economies from rapid technological change by modernizing stable, established niches with high barriers to entry (Hollingsworth 2000; Katzenstein 1984; Streeck 1991). Indeed, patient capital, generous social protections, and defensive industrial policies supported gradual upmarket movement in industries such as Danish food processing and Finnish forestry throughout the early postwar period. At the same time, the Danish and Finnish experiences suggest that conservative corporatist strategies may prove too expensive when small states are forced to grapple with rapid structural change.

The Irish case, however, reveals that even the most acute economic crises do not necessarily generate convergence on a liberal economic model. When policy-makers are strong enough to threaten influential societal actors but too weak to absorb the costs of unilateral reform, they can use concertation or policy co-operation to facilitate market-based reform (Baccaro and Lim 2007; Ebbinghaus and Hassel 1999; Rhodes 1998). Countries may thus react to rapid technologi-cal change by promoting, rather than dismantling, institutionalized cooperation among organized economic actors. Neo-corporatism becomes an instrument for advancing pro-market reform. These "competitive" corporatist pacts have coun-terintuitive implications for economic adjustment. In Ireland, lower spending, wage moderation, and tax reductions actually facilitated rapid movement into new high-tech industries. At the same time, Irish vulnerability to cost competi-tion highlights the disadvantages associated with a purely market-oriented path-way to high-tech markets.

In fact, the Danish and Finnish cases point to a final economic trajectory based on the conversion of industry-labor, private-public, or interfirm coordination in the act of production. These countries relied on institutionalized cooperation not only to dismantle conservative corporatist institutions but also to identify and invest in disruptive new inputs such as risk capital, skills, and research. In dramatically increasing public- and private-sector investment in these areas, these countries furnished firms with resources that they could use to enter new high-tech industries. Furthermore, these countries entered knowledge-intensive activities within high-tech industries, minimizing their vulnerability to the dot-com crash at the turn of the century and their subsequent reliance on nontrad-able services such as residential investment.

At the same time, the Danish, Finnish, and Irish cases raise questions about the broader applicability of this theoretical framework. Do institutional inno-vations in a handful of small wealthy states accurately reflect broader trends in contemporary capitalisms? To what extent do the conservative corporatist institutions of the 1960s and 1970s remain relevant today? Have other countries experimented with competitive corporatism, or is social partnership unique to Ireland? And is it possible to generalize arguments about creative corporat-ism beyond the two, potentially idiosyncratic cases of Denmark and Finland? I address each of these questions by extending my theoretical framework to a broader universe of cases in western Europe and beyond. More specifically, I identify examples of conservative corporatism in continental and Nordic Eu-rope, discuss episodes of competitive corporatism in the Netherlands and along

Europe's southern and eastern periphery, and provide evidence of creative corporatist reform in Sweden and East Asia.

Generalizing the argument in this fashion supports two points. First, capitalist diversity is by no means limited to the three small economies that inform this book. The tripartite distinction between conservative, competitive, and creative corporatism provides a useful framework for analyzing capitalist diversity throughout western Europe and beyond. Second, this expanded universe of cases in turn enables me to test claims about the relationship between different neo-corporatist subtypes, investment in disruptive new inputs, and high-tech competition. In this chapter, I provide additional evidence that conservative corporatism can delay restructuring, while competitive and creative corporatism support significant but divergent positions in emerging high-tech markets. The concluding chapter uses this same universe of cases to revisit arguments about institutional innovation and, by extension, the future of neo-corporatism.

In generalizing the argument to a broader universe of cases, I am not suggesting that countries conform perfectly to neo-corporatist subtypes. On the contrary, I have emphasized and exploited within-case variation, as neo-corporatist subtypes are more pronounced in some domains and less pronounced in others. For example, creative corporatism is particularly pronounced in Finnish innovation policy, as policymakers have converted a tradition of private-public and interfirm coordination to invest in R & D. Finland has done so, however, in part by maintaining relatively conservative social policies. Other countries may be characterized by similar variation across policy domains, regions, and sectors. Similarly, these conservative, competitive, and creative corporatisms are not frozen in place. On the contrary, this tripartite framework illuminates how neo-corporatist economies change over time.

Conservative Corporatism in Central Europe

A cursory reading of this book might suggest that conservative corporatism is a relic of the 1960s or 1970s. Patient capital, generous social benefits, and defensive industrial policies inhibited adaptation to disruptive economic shocks in Denmark and Finland during the 1980s, making a bad situation even worse. Danish and Finnish stakeholders dramatically reduced or eliminated patient capital, traditional social protections, and defensive industrial policies as traditional instruments inhibited adjustment to competency-destroying shocks during the 1980s. Conservative corporatist bargains, however, continue to play an important and constructive role in several European economies such as Germany, Austria, and Norway.

Certainly, each of these countries has changed over the last three decades. Austria, Germany, and Norway have each witnessed increasing restrictions on state aid (E. Moen 2011, 148–49), greater reliance on decentralized equity markets (Deeg 2005, 336), and less generous social benefits (Vail 2010, 110). As the concluding section relates, these countries have also promoted supply-side investment in early stage risk capital (Adelberger 1999, 2), human capital (Culpepper 2007, 625), and research (Gergils 2006, 241). Without denying the significance of these developments, it is important to recognize that these continental economies have not dismantled conservative corporatist instruments as rapidly or extensively as Denmark or Finland, and they have certainly not relied as heavily on foreign investment, fiscal austerity, and tax competition as Ireland. Furthermore, these countries have not struck prominent tripartite bargains to boost investment in disruptive new inputs, and the agreements that they have reached have generated more modest increases in early stage risk capital, human capital, and research.

Consider Germany, which many analysts continue to characterize in conservative corporatist terms (Goyer 2006; Kitschelt and Streeck 2004). Like other EU member states, the German government respects restrictions on state aid, and in fact it eschewed activist industrial policies such as credit rationing or nationalization (Vail 2010; Wood 1997). German firms, however, relied heavily on large long-term loans to defend and upgrade established operations (Hollingsworth 2000; Streeck 1997). While German firms were not as dependent on bank-based capital as their Finnish counterparts during the early postwar period, Germany was slower to reform its financial system. By the height of the dot-com boom in the late 1990s, Germany was characterized by significantly greater ownership concentration and more extensive cross shareholdings than Finland. The discrepancy with Denmark and Ireland, with more decentralized financial systems, is even more striking (Faccio and Lang 2002).

The German financial system evolved during the 1990s toward a more flexible and decentralized ownership structure based on individual shareholders (Cioffi 2010; Deeg 2010). At the same time, it is worth noting that Germany only enacted major corporate control, tax, takeover, and transparency reforms between 1998 and 2002, almost a decade later than their Finnish counterparts (Deeg 2005, 335). They also never experienced the type of massive financial crisis that accelerated the liberalization of the Finnish financial system. Although Germany now rivals (and by some measures exceeds) Finland in measures of formal shareholder protection, convergence in stock market capitalization and ownership dispersion has occurred more slowly. This may be partly because, while Germany has increased shareholder protections, stakeholders have retained some influence over corporate strategy (Cioffi 2010, 238). This is most visible in the case of organized labor, which, in contrast to Nordic Europe, resisted more comprehensive corporate governance reform (163–64). Continued representation on corporate supervisory boards has in turn influenced corporate strategy, attracting international investors such as pension funds with long time horizons and discouraging investment by short-term investors such as hedge funds or mutual funds (Goyer 2006, 421–22).

Codetermination in turn reflects Germany's continued commitment to rewarding and defending investment in specialized skills through generous social protections. Although Germany never embraced the countercyclical fiscal policies or full-employment guarantees that characterized Nordic Europe (Allen 1989; Scharpf 1984), the country has nonetheless relied on relatively generous unemployment benefits and employment regulations to protect core workers. A 2003 OECD index of employment protection, for example, revealed that Germany placed significantly greater restrictions on the right of employers to fire employees (2.5) than did Finland (2.1), Denmark (1.8), or Ireland (1.3). As a result, average job tenure, for example, is among the longest in the OECD at 10.3 years, exceeding Finland (10.1 years), Ireland (9.4 years), and Denmark (8.5 years) (OECD 2004, 117).

Of course, German social policy, like its financial system, has evolved. The 2004 Hartz IV reform transformed German unemployment benefits, limiting access to more generous employer-employee subsidized unemployment benefits to twelve months and forcing recipients to collect less-generous state-financed benefits after that period has expired (Vail 2010, 110). As with reform of the German financial system, however, policymakers introduced comprehensive social policy reforms almost a decade later than their Danish counterparts. Furthermore, it remains unclear how comprehensive the Hartz IV reform is. The Hartz reform agenda only tackled employment protection in enterprises with fewer than ten employees, and analysts note that it may have stabilized the generous system of employer-employee financed unemployment benefits by segmenting workers into core and noncore employees (Palier and Thelen 2010). Indeed, German policymakers responded to the 2007–9 financial crisis by introducing short-term work arrangements to subsidize the retention of established employees (Weishaupt 2010).

The Hartz IV reforms underscore a further distinction between the German case, on the one hand, and the Danish and Finnish case, on the other. Germany has not only witnessed a later and more gradual shift away from conservative corporatism, but it has also invested less aggressively in the types of inputs that define creative corporatism. For example, stakeholders have not struck peak-level deals like those of the Finnish Science and Technology Policy Council or the Danish Zeuthen Commission. While the Schroder administration promoted investment in employment training and counseling for young people through the Alliance for Jobs, the initiative collapsed and active labor market measures were criticized following a series of scandals in 2002 (Vail 2010, 109). The resulting Hartz agenda instead promoted activation through social-benefit retrenchment (110). As a result, Germany spent significantly less in 2005 on active labor market policies (excluding public employment) as a share of GDP (0.60%) then Denmark (1.28%) or even Finland (0.73%) (Eurostat 2011). While it is worth noting that Germany has increased investment in apprenticeships in response to the 2007–9 economic difficulties, it continues to invest less than its Nordic counterparts in university education, an important source of general and transferrable skills (Ansell 2008).

Investment in other domains, where there is no analogue to the apprenticeship system, has been even more modest. For example, while the German financial system has finally converged (and in some ways surpassed) Denmark's and Finland's in formal shareholder protections, investment in early stage risk capital represented only 0.02 percent of GDP in 2007, as opposed to 0.04 percent of GDP in Finland and 0.05 percent of GDP in Denmark (Eurostat 2011). Similarly, Germans invested significantly less in R & D (2.53% of GDP) in 2007 than did Finland (3.47%). While German investment in R & D does exceed Denmark's (2.48%), it is worth noting that large countries such as Germany are perceived to enjoy an advantage in capital-intensive R & D (Kristensen and Levinsen 1983). In fact, as recently as 1992, Germany invested *more* in R & D (2.35% of GDP) than either Finland (2.11%) or Denmark (1.64%). Germany has thus failed to keep pace with its Nordic peers in research expenditure. Furthermore, analysts note that public programs that are designed to support R & D have targeted larger, established enterprises rather than new growth-oriented firms (Veugelers 2009, 5).

This relatively conservative orientation had predictable implications for economic adjustment. In 2007, even following the Hartz IV and financial reforms, Germany continued to lag behind Finland in the share of high-tech exports (13.0% and 17.5%, respectively), the share of high-tech employment (5.18% and 6.71%, respectively), population adjusted measures of high-tech patenting (38.9 and 86.3 application per million inhabitants, respectively), and high-tech patenting specialization (13.2% and 34.0%, respectively) (Eurostat 2011). While German high-tech exports, employment, and patenting are comparable to Denmark's, Germany's achievements are more modest for several reasons. Germany has always enjoyed an advantage in capital-intensive high-tech industries relative to smaller states such as Denmark (Kristensen and Levinsen 1983). As noted, Denmark is virtually excluded from the aerospace industry, which represents 15 percent of German exports (Eurostat 2011). Furthermore, German success in other high-tech markets is often based on the capacity of incumbent multinationals such as a Siemens to defend established niches such as engineering (Dalum, Fagergberg, and Jørgensen 1988).

New entrepreneurial high-tech firms have challenged this popular image of a low- or medium-tech Germany. Industry surveys, however, reveal that high-tech firms are competing in relatively stable niches with high barriers to entry such as platform biotechnology and enterprise software. Germany is conspicuously underrepresented relative to Denmark or Sweden in radically innovative subsectors such as therapeutic biotechnology or middleware software (Casper 2007, 141). In other words, even entrepreneurial high-tech firms appear to use long-term employment relations and cumulative research agendas to excel in incremental innovation (154). Although this characterization does not apply to all high-tech firms, analysts suggest that radically innovative enterprises have succeeded by circumventing rather than leveraging national economic institutions. For example, entrepreneurs have secured financing by importing venture capital from liberal market economies such as Britain and the United States; they have circumvented restrictive labor market regulations by striking atypical working contracts; and they have fostered closer ties with universities at the regional level (Herrmann 2009, 17–19; Lange 2009, 203). These firm-level studies suggest that radical innovation-based competition is possible within the confines of a conservative corporatist economy, particularly in a large country such as a Germany that is differentiated by regions and sectors (Crouch 2005; Herrigel 1996). At the same time, these studies underscore the relative paucity of resources available within a predominantly conservative corporatist economy.

This conservative and incremental orientation is even more pronounced in smaller continental European economies such as Austria and Norway. Austrian firms were even more dependent than their German or Finnish counterparts on bank-based finance during the early postwar period (Hyytinen et al. 2003, 388). Although Austria, like Germany, liberalized its financial system, it ranked closer to Germany than Finland in measures of ownership concentration (Faccio and Lang 2002, 380) and stakeholder protection (389). This eroding but significant supply of patient capital is complemented by comparatively stringent employment protections, even following labor market liberalization in the late 1990s (OECD 2004, 117), and heavy reliance on passive labor market policies such as early retirement for unproductive workers (Sherwood 2006, 3).

Like Germany, Austria has also invested comparatively less in disruptive new inputs. While Austria targeted human capital, it did so by expanding its existing vocational training system rather than expanding university education (Culpepper 2007, 625). Meanwhile, the country continues to trail Denmark (and Finland) in active labor market expenditure and participation in continuing education. The discrepancy in the share of GDP devoted to early stage risk capital (0.01%)

is even more striking (Eurostat 2011). As a result, Austria is even less specialized in high-tech markets than its larger neighbor, in 2007 trailing not only Denmark and Finland but also Germany in the share of high-tech exports (11.1%), the share of high-tech employment (3.94%), and population-adjusted measures of high-tech patenting (33.6 applicants per million inhabitants) (Eurostat 2011).

The Norwegian case is the most interesting, however, because it suggests that conservative bargains are not limited to historically Catholic continental European economies that are coordinated at the sectoral level. Like Denmark and Finland, Norway possesses an ethnically and religiously homogenous population, a large public sector, and a strong social democratic party. Unlike Denmark and Finland, Norway has retained several conservative corporatist features. First, although the Norwegian financial system has changed, banks were not as heavily affected by the downturn of the early 1990s as their Finnish counterparts. As a result, stock market capitalization as a share of GDP is more modest, shareholder protections are weaker (Hyytinen and Pajarinen 2003, 27), and ownership is more concentrated (Faccio and Lang 2002, 380). Furthermore, although Norway sharply reduced expenditure on state aid during the 1980s and 1990s (E. Moen 2011, 148–49), it replaced industrial policies with progressively more generous social measures. For example, Norway spends twice as much on passive measures such as early retirement than its Nordic peers and three times as much on sick leave (Kristensen 2011, 32).

In defending conservative corporatist bargains, Norway also invested less aggressively in disruptive new inputs. For example, while the Norwegian state invests as much as Finland in R & D in absolute terms (E. Moen 2011, 176), it lags behind in research spending as a share of GDP, and policymakers actually rolled back research programs during the 1990s (Wicken 2009, 108–11). Like Germany, research support has targeted existing low- and medium-technology industries like oil extraction, maritime exploration, and shipbuilding rather than emerging technologies like information, communications, or biotechnology (Grønning, Moen, and Olsen 2008, 281). Partly as a result of these developments, the share of GDP devoted to R & D is among the lowest in the OECD at 1.5 percent of GDP (Eurostat 2011). Similar developments prevail in education, where policymakers expanded tertiary enrollment but failed to integrate initiatives with private-sector needs (E. Moen 2011, 176). Norway in fact *reduced* spending on active labor market measures after the early 1990s (177). Furthermore, the *share* of active labor market expenditure devoted to training decreased, from 36 percent in 1990 to 6 percent by the end of the decade (OECD 2011).

Although university-educated entrepreneurs are launching innovative ventures at the margins of the Norwegian economy (E. Moen 2011, 180–81), the economy has not diversified as rapidly as in Denmark, Finland, or Sweden. For example, in 2007 its share of high-tech exports (3.3%) trailed not only Finland (17.5%) and Denmark (11.7%) but would have placed Norway second to last behind Poland (3.0%) in the European Union (Eurostat 2011). While Norway ranks more favorably in measures of high-tech employment (4.28% of the labor force), it again trails Finland (6.71%) and Denmark (5.27%). A similar picture prevails in the number of high-tech patent applications per million inhabitants (11.7), where Norway lags behind not only Finland (86.3) and Denmark (40.1) but also Germany (38.9) and Austria (33.6) (Eurostat 2011). Norway's weak position in high-tech markets is particularly striking, not only because of its ideological and institutional similarity to the other Nordic countries, but also because it benefited from the Nordic Mobile Telephone standard of the 1980s. Norway not only failed to cultivate a flagship multinational like Ericsson or Nokia, but it also struggled to replicate the cluster of dynamic, small and medium-sized enterprises that characterized northern Denmark.

Demonstrating that conservative corporatist institutions inhibited high-tech competition in Austria, Germany, and Norway does not suggest that these economies are intrinsically inferior to their competitive or creative counterparts. Indeed, previous chapters identified significant risks associated with competitive and creative corporatist reforms, including vulnerability to cost competition in Ireland and disruptive technological innovation in Finland. The persistence of conservative corporatism in Austria, Germany, and Norway reflects their capacity to insulate themselves from these competitive pressures. Norway is endowed with an exceptionally scarce natural resource. Austria and Germany, meanwhile, compete in comparatively sophisticated medium-technology industries with high barriers to entry such as automotives and machine tools. Neither was as dependent on low-tech resource-extractive industries such as food processing and paper making as Denmark, Finland, and Ireland.

Competitive Corporatism in Southern and Eastern Central Europe

Of course, not all countries are so fortunate. Other countries, confronting more disruptive shocks, could not afford to defend established industries. As a result, these countries pursued very different strategies during the 1980s and 1990s. One such strategy was competitive corporatism, adapting institutionalized cooperation to exchange wage restraint for pro-market reform, including fiscal austerity, tax reductions, social-benefit restructuring, and labor market deregulation (Ebbinghaus and Hassel 1999; Rhodes 1998; Siegel 2005). Such strategies were not limited to Ireland. The earliest and most successful example of "competitive" corporatism was a Central European country, the Netherlands, where stakehold-ers struck an innovative bargain at Wassenaar in 1982, five years before the Pro-gram for National Recovery (Visser and Hemerijck 1997, 81).

The 1982 Wassenaar agreement represented a watershed in Dutch industrial relations, as a center-right government threatened to freeze wages and social se-curity benefits and reduce work time (Visser and Hemerijck 1997, 100). The social partners, and trade unions in particular, reached a bipartite agreement to reduce wage-cost growth in order to avoid government intervention in the labor market and to boost competitiveness. This emphasis on wage moderation persists to 2011, even following the decentralization of wage bargaining in 1993. For example, the social partners responded to the dot-com crisis by relying on a centrally coordinated wage freeze in 2003 (Hassel 2007, 252).

The Netherlands was not the only country that sought to restrain wage growth during the 1980s and 1990s. What made Dutch neo-corporatism so "competi-tive" was the decision to link wage restraint to budget cutbacks and social-benefit restructuring (Hemerijck 2003, 54) instead of traditional conservative corporat-ist measures, countercyclical spending packages, more generous social benefits, or full-employment guarantees (Scharpf 1984). For example, the government froze unemployment benefits and reduced replacement rates during the second half of the 1980s (Hemerijck 2003, 59). It also reduced reliance on other pas-sive labor market strategies such as disability insurance, by increasing employer contributions, penalizing abuse, and partially privatizing the disability-insurance system (60).

Retrenchment extended to other domains. For example, the government dra-matically reduced expenditure on traditional industrial subsidies (Verspagen 2008, 350). At the same time, the government defended its historically generous treatment of certain forms of corporate revenue, including foreign-earned roy-alties, dividends, and interest (Browning 2007; Kessler and Eicke 2008). Indeed, the government responded to increasing competition by Britain and low-cost, low-tax eastern central European countries by reducing its top corporate tax rate to 25.5 percent in 2007 and to 24 percent by 2011, among the lowest in western Europe (after Ireland). The government has used tax incentives to attract foreign innovation as well as investment, broadening its historically generous treatment of royalties to cover intellectual property as well in 2007 (Kessler and Eicke 2008).

While proponents note that the Netherlands has also targeted disruptive new inputs, investment is more modest than in Denmark or Finland. For example, the Netherlands expanded active labor market programs, but "flexicurity" relied more heavily on labor market deregulation than Danish-style labor market poli-cies (Viebrock and Clasen 2009, 315). Like Ireland, active labor market expen-diture was based in large measure on employment subsidy schemes rather than training, and the latter has been criticized in terms of its effectiveness (Hemerijck 2003, 64; OECD 2004). Consequently, the share of the Dutch population that participated in continuing education in 2007 (26.8%), while high by European standards, was significantly lower than in either Denmark (40.9%) or Finland (33.9%) (Eurostat 2011). Furthermore, in sharp contrast to either Denmark or Finland, public expenditure on education as a share of GDP has been virtually flat since the mid-1980s (Verspagen 2008, 329). Public investment in other inputs such as research actually declined over this period (328), with the result that the Netherlands invested less than 2 percent of its GDP in R & D in 2007 (Eurostat 2011).

The competitive corporatist bargains described here were extremely successful in boosting corporate profitability, growth, and employment. Economic recovery was based in large measure, however, on the increasing number of part-time jobs (Visser and Hemerijck 1997, 42). Furthermore, analysts attribute roughly half of the job creation during the 1980s and 1990s to wage moderation (113), while productivity growth played a much less significant role (26–28). As a result of these developments, some observers have criticized the Netherlands for pursuing a low-end strategy based on cost competition rather than innovation (Verspagen 2008, 324).

As in Ireland, this low-cost strategy has not inhibited high-tech competition and may have facilitated it by securing macroeconomic stabilization, a competitive cost structure, a more dynamic labor market, and a larger, more liquid pool of domestic and foreign capital. The Netherlands exceeded Denmark in population-adjusted measures of high-tech patenting, and Denmark and Finland in the share of high-tech exports in 2007 (Eurostat 2011). Dutch patenting and exports in high-tech markets, however, is based in large measure on large century-old multinational conglomerates such as Philips and their capacity to defend established niches in electronics and health care. For example, the Netherlands lags behind Denmark and Finland in the share of the labor force employed in both high-tech manufacturing and services (Eurostat 2011). Furthermore, research intensity and patenting activity both declined over the course of the 1980s and 1990s (Verspagen 2008, 324).

Although the Netherlands and Ireland are the most prominent examples of competitive corporatism, the concept of competitive corporatism helps explain the resurgence of neo-corporatist bargaining in other historically noncorporatist countries along the European periphery. Competitive corporatist pacting was particularly popular, if less successful, in the Mediterranean region during the 1990s. Here, countries with little tradition of bipartite or tripartite cooperation confronted sizeable trade unions over the implementation of the Maastricht criteria and the adoption of the euro. As in the Netherlands and Ireland, neo-corporatist bargaining in these countries focused mainly, and in some cases exclusively, on wage restraint, as countries attempted to contain costs with a pegged, and subsequently common, currency (Hancké and Rhodes 2005; Hassel 2007). Portuguese employers and trade unions struck incomes agreements to regulate wages as early as the 1980s (Royo 2002), while the Italian social partners agreed to abolish the *scala mobile* and restructure collective wage bargaining in 1990s (Regini and Regalia 1997). Even Spain, which never adopted a formal incomes policy, attempted to promote greater coordination in wage bargaining (Perez 2000).

Wage moderation was in turn linked to fiscal austerity, particularly to the extent that agreements were struck in the shadow of the restrictive Maastricht criteria. In Italy, for example, unions agreed to restructure social benefits, reducing pension payments and tightening eligibility requirements (Baccaro 2002). The Spanish social partners, which did not negotiate over wages, reached a similar agreement to reform pensions in 1996. To the extent that agreements extended beyond fiscal policy, they often expanded market competition. A 1997 Spanish agreement relaxed dismissal costs for permanent workers, while the social partners agreed to expand part-time work in 1998 (Royo 2002). While all three countries reached agreements addressing training, continuing education was not as central to the reform process as it was in Denmark, and the countries lagged behind even the Netherlands and Ireland in the share of GDP devoted to active labor market policies (Eurostat 2011). As a result, analysts have emphasized instead their capacity to regulate wages (Perez 2000), moderate social spending (Baccaro 2002), or deregulate labor markets (Rhodes 1998).

Investment in new supply-side resources, on the other hand, was comparatively modest. This was particularly true of Italy, which deregulated working contracts and reformed its pension system but did not significantly increase expenditure on active labor market measures (Bonoli 2010; Lodovici and Semenza 2008). Gains in research were even more limited, as Italy devoted approximately the same share of GDP, 1.1 percent, to R & D in 1985 and 2005. Investment in early stage venture capital markets was also comparatively low at 0.02 percent of GDP in 2007 (Eurostat 2011). Portugal and Spain did invest more in research and training over the course of the 1990s, but the increase was from extremely low levels. The 0.51 percent and 0.63 percent of GDP devoted to active labor market measures represents significant improvement relative to 1998, but the countries continue to lag behind Denmark (1.1% of GDP) and Finland (0.706% of GDP), with significantly lower unemployment rates. Furthermore, the share of active labor market expenditure devoted to training declined in both countries during this time period (Eurostat 2011). Similar developments prevailed in research. Portuguese and Spain investment in research increased significantly to 1.2% and

1.3% of GDP, respectively, by 2007, but it remained well below the EU average of 1.9 percent (Eurostat 2011).[1] Venture capital markets were equally underdeveloped in Portugal and Spain, as the share of GDP devoted to early stage venture capital investments was 0.03 percent and 0.01 percent, respectively.

Unlike those in the Netherlands and Ireland, Italian, Portuguese, and Spanish social pacts were not strikingly successful in liberalizing their economies. While the agreements enabled the countries to adopt the euro, labor market regulation remained significantly more restrictive than in either the Netherlands or Ireland; the social partners struggled to reduce costs within a common currency; and, by the end of the 1990s, the countries had largely abandoned neo-corporatism (Avdagic 2010). Absent either the dramatic market-based reforms that characterized the Netherlands and Ireland or the significant investment in disruptive new inputs in Denmark and Finland, these countries struggled to enter new high-tech markets. The share of high-tech exports increased from 5 percent to 7 percent in Portugal between 1995 and 2005, and they remained flat at 7 percent in Italy and 5 percent in Spain. The share of the labor force employed in high-tech industries increased modestly in Italy, Portugal, and Spain, but it remains well below the EU average at 4.3 percent, 3.4 percent, and 2.3 percent respectively (Eurostat 2011). In fact, economic performance as a whole deteriorated, as the countries faced sluggish growth, mounting unemployment, and increasingly severe fiscal crises after 2007.

The most successful efforts to duplicate Dutch and Irish economic strategies occurred not along the Mediterranean but in the transitional economies of eastern central Europe. Developments in eastern central Europe are significant in that they reveal that countries outside of western Europe, including states with limited tradition of private-public or industry-labor cooperation, can also rely on neo-corporatist strategies to manage adjustment. Furthermore, successful market reform can in turn accelerate movement into new high-tech industries. At the same time, purely market-based strategies support movement into relatively low-end activities, increasing vulnerability to cost competition.

The post-Communist countries of eastern central Europe would appear to be unlikely candidates for neo-corporatist governance. Eastern central European countries are often depicted as an example of convergence toward a liberal market economy, with limited reliance on state intervention or institutionalized cooperation among organized actors (Åslund 2010). This is particularly true of the former Soviet republics of Estonia, Latvia, and Lithuania, where predomi-

---

1. Portuguese investment in research increased particularly sharply following the government's decision to implement a Finnish-style "technological shock" through the more favorable tax treatment of research and development.

nantly Russian losers in market competition exercised limited political influence. The Baltic states could thus rely on unilateral reform to reduce state aid, social benefits, and taxation (Bohle and Greskovits 2007, 450). Other post-Communist states, however, adopted a distinctively negotiated strategy, with periodic recourse to tripartite bargaining. In central Europe, where socialism was not as heavily discredited and identity politics were less salient, policymakers attempted to diffuse the costs associated with post-Communist liberal reforms by striking deals with weak but sizeable trade unions. Hungary launched the tripartite Council for Interest Reconciliation as early as 1988. The council emerged as a forum for policy concertation and wage coordination in the wake of a taxi drivers' strike in 1990, negotiating a four-year pact governing compensation, social policy, and fiscal expenditure (Cox and Mason 2000, 334–35). By then, the Czech Republic had launched its own Council of Economic and Social Agreement to govern public-sector wages and consult on economic policy (Pollert 1997, 87). In 1994, Poland experimented with analogous forums to coordinate employment relations and social policy (Iankova 2002, 6). While national policymakers in all three countries marginalized peak-level councils in subsequent years, local officials, employer associations, and trade unions continued to rely on periodic negotiations at the regional and sectoral level over the course of the decade (6).

Neo-corporatist bargaining, where it occurred, was highly "competitive" in content. Policymakers not only relied on bipartite and tripartite bargaining to restrain wage costs but, more important, relied on neo-corporatist institutions to advance pro-market reform. Neo-corporatist councils agreed to stabilize finances, restructure social benefits, reduce state aid, liberalize external trade, and re-regulate workplace relations (Iankova 2002, 12). Indeed, negotiations were so heavily tilted toward market-based reform that some scholars dismissed eastern central Europe bargaining as "illusory" corporatism (Ost 2000).[2] By the time they entered the European Union in 2004, the Czech Republic, Hungary, and Poland boasted moderate labor costs, modest fiscal deficits, and highly competitive corporate tax rates (Eurostat 2011).

Investment in disruptive new inputs remained more modest. For example, while social pacts addressed training (Iankova 2002, 12), the Czech Republic, Hungary, and Poland invested less in active labor market measures (0.012%, 0.183%, and 0.404% of GDP, respectively) in 2007 than Denmark (1.02% of GDP) or even Finland (0.672%). The discrepancy is even more striking when one controls for unemployment, which was higher in Hungary and Poland than

---

2. It is worth noting that the Czech Republic, Hungary, Poland, and particularly Slovenia developed more generous social safety nets than the Baltic countries, which relied more heavily on unilateral reform (Bohle and Greskovits 2012).

either Denmark or Finland (Eurostat 2011). These countries also invested less in research, which was never targeted in social pacts. By 2007, R & D as a share of GDP ranged from 0.57 percent of GDP in Poland to 1.54 percent of GDP in the Czech Republic. In all three countries, R & D expenditure as a share of GDP actually *declined* during the 1990s and has yet to return to 1991 levels (Eurostat 2011; OECD 2004). Investment in early stage risk capital is even more modest at less than 0.001 percent of GDP throughout the decade (Eurostat 2011). Countries thus relied on neo-corporatist bargaining to implement market reform rather than to expand social protections or invest in experimental inputs.

These competitive corporatist pacts had familiar implications for economic adjustment. Implementing more sweeping pro-market reform than either their central or southern European counterparts enabled eastern central European countries to attract foreign direct investment in a wide range of new, often high-tech, industries (Nölke and Vliegenthart 2009). Restructuring was particularly rapid in Hungary, where the share of high-tech exports increased from 4.8 percent in 1995 to 19.7 percent by 2005 (Eurostat 2011).[3] Indeed, eastern central European countries were so successful in replicating Ireland's low-tax, cost-competitive strategy that they undermined Ireland's traditional status as a favored export platform (Cowell 2003).

While eastern central European countries thus illustrate the enduring relevance of neo-corporatist bargaining as an instrument of liberalization and the transformative potential of market-based reform, they also are examples of the limitations associated with competitive corporatist strategies. Eastern central European countries such as Hungary have assumed a leading position in high-tech markets, but high-tech competition is based on comparatively low-end assembly activity, and these countries are behind on measures of knowledge generation. For example, in 2007, Hungary filed only 3.8 patent applications to the European Patent Office per million inhabitants as opposed to 86.3 for Finland, 40.1 for Denmark, and 17.7 for Ireland. The Czech Republic and Poland filed even fewer patents. Hungary also trailed Denmark, Finland, and Ireland in the ratio of high-tech patent applications to all patent applications, despite its ostensibly high-tech industrial structure (Eurostat 2011).

Interestingly, this comparatively low-end orientation is in some respects even more pronounced in the countries that pursued unilateral market reform. Estonia, Latvia, and Lithuania also attracted significant foreign direct investment but were considerably less specialized in complex exports (Bohle and Greskov-

---

3. Estonia enjoyed an even more dramatic, if short-lived, shift into high-tech markets. Investment by Finnish IT firms helped to lift the share of high-tech exports from 4.1% in 1995 to 25.1% by 2000 (Eurostat 2011).

its 2007, 459). Indeed, Estonia's leading position in high-tech markets, which represented over a quarter of all exports in 2000, withered to 10.3 percent of exports by 2005, trailing both the Czech Republic and Hungary (Eurostat 2011). By then, all three Baltic countries had experienced significant deindustrialization and were relying on foreign investment in nontradable services, most notably residential investment, rather than export-oriented production. As a result, the three economies were particularly hard hit by the 2007–9 economic crisis and the resulting contraction of international credit markets (Bohle and Greskovits 2012). As in Ireland, these economies have responded to the financial crisis by successfully reducing fiscal deficits and wage costs (Åslund 2010). While this may attract foreign direct investment and revitalize the economy, it also runs the risk of exacerbating their vulnerability to cost competition.

Creative Corporatism in Northern Europe and East Asia

Of course, "competitive" corporatism is not the only way countries have adapted neo-corporatist institutions. Denmark and Finland adapted institutionalized cooperation among organized actors to perform very different functions, facilitating investment in disruptive new inputs and movement into more knowledge-intensive high-tech activities. Denmark and Finland are not the only countries to adapt institutionalized cooperation in this way. We observe similar, if less dramatic, developments in Sweden. Indeed, the Swedish case adds significant analytic value by demonstrating how stakeholders can adapt different forms of cooperation to meet new challenges. In Sweden, the state had played a less direct role in economic development relative to Finland, and enterprises resisted ambitious industrial policies (Pontusson 1984, 13). Meanwhile, labor market cooperation foundered over solidaristic wage bargaining and the controversial wage earner funds of the 1980s (Vartiainen 1998b). Both industry and labor, however, identified a potentially constructive role for jointly managed pension funds in channeling early and late-stage risk capital to new growth-oriented firms. Institutionalized cooperation in financial markets supported the most robust European venture capital market outside of Britain (Eurostat 2011).

Sweden was not always known for its large venture capital market. On the contrary, the country relied on conservative corporatist institutions throughout the postwar period. While Sweden's Labor Market Administration anticipated Danish investments in training by several decades, employment protection was considerably higher in Sweden than in Denmark (OECD 2004, 117). The financial system was even more conservative, with universal banks extending large, long-term loans to established enterprises, linking the latter within a handful of encompassing industrial blocs (Magnusson 2000, 217–18). While the state assumed a less direct role in directing economic development relative to Finland, the tax code effectively subsidized the universal banks and large established firms (Steinmo 2010, 51). Collectively, long-term loans and favorable tax treatment encouraged industrialization in resource-extractive industries such as forestry, mining, and related engineering industries (Porter 1990, 342).

Like Denmark and Finland, Sweden's position in low- and medium-tech markets proved increasingly problematic during the 1970s. Traditional resource-extractive industries were the most heavily affected by new economic challenges (Magnusson 2000, 260), but engineering-based industries and even high-tech niches such as computers and telecommunication equipment lost significant market share (Porter 1990, 354). Efforts to upgrade troubled industries such as shipbuilding with nationalization and subsidization saddled the government with significant financial liabilities, but it did little to facilitate adjustment. By the end of the decade, growth had stagnated and Sweden was grappling with mounting fiscal and current-account deficits (Magnusson 2000, 261). While repeated currency devaluations and financial deregulation forestalled a more several economic crisis, inflationary pressures and financial speculation further eroded Swedish competitiveness over the course of the 1980s (Edquist and McKelvey 1998, 141). Sweden's increasingly tenuous position in international markets culminated in the economic crisis of the early 1990s, in which output plunged by 6 percent and unemployment reached 8 percent (Eurostat 2011). By then, Swedish voters had elected a center-right government that appeared committed to dismantling neo-corporatism.

Indeed, Sweden eliminated or adapted ostensibly core conservative bargains over the course of the 1980s and 1990s. Governments had reduced expenditures on state aid as early as 1982, virtually eliminating traditional industrial subsidies. As in Finland, the economic crisis of the early 1990s weakened the universal banks and loosened the hitherto dense network of cross holdings that characterized Swedish finance (Henrekson and Jakobsson 2003). The shift away from conservative corporatism was even more pronounced in labor markets, where employers unilaterally withdrew from all tripartite boards in the early 1990s (Pontusson and Swenson 1996). The center-right government simultaneously cut government expenditures and social expenditures, reducing benefit levels, introducing a waiting period, and increasing employer contributions (Jochem 2003, 125). Analysts pronounced the demise of the Swedish model, differing only in whether it had converged on liberal Anglo-Saxon capitalism (Henrekson and Jakobsson 2003) or continental German-style corporatism (Iversen and Pontusson 2000).

Neither characterization is correct, however, as stakeholders struck the same creative corporatist bargains that characterize Denmark and Finland. As in Finland, a center-right government that assumed power in 1991 entered with a mandate to dismantle traditional neo-corporatist institutions. At the same time, the government confronted a powerful trade union movement and, unlike Finland, required Social Democratic Workers' Party (SAP) support to pass austerity legislation through the national legislature (Anderson 2004, 295). The Carl Bildt administration thus introduced a series of supply-side investments to limit societal and political opposition. The Social Democratic administration that assumed power in 1994 took a similar approach to adjustment, targeting disruptive new inputs such as skill acquisition and venture capital, in consultation with organized economic actors.

Creative corporatism was more modest in innovation policy, where the state had always played a contested role (Pontusson 1984, 13). That said, the Social Democratic administration that dismantled defensive industrial policies during the early 1980s launched the National Microelectronics Program, which was targeted specifically at information technologies. While more limited than Tekes in Finland, the program was similar in that it targeted experimental R & D rather than technological diffusion within established industries (Jamison 1991, 306). The center-right administration that assumed power in 1991 adopted a similar strategy, diffusing the political fallout over the liquidation of the wage earner funds by reallocating the revenues to three new research foundations, the Swedish Foundation for Strategic Research, the Knowledge Foundation, and the Foundation for Strategic Environmental Research (Gergils 2006, 320–21). The Social Democratic administration that followed placed less importance on research, but it established a peak-level innovation policy agency (Vinnova) modeled after Tekes in 2001 (321).

The Social Democratic administration's attention was instead focused on human capital investment, which grew dramatically over the course of the 1990s. Sweden continued to rely on active labor market policies, most notably the Kunskapslyftet, or Adult Education Initiative, which enrolled over 3 percent of the labor force during the mid-1990s (Eurostat 2011; Steinmo 2010, 71). Policymakers devoted even greater attention to higher education (Ansell 2008), where Sweden had historically invested relatively little (Porter 1990, 343–44). The center-right government not only expanded university enrollment but dramatically increased financial support for higher education. Public expenditure on higher education as a share of GDP doubled between 1990 and 2000, surpassing even the United States (where investment as a share of GDP fell) (Steinmo 2010, 71).

The most dramatic example of institutional conversion, however, was the largely neglected process of converting patient capital into early stage risk capital over the course of the 1980s and 1990s. The same Social Democratic government that eliminated traditional industrial subsidies during the early 1980s simultaneously sought to increase the supply of risk capital for new growth-oriented firms. Financial deregulation and the establishment of an over-the-counter market created more exit opportunities for private venture capital investors, but the government also sought to increase the supply of risk capital by funding thirty regional investment companies (Andersson and Napier 2005, 60). It also sought to mobilize the formidable resources invested in Sweden's jointly managed pension funds. These funds had played an integral role in the Swedish economy since the early postwar period as an instrument to moderate wage claims and subsidize capital-intensive firms (Pontusson 1984). While the Social Democratic administration is most famous for launching the Wage Earner Funds to collectivize the ownership of large firms, it also encouraged pension funds to channel capital to small and medium-sized enterprises, raising the ceiling on unlisted equity investments in 1983. Pension funds subsequently emerged as leading financiers in the early 1980s (Andersson and Napier 2005, 63).

The center-right Bildt administration naturally liquidated the Wage Earner Funds but continued to prioritize public and pension fund investment in early stage risk, as funding for small and medium-sized enterprises contracted. In addition to additional financial and tax reform, the government redirected revenue from the Wage Earner Funds to launch two public venture capital funds in 1992 (Gergils 2006, 338). Those funds were privatized in 1995, but they were replaced by the conversion of Industrifonden, or Industry Fund, into a dedicated venture capital investor in 1996 (339). The government also engaged public pension funds even more explicitly, establishing the Sixth AP Fund, which was devoted exclusively to venture capital. By the end of the decade, analysts characterized the Swedish national pension fund system as a "giant" in the venture capital market (362), with even more venture capital raised than in Denmark (Hyytinen and Pajarinen 2003a, 39). Pension fund investments, meanwhile, were complemented by a broad range of initiatives in early stage venture capital (Andersson and Napier 2005, 65; Gergils 2006, 332).

Far from inhibiting the formation of a viable risk capital market, this pattern of public-sector intervention and pension fund involvement dramatically increased venture capital availability. In 1991, Sweden invested only 0.009 percent of GDP in venture capital, trailing France, Germany, Italy, the Netherlands, and Spain. By 2007, Sweden was devoting 0.223 percent of GDP to venture capital investment, second only to the United Kingdom within the European Union. Gains in early stage capital markets, targeted toward new enterprises, were even more impressive. Here, investment increased from 0.001 percent (less than a quarter of British levels) to 0.68 percent of GDP, ahead of the United Kingdom (0.21% of GDP) and the United States (0.066% of GDP) (Eurostat 2011).

Investment in venture capital and other supply-side resources supported industrial renewal and rapid economic growth over the course of the 1990s. Per capita GDP growth approached 5 percent, while unemployment fell to 5 percent by 2001 (Eurostat 2011). Economic growth was based in part on movement into new high-tech industries, including biotechnology, software, and telecommunication equipment. Swedish high-tech industry, which had declined in earlier decades (Porter 1990, 354), recovered sharply, and the share of high-tech exports more than doubled between 1987 and 2000 (Braunerhjelm and Thulin 2006, 26). While the widespread off shoring of manufacturing activity led the share of high-tech exports to decline sharply from 18.7 percent to 14.2 percent between 2000 and 2005 (Eurostat 2011), this did not necessarily signal a decline in innovative activity (Bitard et al. 2008). On the contrary, Sweden led the EU in share of employment in knowledge-intensive high-tech services and ranked second after Finland in per capita high-tech patent applications and the share of high-tech patents (Eurostat 2011). These knowledge-intensive services represent a potentially more viable source of productivity growth and employment, as physical assembling and manufacturing activity was transferred to eastern Europe and Asia.

Sweden's transformation into a high-tech contender revolved in part around Ericsson, an incumbent telecommunications producer. Indeed, some analysts contend that restructuring was based on leading multinationals, chiefly Ericsson, and their ability to create knowledge, human capital, and entrepreneurship (Casper and Glimstedt 2001, 280). Yet this argument obscures the way in which Ericsson actively relied on collective resources to revitalize its deteriorating position in telecommunications markets. First, Ericsson benefited from research support, including procurement and pressure from the public telephone operator, Televerket (Lindmark et al. 2006, 57). Second, investments in higher education eliminated a bottleneck to high-tech growth by reversing a long-standing shortage in the availability of engineers and IT professionals (Jacobsson, Sjöberg, and Wahlström 2001). Like Nokia, Ericsson could rely on an expanding pool of engineering to scale research operations during the 1990s. Meanwhile, robust venture capital markets fueled the formation of new small and medium-sized enterprises (Glimstedt and Zander 2003, 147), which in turn developed complementary mobile software (Casper 2007, 171).

Nor was restructuring limited to Ericsson or telecommunications. The software industry expanded dramatically during the second half of the 1990s. Surveys revealed that in some subsectors, such as interactive media, over half of the firms were established after 1995 (Sandberg and Augustsson 2002). While the interactive media and telecommunications industries both contracted sharply in the wake of the dot-com crash, Swedish software firms have diversified into radically innovative subsectors, including not only middleware (Casper 2007, 141) but also Internet-based activity more commonly associated with start-ups from large liberal economies. For example, Swedish firms have successfully entered advertising (Tradedoubler), database management (MySQL), communications (Skype), and music distribution (Spotify). These developments place Sweden in an enviable position, even as high-tech manufacturing continues to stagnate.

Sweden was not the only country to experiment with creative corporatist measures during the 1990s. On the contrary, the concept illuminates developments outside of Nordic Europe and western Europe more generally, particularly when one broadens the concept of neo-corporatism to encompass both labor and industry organization (Katzenstein 1984; Pempel and Tsunekawa 1979). More specifically, Finland's capacity to convert private-public and interfirm coordination illustrates how East Asian countries such as South Korea and Taiwan could adapt state-industry ties to achieve comparable gains in emerging high-tech industries. As in Finland, traditional patterns of collaboration facilitated rapid industrialization in low- and medium-technology industries, but this proved increasingly dysfunctional by the 1990s. In dismantling postwar industrial policies, however, East Asian policymakers simultaneously worked with industry to boost investment in disruptive new inputs such as research.

East Asia appears to be an unlikely candidate for creative corporatism. Analysts commonly attribute East Asian industrialization to the autonomy of the "developmental" state (Amsden 1992; Johnson 1982) and the corresponding weakness of the region's producer associations (Hommen and Edquist 2008). This is particularly true of the trade union movement, which was marginalized throughout the postwar period (Lee 1997, 107) and only intermittently engaged in policy concertation (Baccaro and Lim 2007). Later literature on the developmental state (Evans 1995), however, conditions bureaucratic effectiveness on states' capacity to "collaborate with organized private sectors" (Doner, Ritchie, and Slater 2005, 328). While South Korea and Taiwan did not rely on organized labor or peak-level employer associations like their Nordic counterparts did, policymakers engaged encompassing sectoral associations and cross-sectoral "industrial families" (335).

Historically, policymakers supported rapid industrialization by investing in supporting infrastructure, distributing technology and channeling capital to industry at subsidized rates, relying on international market competition and industry associations to effectively monitor these initiatives. As in Finland, these policies encouraged rapid industrialization within low- and medium-technology capital-intensive industries including steel, shipbuilding, and automobile production (Amsden 1992; Amsden and Chu 2003; Doner, Ritchie, and Slater 2005; Wade 1990). This strategy proved increasingly problematic as increasing labor costs placed a premium on technological innovation (Krugman 1994). Japanese growth stagnated in the early 1990s (Katz 1998), while the other East Asian countries experienced an even more acute financial and economic crisis later in the decade (Wade 2000).

The 1997–98 Asian financial crisis precipitated far-reaching reforms, both because of the magnitude of the economic downturn as well as the conditions attached to International Monetary Fund assistance. For example, South Korea privatized publically owned enterprises, dramatically reduced state aid, and liberalized its financial system to eliminate implicit public-sector guarantees (Hyun-Chin and Jin-Ho 2006, 14). Market-based reform, however, did not necessarily mark convergence on a liberal economic model. While industry-labor relations have remained contentious (Baccaro and Lim 2007), state-industry relations are characterized by continued cooperation. The government has worked with private-sector actors to dramatically boost investment in IT-based infrastructure (Lee 2009, 567) and research (Lim 2008, 116). Interestingly, like Finland, achievements in human capital investment are more modest. For example, while the government successfully increased investment in higher education (Lim 2008, 114), retraining initiatives have proven less effective (Park 2007, 417).

Investments in disruptive new inputs, most notably research, have facilitated entry into new high-tech industries from televisions to telecommunication equipment. The share of high-tech exports in South Korea increased from 23.2 percent in 1997 at the beginning of the Asian financial crisis to 28.7 percent by 2006. Furthermore, South Korea's relatively high-tech export profile does not reflect the low-cost assembly activity that prevails in eastern central Europe and China. Between 1997 and 2006 the number of high-tech patent applications per million citizens increased from 7.14 to 47.27, which would place South Korea fourth in the European Union after Finland, Sweden, and the Netherlands (Eurostat 2011). Just as Ireland was undercut by rivals in eastern central Europe, Nokia is in danger of ceding leadership in mobile communications to South Korean firms relying on strikingly similar inputs. Nor is the South Korean experience unique within East Asia. Analysts note that Taiwanese policymakers have also collaborated with industry networks to compete on the basis of rapid technological innovation in high-tech industries (Breznitz 2005).[4]

The Swedish and South Korean cases thus provide additional evidence of how neo-corporatist bargaining can accelerate industrial restructuring and support competition in rapidly evolving high-tech industries. Neo-corporatist bargaining continues to support incremental innovation in countries as diverse as Austria, Germany, and Norway, but it can be adapted to perform much more

---

4. Like Finland, however, these East Asian countries have witnessed more modest returns in biotechnology (Wong 2011).

disruptive functions. While adaptation entailed significant liberalization in Sweden and South Korea, it did not reflect convergence on a liberal economic model. On the contrary, we observe increasing collaboration among policymakers and organized producer associations in early stage risk capital, skill acquisition, and research. As in Denmark and Finland, disruptive new inputs enabled firms to enter new high-tech industries, competing in more knowledge-intensive activities relative to those of more market-oriented rivals such as the Netherlands, Hungary, and Estonia. This creative corporatist strategy thus represents an attractive strategy for conservative and competitive corporatist countries alike. The concluding chapter uses this expanded universe of cases to explore the prospects for institutional innovation in other countries.

CONCLUSION
Explaining Institutional Innovation

Economic globalization and technological change has clearly failed to induce convergence on a liberal economic model in which policymakers unilaterally implement sweeping pro-market reforms. How do we explain this variation? When do countries defend conservative corporatist institutions, and under what circumstances do they abandon them? And when do countries adapt neo-corporatist institutions to achieve competitive or creative objectives? The expanded universe of cases described in this book provides an ideal foundation for explaining variation in contemporary political economy and, in so doing, contributes to our understanding of how institutions change (and persist) over time. Stated most concisely, I identify a larger scope for institutional innovation, and institutional conversion in particular, by combining insights from the hitherto distinct literatures on concertation and coordination.

The literature on concertation reveals that neo-corporatist adaptation is shaped by a unique distribution of power in which policymakers are strong enough to threaten societal actors, most notably trade unions, but too weak to implement reforms on their own (Baccaro and Lim 2007; Rhodes 1998). Economic crises and external constraints are instrumental in "hardening" policymakers and weakening societal actors (Sala 1997). Countries that do not experience crises, such as Austria or Norway, face few incentives to adapt conservative corporatist institutions. Similar dynamics prevail in Germany, where societal actors are insulated from deteriorating economic performance by a federal and constitutionally constrained government (Ebbinghaus and Hassel 1999). These safeguards enabled trade unions to block neo-corporatist reform or, more precisely, redirect it to the periphery of the political system through an incremental process of dualization (Palier and Thelen 2010). By contrast, particularly strong policymakers can dismantle neo-corporatist institutions altogether (Hassel 2007, 58), leading to unilateral liberalization as in the United Kingdom, Estonia, and Latvia.

While the literature on concertation explains countries adapting neo-corporatist institutions, it says relatively little about how they adapt them. Here, literature on coordination or collaboration in the act of production yields valuable insight into employer preferences and behavior. Countries with a weak or nonexistent tradition of coordination, such as Ireland, the Netherlands, Italy, and the post-Communist countries of eastern central Europe, will have a more difficult time convincing firms to share sensitive information about capital requirements, skill profiles, and product portfolios. Indeed, they may struggle to convince firms that state actors, trade unions, or other firms can contribute meaningfully to the construction of these resources. Cooperation is thus more likely to privilege policies that only indirectly affect production, including wage restraint, fiscal retrenchment, and pro-market reform.

Countries with extensive coordination, such as Denmark, Finland, and Sweden, are more likely to strike deals to invest in disruptive new inputs, as stakeholders can more easily convince firms to strike peak-level agreements and participate in lower-level implementation (see table 7.1). In addition to visually illustrating the interplay between concerted reform and coordination, the table situates Austria, Denmark, Estonia, Finland, Germany, Ireland, Latvia, the Netherlands, Italy, Norway, Sweden, and the United Kingdom within this framework. In the remainder of the conclusion I develop the argument, moving counterclockwise from conservative corporatism to creative corporatism.

In explaining varying patterns of institutional change and neo-corporatist bargaining, I also address the prospects for neo-corporatist innovation in the future. Contrary to theories of liberal convergence, economic globalization and rapid technological change may make countries, even predominantly market-oriented economies, even *more* likely to strike competitive corporatist pacts. Creative corporatist arrangements are also likely to feature prominently as countries

TABLE 7.1   Neo-Corporatist (and Non-Corporatist) Outcomes

	NO CONCERTED REFORM (UNEVEN VULNERABILITY)	CONCERTED REFORM (MUTUAL VULNERABILITY)
COORDINATION (COLLABORATION IN PRODUCTION)	Conservative corporatism	Creative corporatism
NO COORDINATION (NO COLLABORATION IN PRODUCTION)	Unilateral liberalization	Competitive corporatism

grapple with disruptive shocks, although this form of institutional conversion is most likely to occur in the countries that have done the least to reform their neo-corporatist institutions and will evolve over time as countries confront disruptive new challenges.

Conservative Corporatism: Coordination without Concerted Reform

The decision to reform neo-corporatist bargaining, or any institutional arrangements, begins with poor economic performance. Countries with stable growth and low unemployment face few incentives to adapt traditional institutions. Austria and Norway, for example, have enjoyed stable growth and successfully defended conservative corporatist bargaining over the last three decades. Austria occupies more stable medium-technology niches such as automotives and machine tools and has benefited from its proximity to relatively fast-growing post-Communist countries in eastern central Europe. It has been able to sustain employment protections, generous social benefits, early retirement, and related schemes with modest but sustainable increases in public debt (Sherwood 2006). Norway, meanwhile, has used its oil wealth to maintain large-scale transfer payments and public-sector employment, including heavy reliance on disability insurance, early retirement, and other passive labor market programs (E. Moen 2011).

Policymakers in Denmark, Estonia, Finland, Ireland, Italy, Latvia, the Netherlands, Sweden, and the United Kingdom, by contrast, all faced severe economic crises between the 1980s and the 1990s. For example, unemployment approached double digits in Denmark, Finland, and Ireland, from a comparatively "low" 8.3 percent in the Netherlands to over 16 percent in Finland and Ireland (Eurostat 2011). Meanwhile, traditional neo-corporatist strategies generated unsustainable fiscal and current account deficits. Denmark, Ireland, and the Netherlands all faced IMF bailouts during the 1980s. Contemporaries perceived deteriorating economic performance as an existential threat, as international intervention threatened to compromise national sovereignty. One Irish contemporary, for example, characterized his country as facing "national bankruptcy."[1] Finland was on sounder fiscal footing, but perceived a more severe geopolitical threat in the form of growing dependence on the Soviet Union (Fellman 2008, 181; Steinbock 2000, 28).[2] Dependence on the Soviet Union was even more pronounced and problematic in the Baltic republics of Estonia and Latvia (Bohle and Greskovits 2012).

---

1. Author interview with former executive, Department of the Taoiseach (14 June 2006, Ireland).
2. Author interview with former executive officer, forestry firm (31 October 2005, Finland).

Societal actors were profoundly vulnerable to these developments. Newly elected center-right governments in all countries challenged trade union resources by threatening to dismantle collective wage bargaining, revise union recognition laws, cut unemployment insurance benefits, or sever the link between social insurance and trade union membership (Baccaro 2002; Bohle and Greskovits 2012; Thomas 2003; Vartiainen 1998b; Visser and Hemerijck 1997). Nor was industry immune to these developments. Firms were sensitive to disruptive economic shifts as a result of their reliance on barter trade and commodities in Finland (Steinbock 2000, 28).[3] The collapse of the universal bank plunged Finnish (and Swedish) firms even deeper into crisis by disrupting financial markets (Honkapohja et al. 1999, 408). Danish firms appeared to suffer from their relatively low technological intensity and mounting tax burden (Jamison 1991, 306).[4] Irish employers, meanwhile, struggled with industrial unrest, wage inflation, mounting taxes, and the uncertainty associated with large fiscal deficits (Thomas 2003, 154).[5]

Stakeholder vulnerability is significant, because it differentiates Denmark, Finland, Ireland, the Netherlands, and Sweden from other conservative corporatist countries facing deteriorating economic performance. Germany, for example, also suffered from stagnant growth and mounting unemployment during the 1990s (Streeck 1997). Stakeholders, however, were largely insulated from deteriorating economic performance in two respects. First, Germany was a large country, and deteriorating economic performance never posed the same threat to its financial or political sovereignty. Germany was never confronted with the threat of intervention by the IMF during the 1980s or 1990s, and policymakers largely ignored the restrictive Maastricht criteria that had strengthened government credibility in countries such as Finland, Ireland, Italy, and the Netherlands in previous decades (Hancké and Rhodes 2005; Rhodes 1998; Sala 1997).[6]

Second, and more important, stakeholders were internally insulated from the threats that precipitated neo-corporatist reform in Denmark, Finland, Ireland, the Netherlands, and Sweden. For example, constitutional restrictions on the government's power to intervene in the labor market enabled trade unions to effectively block political and economic reform (Ebbinghaus and Hassel 1999). Meanwhile, the large firms that dominated neo-corporatist bargaining were not

---

3. Author interview with former executive officer, forestry firm (31 October 2005, Finland).

4. Author interview with former director, Danish Technological Institute (6 December 2005, United States).

5. Author interviews with former director, Irish Business and Employers Confederation (24 May 2006, Ireland) and director, Irish Training and Employment Authority (2 June 2006, Ireland).

6. The same was true of East Asian states such as Japan, which largely defended traditional conservative corporatist bargains (Levy, Miura, and Park 2006). Unlike their smaller neighbors such as South Korea, Japan was never bailed out by the IMF.

exposed to the same low-tech, resource-extractive niches. Firms were positioned in more stable medium-technology industries such as automotives, chemicals, and machine tools, while their sponsors, the universal banks, remained solvent throughout the 1990s and 2000s (Manow and Seils 2000).

As the largest nonliberal economy in western Europe, Germany has exercised a disproportionate influence in how political scientists conceptualize change. The country's highly decentralized federal political structure (Katzenstein 1987; Scharpf 1988) encouraged political scientists to emphasize the path-dependent reproduction of national political and economic institutions (Katzenstein 1978; Kitschelt and Streeck 2004; Zysman 1994). This incremental orientation is even more pronounced in the varieties of capitalism literature, where increasing returns to coordination across different policy domains are perceived to generate stable institutional equilibriums in Germany and other coordinated market economies (Hall and Soskice 2001). Political gridlock is perceived to enhance coordination by preventing policy-makers from dismantling social protections (Wood 1997). Those more secure protections in turn support incremental up-market movement within established low- and medium-tech industries (Hall and Soskice 2001).

An increasing number of scholars have criticized this narrowly path-dependent interpretation by identifying how German institutions change over time. Indeed, we observe potentially significant changes in financial markets (Deeg 2010) and social policy (Vail 2010). Germany's fragmented political structure, however, leads scholars to emphasize comparatively incremental processes of hybridization (Crouch 2005) by which new market-friendly measures are gradually layered atop traditional patterns of coordination (Streeck and Thelen 2005, 24). Reform, to the extent it occurs, unfolds at the margins of German society through the incremental dualization into more and less coordinated spheres (Deeg 2010; Palier and Thelen 2010).

This literature represents a significant breakthrough because it redresses the narrowly path-dependent character of the early varieties of capitalism literature (Hall and Thelen 2009). It also yields valuable insights into the contemporary German economy and how it is evolving (Deeg 2010; Vail 2010). At the same time, the growing German-influenced literature on incremental institutional change obscures more radical institutional and economic shifts in other countries. For example, Britain implemented far-reaching pro-market reforms during the early 1980s (Levy, Kagan, and Zysman 1997), while the post-Soviet Baltic republics of Estonia and Latvia orchestrated an even more implausible transformation from state-led planning to unadulterated neoliberalism (Bohle and Greskovits 2007; Bohle and Greskovits 2012). In both cases, market reform facilitated rapid restructuring away from low- and medium-tech industry toward new high-tech industries and services.

Unilateral Liberalization: Neither Concertation nor Coordination

Unilateral liberalization reflected a very different distribution of power, characteristic of many historically liberal market economies such as Australia, New Zealand, and the United Kingdom. In contrast to continental European economies such as Austria, Germany, and Norway, organized industry and labor associations played little role in politics and production and were poorly positioned to resist liberal reforms. Banks exercised less control over industry, employer confederations were less encompassing, trade union density was lower, and unions were more fragmented than in their continental European counterparts (Levy, Kagan, and Zysman 1997).

Political institutions enhanced policymaker influence relative to societal actors. In the United Kingdom, for example, a clear single-party parliamentary majority and a unitary state with few constitutional safeguards insulated Margaret Thatcher from industry and trade union resistance (Levy, Kagan, and Zysman 1997).[7] Policymakers were thus free to respond to devastating financial crises by following the prevailing (liberal) ideas of the time, retrenching state expenditure, deregulating labor markets, liberalizing financial markets, and weakening organized actors (Levy, Kagan, and Zysman 1997; Schwartz 1994). While historical institutionalists have argued that the Anglo-Saxon countries were "restoring" preexisting liberal institutions (Levy, Kagan, and Zysman 1997), this framework can also explain strikingly discontinuous institutional changes, such as the decision to abandon state-led planning for unfettered market competition in the post-Soviet Baltic republics (Bohle and Greskovits 2007; Bohle and Greskovits 2012).

While countries such as Estonia and Latvia lacked the political and economic institutions of their Anglo-Saxon counterparts, policymakers wielded significant power over severely weakened societal actors. The post-Soviet Baltic republics faced much deeper economic crises following the collapse of the Soviet Union during the early 1990s (Bohle and Greskovits 2007, 460). Furthermore, direct rule discredited nonmarket strategies and the actors associated with them. For example, policymakers were quick to eliminate support for established industries

---

7. The same was true, to a lesser extent, of France, which also implemented significant market-oriented reforms during this period (Levy 1999; Vail 2010).

to reduce dependence on Russia, while Russian-speaking trade union members were viewed with suspicion and actively disenfranchised (Bohle and Greskovits 2007, 451). Nor could societal actors rely on well-organized opposition parties to oppose market-based reform (O'Dwyer and Kovalčík 2007, 3). Consequently, the Baltic countries pursued sweeping market reforms within the region, liberalizing financial markets, dismantling state aid, retrenching social spending, and reducing or even eliminating corporate taxation (Bohle and Greskovits 2007, 448; O'Dwyer and Kovalčík 2007, 11).

Comprehensive market reform facilitated rapid movement into new industries, from British biotechnology to Estonian telecommunication equipment (Casper 2007; Nölke and Vliegenthart 2009). At the same time, this model of unilateral liberalization remains limited for two reasons. First, restructuring could also lead to rapid deindustrialization (Bohle and Greskovits 2007, 459). After all, liberal supremacy in high-tech markets is based in part on the impressive performance of the United States, a large economy that enjoys a significant advantage in standard setting (Dalum, Fagerberg, and Jørgensen 1988) and that has the world's largest defense sector (Leslie 2000).[8] Other liberal economies such as Austria, Canada, and New Zealand, by contrast, moved into comparatively low- and medium-technology resource-extractive industries such as mining and agriculture. Even ostensibly high-tech leaders such as Britain and Estonia (as well as the United States) struggled to defend high-tech niches in the wake of the dot-com crash and relied on nontradable services to support growth and employment. Second, and more important, policymakers in other countries simply lacked the capacity to unilaterally dismantle nonliberal economic institutions. Policymakers in these countries had to rely on a very different strategy to promote growth and restructuring.

Competitive Corporatism: Concertation without Coordination

In fact, not all institutional change reflected movement away from neo-corporatism. Most intriguingly, Ireland, Italy, the Netherlands, Portugal, Spain, the Czech Republic, and Hungary all experimented with neo-corporatist bargaining after 1980 (Hancké and Rhodes 2005; Hassel 2009; Iankova 2002; Rhodes 1998). The turn toward neo-corporatist bargaining in these countries is particu-

---

8. The United States also relied quite heavily on nontradable services in the wake of the dot-com crash.

larly surprising because all possessed a relatively weak or conflicted tradition of cooperation among firms, trade unions, and the state. As described in chapter 2, Ireland relied primarily on liberal market-based institutions to govern financial and labor markets and failed to sustain neo-corporatist bargaining during the 1970s (Hardiman 1988). Italian neo-corporatism similarly foundered with fragmented and polarized interest groups and an unsupportive government (Regini 1984). Conditions were hardly more auspicious in early postwar Portugal, Spain, the Czech Republic, or Hungary, where repressive fascist or Communist regimes used state-industry and industry-labor cooperation to channel popular demands (Ost 2000; Royo 2002; Schmitter 1974).

This characterization extends even to the Netherlands. While the Dutch *poldermodel*, relying on consensual negotiations among distinct social pillars or blocs, represented one of the earliest examples of institutionalized cooperation (Lijphart 1968), this pattern of institutionalized cooperation revolved primarily around Catholic, Protestant, and social democratic political blocs rather than economic actors (Verspagen 2008, 321). Organized actors such as trade unions and employer associations played a less central role. Furthermore, the poldermodel declined in salience in the postwar period, just as countries like Austria, Denmark, Finland, and Sweden were developing more encompassing forms of neo-corporatism (321). Collective wage bargaining was never as centralized or as encompassing in the Nordic countries, and in fact it appeared to collapse during the 1970s (Visser and Hemerijck 1997, 93).

By the 1990s, however, all of these countries were engaging trade unions and employer associations in peak- and lower-level negotiations over wages, public spending, social policy, labor market regulation, and other policy domains (Hancké and Rhodes 2005; Hassel 2009; Iankova 2002; Rhodes 1998). The aforementioned distinction between neo-corporatist continuity in Germany and liberal reform in Britain and the United States (Albert 1993; Hall and Soskice 2001; Kitschelt et al. 1999) yields little insight into this outbreak of cooperation along the European periphery. Why would countries such as Ireland, Italy, the Netherlands, or Hungary, with little history of institutionalized cooperation, experiment with neo-corporatist bargaining when their Anglo-Saxon and Baltic counterparts were actively dismantling it?

Like Britain, Estonia, and Latvia, these countries faced acute economic crises, including sluggish growth, mounting unemployment, serious balance-of-payment deficits, and the specter of IMF intervention. In Ireland, the Netherlands, and southern and eastern central Europe, center-right governments assumed power with a mandate to weaken societal actors and enact sweeping market reforms. In many cases, however, policymakers eschewed unilateral liberalization. Instead, they engaged societal actors, most notably trade unions. In doing so, they not only attempted to reduce wage costs (Hancké and Rhodes 2005; Hassel 2007) but also to diffuse the costs associated with polarizing pro-market reforms (Baccaro 2002; Ebbinghaus and Hassel 1999; Rhodes 1998).

Policymakers pursued a neo-corporatist strategy because they faced a radically different political environment. In fact, policymakers presiding over fragmented proportional parliamentary systems were almost as vulnerable as the stakeholders that they threatened. For example, Italian policymakers did not possess a parliamentary majority (Baccaro 2002, 417), while the Irish Fianna Fail administration cooperated with the opposition Fine Gael party to retrench public spending (Thomas 2003, 166). Experiments with unilateral liberalization provoked fierce social resistance, such as the 1990 Hungarian taxi drivers' strike (Cox and Mason 2000, 334) and, in the case of Italy, a prompt electoral defeat (Baccaro 2002, 414). In short, policymakers were powerful enough to threaten core stakeholders and successfully dismantle important neo-corporatist institutions, yet they paid a heavy price for doing so and preferred to negotiate market-enhancing reforms (Baccaro and Lim 2007).

The literature on concertation thus challenges and expands the dichotomous distinction between neo-corporatist continuity and liberal reform by illustrating how historically noncorporatist countries can actively develop neo-corporatist institutions. More specifically, it suggests that vulnerable policymakers and societal actors can create cooperation from scratch, layering neo-corporatist forum atop comparatively liberal or disorganized societies (Iankova 2002; O'Donnell 2001). At the time, the literature on competitive corporatism and concertation more generally illuminates the limits of institutional innovation within a liberal market economy. The competitive corporatist pacts I have described were most effective in assembling a coalition to redistribute the costs and benefits associated with a particular reform. During the 1960s and 1970s, governments offered social concessions to induce wage restraints (Regini 1984). By the 1980s and 1990s, trade unions were ratifying fiscal retrenchment, labor market deregulation, and related market-based measures to forestall more damaging unilateral reforms (Ebbinghaus and Hassel 1999; Hassel 2009; Rhodes 1998).

Countries with a weak or conflicted tradition of cooperation in the act of production, however, struggled to promote private-public, interfirm, or industry-labor cooperation in collective investment. This is not surprising—collaboration in investment required firms to share far more sensitive information about their financial needs, competencies, and technologies. Firms that had no tradition of cooperation with one another or other actors had less confidence in the gains to be achieved through collective action and were more sensitive to the associated costs. As a result, neo-corporatist agreements rarely addressed education, training, research, venture capital, or similar inputs, and when they did (as in the case of Ireland) private-sector investments remained relatively modest (Bohle and Greskovits 2012; Bonoli 2010; Hassel 2009; Visser and Hemerijck 1997).

While the Czech, Dutch, Hungarian, Irish, Italian, Portuguese, and Spanish cases thus suggest that it is possible to layer neo-corporatist forums atop relatively liberal and pluralist institutions, these efforts were more successful in achieving distributive outcomes. In the case of competitive corporatism, wage restraint, fiscal austerity, and market-based reform accelerated movement into new high-tech industries. At the same time, distributive deals did not necessarily stimulate deeper collaboration in the sensitive area of production. Furthermore, limited investment in disruptive new inputs such as risk capital, training, and research heightened vulnerability to cost competition and competency-destroying shocks. As a result, competitive corporatist bargains were considerably less stable than their conservative or creative corporatist counterparts. Irish social partnership collapsed when unions were no longer willing to absorb externally mandated austerity measures in the wake of the financial crisis, and negotiations broke down even earlier in the Czech Republic, Hungary, Italy, Portugal, and Spain.

Creative Corporatism: The Concerted Reform of Coordination

Of course, institutional innovation was not limited to market-based reform. Denmark, Sweden, and Finland adapted neo-corporatist institutions to invest in disruptive new inputs. Like Ireland, Italy, Portugal, Spain, and eastern central Europe, these three Nordic countries confronted acute economic crises during the 1980s and 1990s (Honkapohja et al. 1999; Huber and Stephens 1998; Schwartz 1994). In each case, governments challenged societal actors, most notably trade unions, with measures designed to weaken organized labor. At the same time, coalition governments were poorly positioned to absorb the costs associated with pro-market reform. The Finnish center-right government of the early 1990s retreated when confronted with the threat of a general strike (Ornston and Rehn 2006, 89), while its Swedish colleagues relied on support by the Social Democrats to pass pro-market reforms (Anderson 2004, 295). This situation of mutual dependence, in which insecure policymakers could threaten weakened societal actors led policymakers, trade unions, and employers alike to negotiate reform.

Denmark, Finland, and Sweden differed from their competitive corporatist counterparts, however, in that each possessed a much stronger tradition of coordination or institutional cooperation in the act of production. In Denmark, policymakers leveraged a long history of industry-labor collaboration in collective wage bargaining, social policy, training, and shop-floor management (Kristensen 1995). In Finland, policymakers could exploit a tradition of private-public collaboration in industrialization and interfirm cooperation within encompassing universal banking blocs (Ornston and Rehn 2006). Swedish industrial relations were strained during the 1980s and 1990s, but policymakers could draw on jointly managed pension funds, which had stabilized the Swedish economy for decades (Pontusson 1984).

This history of constructive collaboration in the act of production enabled policymakers to move beyond distributive bargaining to tackle sensitive issues such as financing, skill formation, and research. Firms were both more willing to value and participate within collective schemes to boost investment when they had a tradition of collaborating with other actors in this space. Finnish firms, which had relied on public credit, patient capital, and price-fixing cartels for decades, were more receptive to public and private appeals regarding the importance of R & D, and more willing to share sensitive information about their product portfolios with policymakers and other firms. As chapter 3 relates, policymakers thus had a relatively easy time finding firms to participate in new technology programs, using peak-level councils, sectoral associations, and informal roundtables to recruit participants. Danish and Swedish policymakers were able to rely on similar instruments to engage firms in training and risk capital.

Industry participation facilitated policy implementation in several ways. First, repeated interaction generated a broad consensus regarding the importance of these disruptive new inputs. Finnish firms were subjected to persuasive appeals by peak-level actors such as the Science and Technology Policy Council, industry association presidents such as Urho Kekkonen, informal roundtables, and course instructors. Local cooperation in turn facilitated monitoring, increased transparency, and raised the costs associated with opportunistic behavior, pressuring firms to contribute to collective ventures.[9] Finally, neo-corporatist networks enabled stakeholders to scale their activities, coordinating educational, risk capital, and research-related initiatives and firm research to support larger and more complex investments. In countries without a strong tradition of coordination, such as Ireland, firms were less willing to share sensitive information or scarce resources and more skeptical about the potential utility of collaboration.

Cross-national analysis of "successful" creative corporatist economies supports claims about the importance of prior coordination. Finland, with its history of interfirm collaboration, successfully engaged firms in new innovation policies, dramatically increasing investment in R & D from one of the lowest to

---

9. Author interview with research director, electronics firm (19 October 2005, Finland).

one of the highest levels in the OECD. At the same time, firms were less enthusiastic about labor market reform, and Finland continues to lag behind Denmark in active labor market expenditure, despite suffering significantly higher unemployment throughout the 1990s and 2000s. Denmark, on the other hand, with its history of labor market cooperation, had a much easier time engaging firms in active labor market policies and now leads the European Union on several measures of continuing education. Danish firms were more skeptical about the utility of new innovation policies, particularly at the national level. Denmark targeted technological innovation less aggressively than did Finland and has not increased investment in R & D as dramatically. Sweden, caught between employer skepticism toward industrial policy, on the one hand, and the breakdown of labor market cooperation, on the other, could engage pension funds to promote restructuring. Small investments in new growth-oriented enterprises did not threaten to devolve into state-led planning nor collective ownership. As a result, Sweden has emerged as an unlikely leader in venture capital, and early stage venture capital markets in particular, but expenditure on research and training increased more modestly.

In boosting investment in disruptive new inputs such as risk capital, skill formation, and research, these creative corporatist bargains had very different implications for economic adjustment. Stated most concisely, they enabled historically low- and medium-tech small states to make big leaps into radically different high-tech industries. For example, Finland broke with its traditional reliance on pulp, paper, and related engineering industries to assume leadership in rapidly evolving telecommunication equipment markets. Denmark and Sweden, meanwhile, relied on new growth-oriented enterprises to enter an even broader range of industries from biotechnology to software. In doing so, these countries not only departed from conservative neo-corporatist bargaining but simultaneously deviated from their traditional reliance on incremental upmarket movement within stable established industries.

The Danish, Finnish, and Swedish experiences thus illuminate the possibility of achieving far more sweeping institutional reforms within densely organized economies than is commonly acknowledged in the literature on comparative political economy. More specifically, it underscores the importance of institutional "conversion" (Streeck and Thelen 2005, 31) as an alternative to incremental processes of layering, dualization, or hybridization (Campbell and Pedersen 2007; Mahoney and Thelen 2009; Palier and Thelen 2010). Countries can strike peak-level deals, adapting neo-corporatist institutions to perform very different functions. Nor is institutional conversion limited to "competitive" pro-market reform (Rhodes 1998). On the contrary, historically neo-corporatist countries are just as likely to adapt neo-corporatist institutions to increase investment in disruptive new inputs. Those investments in turn enable countries to break with path-dependent industrial trajectories, making big leaps into new industries.

At the same time, these big institutional and economic leaps are path-dependent leaps, as they require and are bounded by prior patterns of coordination. Denmark, Finland, and Sweden each relied on institutionalized cooperation in production to boost investment in disruptive new inputs. Furthermore, inherited patterns of coordination bounded adjustment in significant ways. Finland was able to radically increase investment in R & D but struggled to promote industry-labor cooperation in training. Partly as a result, Finland has excelled in patenting but has a more modest record in labor market performance and nontechnological innovation. Denmark, by contrast, has relied on training to accelerate the redistribution of labor to emerging high-tech industries, but it has struggled to compete in more capital-intensive industries such as network equipment and mobile handsets. The concept of institutional conversion thus broadens our understanding of how countries have adapted institutions in strikingly discontinuous ways, while illustrating how existing patterns of coordination continue to bind and influence actors.

The Future of European Corporatism

This discussion of the forces shaping institutional continuity and change offers some insights into the future of European corporatism. Most obviously, it suggests that convergence on a liberal economic model is unlikely, even as economic internationalization and technological competition intensifies. Far from weakening institutionalized cooperation among organized actors, economic crises may reinforce or even increase reliance on neo-corporatist institutions. Enduring reliance on institutionalized cooperation need not reflect institutional or economic continuity, although some conservative corporatist economies such as Austria, Germany, and Norway have proven relatively resilient in the face of rapid technological innovation and economic internationalization (Goyer 2006; E. Moen 2011; Sherwood 2006). Instead, it may reflect significant institutional change, as countries layer neo-corporatist forums atop liberal institutions or convert coordination to achieve new ends.

Institutional innovation is most striking in the predominantly liberal, decentralized economies along Europe's western, southern, and eastern periphery. Indeed, the preceding analysis suggests that neo-corporatist pacts are surprisingly easy to reach when vulnerable policymakers confront weakened stakeholders (Baccaro 2003; Natali and Pochet 2009; Rhodes 1998). Neo-corporatist strategies are thus likely to remain relevant, even within increasingly market-oriented societies. Indeed, neo-corporatist bargaining was most successful in one of Europe's most liberal economies, Ireland, as policymakers attempted to restrain wages, state spending, and taxation to create a more market-friendly environment for foreign direct investment.

At the same time, there are clear limits to institutional innovation in Ireland and other historically noncorporatist economies. Policymakers have proven much more successful in using threats, side payments, and persuasive appeals to reach negotiated settlements regarding wage levels, fiscal retrenchment, and labor market deregulation. By contrast, policymakers have had a more difficult time promoting collective investment in disruptive new inputs such as risk capital, training, and research, which requires firms to share valuable information about their financial needs, human capital, and technological portfolios. As a result, competitive corporatist economies face formidable challenges, even when they enter new high-tech industries. While wage restraint and market-based reform can facilitate rapid restructuring, they can also attract firms competing in relatively low value-added activities. Competitive corporatist deals can thus increase vulnerability to cost competition, heighten reliance on nontradable services, and exacerbate a country's exposure to international financial crises.

As chapter 5 relates, Irish policymakers are aware of and have attempted to address these challenges by experimenting with creative corporatism. For example, stakeholders have constructed new bodies such as Science Foundation Ireland to promote private-public and interfirm collaboration in technological innovation. Policymakers in other competitive corporatist economies, such as the Netherlands, have launched parallel training schemes. Such initiatives, however, have proven difficult even in the most successful cases. Competitive corporatist economies not only have difficulty engaging relevant stakeholders but find themselves constrained by their earlier reliance on wage restraint, fiscal retrenchment, and market-based reform.

Meanwhile, the 2007–9 financial crisis threatens to reinforce their reliance on wage restraint and fiscal retrenchment. These deflationary measures further undermine the prospects for creative corporatist bargaining by reducing the resources that can be invested in disruptive new inputs. In fact, the financial crisis has weakened competitive corporatist bargaining, as unprecedented, externally mandated spending cuts eliminate the tradeoffs that supported early bargaining rounds. While Fianna Fail's devastating electoral defeat in 2011 suggests that governments may attempt to strike a deal with societal actors, and trade unions in particular, in the future, the prospects for creative corporatist bargaining appear bleak.

Indeed, I suggest that while it is relatively easy to create concertation or cooperation in policymaking (Baccaro 2003; Hassel 2009; Rhodes 1998), coordination or cooperation in production is much harder to induce (Hall and Soskice 2001). Creative corporatism in Denmark and Finland leveraged a century-old tradition of collaboration in production that was integrally linked to the construction of the nation-state. Those patterns of coordination proved remarkably resilient to subsequent changes in the size and influence of different societal actors, such as the rise of the trade union movement and subsequent expansion of the public sector in Finland. This is not to suggest that it is impossible to create coordination, but rather that it is more easily forged during critical junctures, specifically the period of geopolitical challenges associated with state-building that required rapid, collective responses. The limited progress in Finnish labor markets and Irish social partnership suggest that constructing coordination in the absence of such a critical juncture is, at best, a challenging and time-consuming endeavor.

This distinction between concertation and coordination explains why competitive corporatist economies from Ireland to the Netherlands, Italy, Portugal, Spain, and eastern central Europe have struggled to extend bargaining from market reform to collective investment. It also underscores the important but limited role of the European Union, which accelerated institutional innovation by limiting recourse to traditional adjustment instruments from price-fixing cartels to deficit spending (Sala 1997) but was only modestly successful in boosting investment in research and training at the European or national levels (Pisani-Ferry and Sapir 2006). The Danish, Finnish, and Swedish cases highlight the challenges associated with engaging firms in collaborative ventures at the European level, as well as asymmetric capacity to boost investment in disruptive new inputs at the national level.

Curiously, the countries that are best positioned to adopt creative corporatism may in fact be the ones that have done the most to conserve traditional neo-corporatist institutions. While traditionally depicted in incremental veto-prone terms (Katzenstein 1987; Kitschelt et al. 1999), these countries are also able to convert a strong tradition of cooperation among trade unions, financial intermediaries, industry associations, sectoral organizations, and other stakeholders to perform new functions. Indeed, we observe experimentation with creative corporatist measures in each of these economies. Austria has invested aggressively in education and training, albeit with an emphasis on protecting specialized skills in existing industries (Culpepper 2007). Germany has attempted, with modest success, to engage financial intermediaries in constructing early stage risk capital markets (Adelberger 1999), and Norway has copied the Finnish Science and Technology Policy Council in a bid to reverse its declining position in high-tech markets and research-intensive activity more generally (Gergils 2006).

Such initiatives remain modest in size and scope, but this could change in the event that any of these countries confronts an acute crisis. Austria may invest much more aggressively in education, with greater attention to noncore workers and general skills, if deteriorating conditions in eastern Europe trigger a severe economic crisis. Norwegian investments in R & D could increase significantly if demand for or the supply of its natural resources begins to decline. Germany may redouble its efforts to invest in early stage risk capital markets at either the national or local level if stakeholders are exposed to greater political or economic pressure. The Danish, Finnish, and Swedish experiences suggest that such shocks can precipitate significant institutional innovation and rapid movement into new, often dynamic industries.

This is not to suggest that creative corporatist innovations solve all problems. Most obviously, movement into new high-tech industries exposes countries to new risks. While creative corporatist economies are more resilient to cost competition, they are vulnerable to disruptive technological and social innovations. Finland's dependence on Nokia is the most striking example of these risks, but the rise and fall of the telecommunication equipment industry in Aalborg, Denmark, suggests that even more diversified regional and national economies are vulnerable to disruption (Stoerring and Dalum 2007).

Furthermore, creative corporatism as a form of institutional conversion constrains adaptation to new challenges. National responses, after all, are limited by the type of cooperation that they can adapt. While Denmark and Finland experimented with a range of strategies to manage adjustment, Denmark ultimately relied on industry-labor investment in continuing education, while Finnish stakeholders privileged interfirm and private-public cooperation in R & D. These strategies, in turn, inhibited adaptation. Finland excelled in technological innovation, but its labor market performance was considerably less impressive (Ornston and Rehn 2006, 89), and it struggled in the area of nontechnological innovation (Ben-Aaron 2010). Denmark, on the other hand, relied on aggressive investments in training to lower unemployment but lagged behind in innovation based on science and technology (Eurostat 2011; Gergils 2006).

These challenges point to a more fundamental problem, the diminishing returns associated with purely supply-side investments. Investments in early stage risk capital do not necessarily generate the managerial skills necessary to identify and develop profitable enterprises (Hyytinen and Pajarinen 2003b; Maula and Murray 2003). Investments in scientific and technological research do not always yield commercial successes, as they do not address critical factors such as design or marketing.[10] And even Danish policymakers concede that training does not

---

10. Author interviews with director, Finnish Funding Agency for Technology and Innovation (20 October 2005, Finland) and former director, Ministry of Finance (11 November 2005, Finland).

always anticipate industrial needs.[11] In other words, investments in risky startups, research, and human capital have not always generated significant income for individual firms or countries as a whole (Edquist and McKelvey 1998).

One reason is that supply-side inputs, by themselves, do not address the important role that demand plays in stimulating innovation, whether through interaction between producers and suppliers or consumers (Hommen and Edquist 2008). Nordic firms have always excelled in this respect, but chiefly because of their close proximity to "lead users" in traditional low-tech markets such as agriculture, mining, and forestry (Lundvall 1992). High-tech competition is more challenging, however, because producers are so far removed from leading markets such as the United States.

Such challenges will not necessarily undermine neo-corporatist bargaining. Neo-corporatist institutions have always proven adept at linking domestic producers to international markets. Finland, for example, leveraged interfirm coordination to shift from Russian to German markets during the interwar period (Fellman 2008, 162). Policymakers are actively restructuring innovation policies to attract foreign venture capital to Finland and internationalize small and medium-sized Finnish enterprises.[12] Internationalization is even more pronounced in Denmark, with its proportionately greater reliance on foreign investment and ownership. These innovations represent an enduring source of diversity and dynamism in comparative political economy, particularly since their capacity to support high-tech competition will expose these countries to even more disruptive shocks in the future.

---

11. Author interviews with director, Research Institute of the Finnish Economy (26 October 2005, Finland) and director, Confederation of Danish Industries (28 February 2006, Denmark).

12. Author interviews with director, Confederation of Finnish Industry (18 October 2005, Finland) and director, venture capital fund (22 November 2006, Finland).

References

Adelberger, Karen E. 1999. "A Developmental German State? Explaining Growth in German Biotechnology and Venture Capital." Berkeley Roundtable on the International Economy Working Paper 134. Berkeley, CA: Berkeley Roundtable on the International Economy.

Aiginger, Karl, Aavo Okko, and Pekka Ylä-Anttila. 2009. "Globalization and Business: Innovation in a Borderless World Economy." In *Evaluation of the Finnish National Innovation System*. 103–46. Helsinki: Taloustieto Oy.

Alasoini, Tuomo. 1999. "Organizational Innovations as a Source of Competitive Advantage: New Challenges for Finnish Companies and the National Workplace Development Infrastructure." In *Transformation toward a Learning Economy: The Challenge for the Finnish Innovation System*, edited by Gerd Schienstock and Osmo Kuusi. 205–19. Helsinki: Finnish National Fund for Research and Development.

——. 2004. "The Flexible Production Model in Finnish Companies: Trends in Production Management, Work Organization and Employment Relations." In *Embracing the Knowledge Economy: The Dynamic Transformation of the Finnish Innovation System*, edited by Gerd Schienstock. 128–44. Cheltenham, UK: Edward Elgar.

Albert, Michel. 1993. *Capitalism against Capitalism*. London: Whurr.

Alderman, Liz. 2010. "Denmark Starts to Trim Its Admired Safety Net." *New York Times*, August 16. http://www.nytimes.com/2010/08/17/business/global/17denmark.html.

Ali-Yrkkö, Jyrki. 2003. "Patterns of the Finnish Merger and Acquisition Activity." In *Financial Systems and Firm Performance: Theoretical and Empirical Perspectives*, edited by Ari Hyytinen and Mika Pajarinen. 177–200. Helsinki: Taloustieto Oy.

——. 2010a. "Introduction and Synthesizing Discussion." In *Nokia and Finland in a Sea of Change*, edited by Jyrki Ali-Yrkkö. 1–8. Helsinki: Taloustieto Oy.

——. 2010b. "The Role of Nokia in the Finnish Economy." In *Nokia and Finland in a Sea of Change*, edited by Jyrki Ali-Yrkkö. 9–36. Helsinki: Taloustieto Oy.

Ali-Yrkkö, Jyrki, Ari Hyytinen, and Johanna Liukkonen. 2003. "Exiting Venture Capital Investments: Lessons from Finland." In *Financial Systems and Firm Performance: Theoretical and Empirical Perspectives*, edited by Ari Hyytinen and Mika Pajarinen. 135–76. Helsinki: Taloustieto Oy.

Ali-Yrkkö, Jyrki, and Pekka Ylä-Anttila. 2003. "Globalization of Business in a Small Country–Does Ownership Matter?" In *Financial Systems and Firm Performance: Theoretical and Empirical Perspectives*, edited by Ari Hyytinen and Mika Pajarinen. 249–67. Helsinki: Taloustieto Oy.

Allen, Christopher S. 1989. "The Underdevelopment of Keynesianism in the Federal Republic of Germany." In *The Political Power of Economic Ideas: Keynesianism across Nations*, edited by Peter Hall. 263–89. Princeton: Princeton University Press.

Allen, Kieren. 2000. *The Celtic Tiger: The Myth of Social Partnership in Ireland*. Manchester, UK: Manchester University Press.

Amin, Ash, and Daminan Thomas. 1996. "The Negotiated Economy: State and Civic Institutions in Denmark." *Economy and Society* 25: 255–81.

Amsden, Alice. 1992. *Asia's Next Giant: South Korea and Late Industrialization.* Oxford: Oxford University Press.

Amsden, Alice, and Wan-Wen Chu. 2003. *Beyond Late Development: Taiwan's Upgrading Policies.* Cambridge: MIT Press.

Andersen, Poul Houman, and Peer Hull Kristensen. 1999. "The Systemic Qualities of Danish Industrialism." In *Mobilizing Resources and Generating Competencies: The Remarkable Success of Small and Medium-Sized Enterprises in the Danish Business System,* edited by Peter Karnoe, Peer Hull Kristensen, and Poul Houman Andersen. 229–331. Copenhagen: Copenhagen Business School.

Andersen, Torben M., Bengt Holmström, Seppo Honkapohja, Sixten Korkman, Hans Tson Söderström, and Juhana Vartiainen 2007. *The Nordic Model: Embracing Globalization and Sharing Risks.* Helsinki: Taloustieto Oy.

Anderson, Karen M. 2004. "Pension Politics in Three Small States: Denmark, Sweden and the Netherlands." *Canadian Journal of Sociology* 29: 289–312.

Andersson, Thomas, and Glenda Napier. 2005. *The Venture Capital Market: Global Trends and Issues for Nordic Countries.* Malmo, Sweden: International Organization for Knowledge Economy Development.

Ansell, Ben W. 2008. "University Challenges: Explaining Institutional Change in Higher Education." *World Politics* 60: 189–230.

Åslund, Anders. 2010. *The Last Shall Be the First: The East European Financial Crisis.* Washington, DC: Peterson Institute for International Economics.

Asplund, Rita. 2003. *Flexibility and Competitiveness: Labour Market Flexibility, Innovation and Organisational Performance.* Helsinki: Taloustieto Oy.

Auer, Peter L. 2000. *Employment Revival in Europe: Labor Market Success in Austria, Denmark, Ireland and the Netherlands.* Geneva: International Labour Organization.

Baccaro, Lucio. 2002. "Negotiating the Italian Pension Reform with the Unions: Lessons for Corporatist Theory." *Industrial and Labor Relations Review* 55: 413–31.

——. 2003. "What Is Alive and What Is Dead in the Theory of Corporatism." *British Journal of Industrial Relations* 41: 683–706.

Baccaro, Lucio, and Sang-Hoon Lim. 2007. "Social Pacts as Coalitions of the Weak and Moderate: Ireland, Italy and South Korea in Comparative Perspective." *European Journal of Industrial Relations* 13: 27–46.

Baldwin, Richard. 2006. *Globalisation: The Great Unbundling(s).* Helsinki: Prime Minister's Office.

Barry, Frank. 2000. "From Periphery to Core? Foreign Direct Investment, Cost Competitiveness and the Transformation of the Irish Economy." *Development Southern Africa* 17: 289–305.

——. 2004. "Export-Platform Foreign Direct Investment: The Irish Experience." *European Investment Bank Papers* 9: 8–37.

Barry, Frank, and Chris van Egeraat. 2008. "The Decline of the Computer Hardware Industry: How Ireland Adjusted." *Economic and Social Research Institute Quarterly Economic Commentary* (Spring): 38–57.

Baygan, Gunseli. 2003. "Venture Capital Policies in Denmark." OECD Science, Technology and Industry Working Paper 2003:10. Paris: Organization for Economic Cooperation and Development.

Ben-Aaron, Diana. 2010. "After Nokia, Can Angry Birds Propel Finland?" *Business Week*, December 2. http://businessweek.com/magazine/content/10_50/b4207 048626069.htm.

Ben-Aaron, Diana, and Kati Pohjanpalo. 2011. "Nokia Wins Apple Patent-License Deal Cash, Settles Lawsuits." *Bloomberg*, June 14. http://www.bloomberg.com/news/2011–06–14/nokia-apple-payments-to-nokia-settle-all-litigation.html.

Bengtsson, Maria, and Kock Soren. 2000. "Coopetition in Business Networks—to Cooperate and Compete Simultaneously." *Industrial Marketing Management* 29: 411–26.

Bergholm, Tapio. 2003. *A Short History of SAK*. Helsinki: Central Organisation of Finnish Trade Unions.

Beuzekom, Brigitte van, and Anthony Arundel. 2006. *OECD Biotechnology Statistics 2006*. Paris: Organization for Economic Cooperation and Development.

Bilton, Nick. 2011. "The Engineer-Driven Culture of Nokia." *New York Times*, February 11. http://bits.blogs.nytimes.com/2011/02/11/for-nokia-design-will-be-key-to-future/.

Bitard, Pierre, Charles Edquist, Leif Hommen, and Annika Rickne. 2008. "Reconsidering the Paradox of High R & D Input and Low Innovation: Sweden." In *Small Country Innovation Systems: Globalization, Change and Policy in Asia and Europe*, edited by Charles Edquist and Leif Hommen. 237–80. Cheltenham, UK: Edward Elgar.

Björkland, Anders. 2000. "Going Different Ways: Labour Market Policy in Denmark and Sweden." In *Why Deregulate Labour Markets?* edited by Gøsta Esping-Andersen and Marino Regini. 148–80. Oxford: Oxford University Press.

Blankenfeld-Enkvist, Gabriela von, Malin Brännback, Riitta Söderlund, and Marin Petrov. 2004. "OECD Case Study on Innovation: The Finnish Biotechnology Innovation System." Turku, Finland: Innomarket.

Bloch, Carter. 2004. "Biotechnology in Denmark: A Preliminary Report." Aarhus: Danish Centre for Studies in Research and Research Policy Working Paper 2004/1., Aarhus: Danish Center for Studies in Research and Research Policy.

Bohle, Dorothee, and Béla Greskovits. 2007. "Neoliberalism, Embedded Neoliberalism and Neocorporatism: Towards Transnational Capitalism in Central-Eastern Europe." *West European Politics* 30: 443–66.

——. 2012. *Capitalist Diversity on Europe's Periphery*. Ithaca: Cornell University Press.

Bonoli, Giuliano. 2010. "The Political Economy of Active Labour Market Policy." *Politics & Society* 38: 435–57.

Boutin, Paul. 2010. "Analysts: How Nokia Lost the USA." *VentureBeat*, February 16. http://venturebeat.com/2010/02/16/nokia-us-cmda/.

Boyle, Nigel. 2004. "Consensus and Institutional Capacity in Irish Policymaking." Paper presented to the 2nd Pan-European Conference on EU Politics. Bologna, Italy: June 24–26.

——. 2005. *Fás and Active Labour Market Policy 1985–2004*. Dublin: Policy Institute.

Brännback, Malin, Markku Jalkanen, Kauko Kurkela, and Esa Soppi. 2005. "Pharma Development in Finland Today and in 2015." Helsinki: National Technology Agency of Finland.

Braunerhjelm, Pontus, and Per Thulin. 2006. "Can Countries Create Comparative Advantages?" Stockholm: Royal Institute of Technology.

Brennan, Niamh. 2006. "Time to Raise the Bar on Corporate Governance." *Sunday Business Post*, March 26.

Brennan, Niamh, and Michael McDermott. 2002. "Are Non-Executive Directors of Irish Plcs Independent?" Dublin: Institute of Directors, University College Dublin.

Breznitz, Dan. 2005. "Development, Flexibility, and R & D Performance in the Taiwanese IT Industry: Capability Creation and the Effects of State-Industry Co-Evolution." *Industrial and Corporate Change* 14: 153–87.

——. 2007. *Innovation and the State: Political Choice and Strategies for Growth in Israel, Taiwan, and Ireland.* New Haven: Yale University Press.

Breznitz, Dan, Mikko Ketokivi, and Petri Rouvinen. 2009. "Demand- and User-Driven Innovation." In *Evaluation of the Finnish National Innovation System.* Helsinki: Taloustieto Oy.

Browning, Lynnley. 2007. "The Netherlands, the New Tax Shelter Hot Spot." *New York Times,* February 4. http://www.nytimes.com/2007/02/04/business/yourmoney/04amster.html.

Calmfors, Lars, and John Driffill. 1988. "Bargaining Structure, Corporatism and Macroeconomic Performance." *Economic Policy* 6:14–61.

Campbell, John L., and John A. Hall. 2006. "Introduction: The State of Denmark." In *National Identity and the Varieties of Capitalism: The Danish Experience,* edited by John A. Hall John L. Campbell, and Øve K. Pedersen. 1–49. Montreal: McGill-Queen's University Press.

Campbell, John L., and Øve K. Pedersen. 2007. "The Varieties of Capitalism and Hybrid Success: Denmark in the Global Economy." *Comparative Political Studies* 40: 307–32.

Carlsson, Bo. 1984. "Industrial Subsidies in the Nordic Countries." In *Economic Growth in a Nordic Perspective.* 221–29. Copenhagen: Det Økonomiske Råd Sekretariat.

Casey, Frank. 2000. *Credit Where Credit Is Due: The Evolution of Business Banking in Ireland.* Dublin: Institute of Public Administration.

Casper, Steven. 2007. *Creating Silicon Valley in Europe: Public Policy towards New Technology Industries.* Oxford: Oxford University Press.

Casper, Steven, and Henrik Glimstedt. 2001. "Economic Organization, Innovation Systems, and the Internet." *Oxford Review of Economic Policy* 17: 265–81.

Castells, Manuel, and Pekka Himanen. 2002. *The Information Society and the Welfare State: The Finnish Model.* Oxford: Oxford University Press.

Christensen, Jesper Lindgaard, Ina Drejer, and Anker Lund Vinding. 2004. "Produktudvikling I Dansk Fremstillingsindustri [Product development in Danish manufacturing]." *ACE Memo* 8. Copenhagen: Ministry of Science.

Christiansen, Hans, Andrea Goldstein, and Ayse Bertrand. 2007. *Trends and Recent Developments in Foreign Direct Investment.* Paris: Organization for Economic Cooperation and Development.

Christiansen, Peter Munk. 1988. *Teknologi Mellem Stat og Marked: Dansk Teknologipolitik 1970–87* [Technology between the state and the market: Danish technology policy]. Copenhagen: Forlaget Politica.

Cioffi, John. 2010. *Public Law and Private Power: Corporate Governance Reform in the Age of Finance Capitalism.* Ithaca: Cornell University Press.

Clinch, Peter, Frank Convery, and Brendan Walsh. 2002. *After the Celtic Tiger: The Challenges Ahead.* Dublin: O'Brien.

Collins, John. 2011. "Microsoft Ireland Profits Rise By 76% to 1.43 Billion Euro." *Irish Times,* April 20. http://www.irishtimes.com/newspaper/finance/2011/0420/1224295068643.html.

Compston, Hugh. 2003. "Beyond Corporatism: A Configurational Theory of Policy Concertation." *European Journal of Political Research* 42: 787–809.

Considine, John, and Eoin O'Leary. 1999. "The Growth Performance of Northern Ireland and the Republic of Ireland: 1960 to 1995." In *Political Issues in Ireland Today,* edited by Neil Collins. 106–25. Manchester, UK: Manchester University Press.

Cowell, Alan. 2003. "Ireland: Once a Celtic Tiger Now Slackens Its Stride." *New York Times,* February 19. http://www.nytimes.com/2003/02/19/business/worldbusienss/19IREL.html.

Cox, Terry, and Bob Mason. 2000. "Interest Groups and the Development of Tripartism in East-Central Europe." *European Journal of Industrial Relations* 6: 325–347.

Cradden, Terry. 1999. "Social Partnership in Ireland: Against the Trend." In *Political Issues in Ireland Today*, edited by Neil Collins. 46–63. Manchester, UK: Manchester United Press.

Crouch, Colin. 2005. *Capitalist Diversity and Change: Recombinant Governance and Institutional Entrepreneurs.* Oxford: Oxford University Press.

Culliton Industrial Policy Review Group. 1992. *A Time for Change: Industrial Policy for the 1990s.* Dublin: Stationary Office.

Culpepper, Pepper D. 2007. "Small States and Skill Specificity: Austria, Switzerland and Interemployer Cleavages in Coordinated Capitalism." *Comparative Political Studies* 40: 611–37.

——. 2008. "The Politics of Common Knowledge: Ideas and Institutional Change in Wage Bargaining." *International Organization* 62: 1–33.

Dahl, Michael S., Christian Ø. R. Pedersen, and Bent Dalum. 2003. "Entry by Spinoff in a High-Tech Cluster." DRUID Working Paper 03–11. Aalborg: Danish Research Unit on Industrial Dynamics.

——. 1992. "Export Specialisation, Structural Competitiveness and National Systems of Innovation." In *National Systems of Innovation: Towards a Theory of Innovation and Interactive Learning*, edited by Bengt-Åke Lundvall. 119–225 London: Pinter.

Dalum, Bent, Christian Ø. R. Pedersen, and Gert Villumsen. 2002. "Technological Life Cycles: Regional Clusters Facing Disruption." DRUID Working Paper 02–10. Aalborg: Danish Research Unit for Industrial Dynamics.

Dalum, Bent, and Gert Villumsen. 2005. "Norcom: History and Present Perspectives." Aalborg, Denmark: Department and Business Studies, University of Aalborg.

Dalum, Bent, Jan Fagerberg and Ulrik Jørgensen. 1988. "Small Open Economies in the World Market for Electronics: The Case of the Nordic Countries." In *Small Countries Facing the Technological Revolution*, edited by Christopher Freeman and Bengt-Åke Lundvall. 113–38. London: Pinter.

Deeg, Richard. 2005. "The Comeback of Modell Deutschland? The New German Political Economy in the EU." *German Politics* 14: 332–53.

——. 2010. "Industry and Finance in Germany since Unification." *German Politics and Society* 28: 116–29.

Department of Finance. 2005 *Budgetary and Economic Statistics.* Dublin: Department of Finance.

Department of the Taoiseach. 1987. *Program for National Recovery.* Dublin: Department of the Taoiseach.

——. 1998. *Partnership 2000.* Dublin: Department of the Taoiseach.

——. 2008. *Building Ireland's Smart Economy.* Dublin: Department of the Taoiseach.

Doner, Richard F., Bryan K. Ritchie, and Dan Slater. 2005. "Systemic Vulnerability and the Origins of Developmental States: Northeast and Southeast Asia in Comparative Perspective." *International Organization* 59: 327–61.

Dossani, Rafiq, and Martin Kenney. 2006. "The Relocation of Service Provision to Developing Nations: The Case of India." In *How Revolutionary Was the Revolution? National Responses, Market Transitions, and Global Technology*, edited by John Zysman and Abraham Newman. 193–216. Stanford: Stanford University Press.

Dunning, John H. 1992. "The Global Economy, Doemestic Governance Strategies and Transnational Corporations: Interactions and Policy Implications." *Transnational Corporations* 1: 7–45.

Durkan, Joe. 1992. "Social Consensus and Incomes Policy." *Economic and Social Review* 23: 347–63.

Ebbinghaus, Bernhard, and Anke Hassel. 1999. "The Role of Tripartite Concertation in the Reform of the Welfare State." *Transfer: European Review of Labour and Research* 5: 64–81.

Economist Intelligence Unit. 2000. *Country Profile: Finland 2000.* London: Economist Intelligence Unit.

Edey, Malcom, and Ketil Hviding. 1995. "An Assessment of Financial Reform in OECD Countries." *OECD Economic Studies* 25. Paris: Organization for Economic Co-operation and Development.

Edquist, Charles, and Bengt-Åke Lundvall. 1993. "Comparing the Danish and Swedish Systems of Innovation." In *National Innovation Systems: A Comparative Analysis*, edited by Richard R. Nelson. 265–98. New York: Oxford University Press.

Edquist, Charles, Terttu Luukkonen, and Markku Sotarauta. 2009. "Broad-Based Innovation Policy." In *Evaluation of the Finnish National Innovation System.* 11–70. Helsinki: Taloustieto Oy.

Edquist, Charles, and Maureen McKelvey. 1998. "High R & D Intensity without High Tech Products: A Swedish Paradox?" In *Institutions and Economic Change: New Perspectives on Markets, Firms and Technology*, edited by Klaus Nielsen and Björn Johnson. 131–49. Cheltenham, UK: Edward Elgar.

Egeraat, Chris Van. 2006. "Spatial Concentration in the Irish Pharmaceutical Industry: The Role of Government Intervention and Agglomeration Economies." Maynooth, Ireland: National Institute for Regional and Spatial Analysis.

EIRO (European Industrial Relations Observatory). 2002. "2001 Annual Review for Ireland." European Industrial Relations Observatory Online. http://www.euro found.europa.eu/eiro/2002/01/feature/ie0201252f.htm.

——. 2004. "2003 Annual Review for Denmark." European Industrial Relations Observatory Online. https://eurofound.europa.eu/eiro/2004/01/feature/dk0401102f. htm.

——. 2007. "New Industry Agreement Marked by Innovative Elements." European Industrial Relations Observatory Online. http://www.eurofound.europa.eu/ eiro/2007/03/articles/dk0703029i.htm

——. 2010. "End of Social Partnership as Public Sector Talks Collapse." European Industrial Relations Observatory Online. http://www.eurofound.europa.eu/ eiro/2009/12/articles/ie0912019i.htm.

——. 2011. "Impact of Government's Four-Year Plan on Minimum Wage and Sectoral Wage Agreements." European Industrial Relations Observatory Online. http:www.eurofound.europa.eu/eiro/2010/12/articles/ie1012029i.htm.

Elanger, Steven. 2010. "Absorbing the Blows That Buffet Europe." *New York Times*, March 8. http://www.nytimes.com/2010/03/08/world/european/08france. html.

Enright, Patrick G. 2001. "A Comparative Study of the Restructuring of the Irish and Danish Dairy Processing Industries: A Regulationist Approach." PhD diss., University of Leicester.

European Commission. 1999. *The Economic and Financial Situation in Finland.* Luxembourg: Office for Official Publications of the European Union.

——. 2003a. *European Competitiveness Report.* Luxembourg: Office for Official Publications of the European Union.

——. 2003b. *European Economy 2002 Review.* Luxembourg: Office for Official Publications of the European Union.

——. 2004. *Joint Employment Report 2003/2004.* Luxembourg: Office for Official Publications of the European Union.

——. 2006. *European Innovation Scoreboard 2005.* Luxembourg: Office for Official Publications of the European Union.

——. 2007. *Biopolis: Inventory and Analysis of National Public Policies That Stimulate Biotechnology Research, Its Exploitation and Commercialization by Industry in Europe in the Period 2002–2005: Final Report.* Luxembourg: Office for Official Publications of the European Union.

——. 2011. *European Economic Forecast: Spring 2011.* Luxembourg: Office for Official Publications of the European Union.

Eurostat. 2011. "Data Explorer." Eurostat. http://epp.eurostat.cec.eu.int/.

Evans, Peter. 1995. *Embedded Autonomy: States and Industrial Transformation.* Princeton: Princeton University Press.

Ewing, Jack. 2010. "Siemens and VW Surge on Roaring Demand from China." *New York Times,* July 30. http://www.nytimes.com/2010/07/30/business/global/30euecon.html.

Expert Group on Future Skills Needs. 2008. *Future Requirement for High-Level ICT Skills in the ICT Sector.* Dublin: Expert Group on Future Skills Needs.

Faccio, Mara, and Larry H. P. Lang. 2002. "The Ultimative Ownership of Western European Companies." *Journal of Financial Economics* 65: 365–95.

Fellman, Susanna. 2008. "Growth and Investment: Finnish Capitalism, 1850s-2005." In *Creating Nordic Capitalism: The Business History of a Competitive Periphery,* edited by Susanna Fellman, Martin Jes Iversen, Hans Sjögren, and Lars Thue. 139–217. New York: Palgrave Macmillan.

Fink, Philipp. 2004. *Purchased Development: The Irish Republic's Export-Oriented Development Strategy.* Munster, Germany: Lit Verlag.

Friedman, Thomas. 1999. *The Lexus and the Olive Tree.* New York: Farrar, Strauss and Giroux.

Fromlet, Pia. 2004. "The Danish Labour Market and Wage Formation Process." Bank of Finland Working Paper 2004/2. Helsinki: Bank of Finland.

FVCA (Finnish Venture Capital Association). 2004. *Yearbook 2004.* Helsinki: Finnish Venture Capital Association.

Gergils, Håkan. 2006. *Dynamic Innovation Systems in the Nordic Countries.* Stockholm: Studieförbundet Näringsliv & Samhälle Förlag.

Gerschenkron, Alexander. 1963. *Economic Backwardness in Historical Perspective.* Cambridge: Cambridge University Press.

Glimstedt, Henrik, and Udo Zander. 2003. "Sweden's Wireless Wonders: The Diverse Roots and Selective Adaptations of the Swedish Internet Economy." In *The Global Internet Economy,* edited by Bruce Kogut. 109–51. Cambridge: MIT Press.

Goldethorpe, John H., ed. 1984. *Order and Conflict in Contemporary Capitalism.* Oxford: Clarendon.

Goyer, Michel. 2006. "Varieties of Institutional Investors and National Models of Capitalism: The Transformation of Corporate Governance in France and Germany." *Politics & Society* 34: 399–430.

Grønning, Terje, Svein Erik Moen, and Dorothy Sutherland Olsen. 2008. "Low Innovation Intensity, High Growth and Specialized Trajectories: Norway." In *Small Country Innovation Systems: Globalization, Change and Policy in Asia and Europe,* edited by Charles Edquist and Leif Hommen. 281–318. Cheltenham, UK: Edward Elgar.

Gunnigle, Peter. 1998. "More Rhetoric Than Reality: Enterprise Level Industrial Relations Partnerships in Ireland." *Economic and Social Review* 29: 179–200.

Gylfason, Thorvaldur, Bengt Holmström, Sixten Korkman, Hans Tson Söderström, and Vesa Vihriälä. 2010. *Nordics in Global Crisis: Vulnerability and Resilience.* Helsinki: Taloustieto Oy.

Hakkarainen, Niilo. 1993. *Oravanpyörässä* [The rat race]. Helsinki: Otava.

Hall, Peter, and David Soskice. 2001. "An Introduction to Varieties of Capitalism." In *Varieties of Capitalism: The Institutional Foundations of Comparative Advantage*, edited by Peter Hall and David Soskice. 1–70. Oxford: Oxford University Press.

Hall, Peter, and Kathleen Thelen. 2009. "Institutional Change in Varieties of Capitalism." *Socio-Economic Review* 7: 7–34.

Hancké, Bob, and Martin Rhodes. 2005. "EMU and Labor Market Institutions in Europe." *Work and Occupations* 32: 196–228.

Hardiman, Niamh. 1988. *Pay, Politics and Economic Performance in Ireland: 1970–1987.* Oxford: Clarendon.

——. 1998. "Inequality and the Representation of Interests." In *Ireland and the Politics of Change*, edited by William Crotty and David E. Schmitt. 122–43. London: Addison Wesley Longman.

Hassel, Anke. 2007. *Wage Setting, Social Pacts and the Euro: A New Role for the State.* Amsterdam: Amsterdam University Press.

——. 2009. "Policies and Politics in Social Pacts in Europe." *European Journal of Industrial Relations* 15: 7–26.

Haughton, Jonathan. 1995. "The Historical Background." In *The Economy of Ireland: Policy and Performance in a Small European Country*, edited by J. W. O'Hagan. 1–48. London: Macmillan.

——. 1998. "The Dynamics of Economic Change." In *Ireland and the Politics of Change*, edited by William Crotty and David E. Schmitt. 27–50. London: Addison Wesley Longman.

Hemerijck, Anton C. 2003. "The Resurgence of Dutch Corporatist Policy Coordination in an Age of Globalization." In *Renegotiating the Welfare State: Flexible Adjustment through Corporatist Concertation*, edited by Frans van Waarden and Gerhard Lehmbruch. 33–69. London: Routledge.

Hemerijck, Anton C., and Mark I. Vail. 2006. "The Forgotten Center: State Activism and Corporatist Adjustment in Holland and Germany." In *The State after Statism: New State Activities in the Age of Liberalization*, edited by Jonah D. Levy. 57–92. Cambridge: Harvard University Press.

Henrekson, Magnus, and Ulf Jakobsson. 2003. "The Transformation of Ownership Policy and Structure in Sweden: Convergence towards the Anglo-Saxon Model?" *New Political Economy* 8: 73–102.

Hermans, Raine, and Terttu Luukkonen. 2002. "Findings of the ETLA Survey on Finnish Biotechnology Firms." ETLA Discussion Paper 819. Helsinki: Research Institute of the Finnish Economy.

Herrigel, Gary. 1996. *Industrial Constructions: The Sources of German Industrial Power.* Cambridge: Cambridge University Press.

Herrigel, Gary, and Volker Wittke. 2004. "Varieties of Vertical Integration: The Global Trend toward Heterogeneous Supply Relations and the Reproduction of Difference in the U.S. and German Manufacturing." In *Changing Capitalism*, edited by Glenn Morgan, Richard Whitley, and Eli Moen. 312–51. Oxford: Oxford University Press.

Herrmann, Andrea M. 2009. *One Political Economy, One Competitive Strategy? Comparing Pharmaceutical Firms in Germany, Italy, and the UK.* Oxford: Oxford University Press.

Hoepner, James. 1999. "The Danish Banking System: Concentration, Local Autonomy and the Financing of Small and Medium-Sized Enterprises." In *Mobilizing Resources and Generating Competencies: The Remarkable Success of Small and Medium-Sized Enterprises in the Danish Business System*, edited by Peter Karnoe, Peer Hull Kristensen, and Poul Houman Andersen. 113–35. Copenhagen: Copenhagen Business School Press.

Hollingsworth, J. Rogers. 2000. "Doing Institutional Analysis: Implications for the Study of Innovations." *Review of International Political Economy* 7: 595–644.

Hommen, Leif, and Charles Edquist. 2008. "Globalization and Innovation Policy." In *Small Country Innovation Systems: Globalization, Change and Policy in Asia and Europe*, edited by Charles Edquist and Leif Hommen. 442–83. Cheltenham, UK: Edward Elgar.

Honkapohja, Seppo, Erkki Koskela, Stefan Gerlach, and Lucrezia Reichlin. 1999. "The Economic Crisis of the 1990s in Finland." *Economic Policy* 14: 399–436.

Honohan, Patrick. 2009. "Resolving Ireland's Banking Crisis." *Economic and Social Review* 40: 207–31.

Höpner, Martin. 2007. "Coordination and Organization: The Two Dimensions of Nonliberal Capitalism." Max Planck Institute for the Study of Societies Discussion Paper 12/07. Cologne, Germany: Max Planck Institute for the Study of Societies.

Huber, Evelyne, and John D. Stephens. 1998. "Internationalization and the Social Democratic Model: Crisis and Future Prospects." *Comparative Political Studies* 31: 353–97.

Hyun-Chin, Lim, and Jang Jin-Ho. 2006. "Between Neoliberalism and Democracy: The Transformation of the Developmental State in South Korea." *Development and Society* 35: 1–28.

Hyytinen, Ari, Iikka Kuosa, and Tuomas Takalo. 2003. "Investor Protection and Financial Development in Finland." In *Financial Systems and Firm Performance: Theoretical and Empirical Perspectives*, edited by Ari Hyytinen and Mika Pajarinen. 65–95. Helsinki: Taloustieto Oy.

Hyytinen, Ari, Laura Paija, Petri Rouvinen, and Pekka Ylä-Anttila. 2006. "Finland's Emergence as a Global Information and Communications Technology Player: Lessons from the Finnish Wireless Cluster." In *How Revolutionary Was the Revolution? National Responses, Market Transitions, and Global Technology*, edited by John Zysman and Abraham Newman. 55–77. Stanford: Stanford University Press.

Hyytinen, Ari, and Mika Pajarinen. 2003a. "Financial Systems and Venture Capital in the Nordic Countries: A Comparative Study." In *Financial Systems and Firm Performance: Theoretical and Empirical Perspectives*, edited by Ari Hyytinen and Mika Pajarinen. 19–63. Helsinki: Taloustieto Oy.

——. 2003b. "Small Business Finance in Finland: A Descriptive Survey." In *Financial Systems and Firm Performance: Theoretical and Empirical Perspectives*, edited by Ari Hyytinen and Mika Pajarinen. 203–47. Helsinki: Taloustieto Oy.

Hyytinen, Ari, Petri Rouvinen, Otto Toivanen, and Pekka Ylä-Anttila. 2003. "Does Financial Development Matter for Innovation and Economic Growth? Implications for Public Policy." In *Financial Systems and Firm Performance: Theoretical and Empirical Perspectives*, edited by Ari Hyytinen and Mika Pajarinen. 379–456. Helsinki: Taloustieto Oy.

Hyytinen, Ari, and Lotta Väänänen. 2003. "Government Funding of Small and Medium-Sized Enterprises in Finland." In *Financial Systems and Firm Performance: Theoretical and Empirical Perspectives*, edited by Ari Hyytinen and Mika Pajarinen. 325–78. Helsinki: Taloustieto Oy.

Iankova, Elena. 2002. *Eastern European Capitalism in the Making*. Cambridge: Cambridge University Press.

ILO (International Labour Organization). 1982. *Yearbook of Labour Statistics*. Geneva: International Labour Organization.

———. 1987. *Yearbook of Labour Statistics*. Geneva: International Labour Organization.

Iversen, Martin J. 2005. *GN Store Nord: A Company in Transition*. Copenhagen: Copenhagen Business School Press.

Iversen, Martin J., and Steen Andersen. 2008. "Cooperative Liberalism: Denmark from 1857 to 2007." In *Creating Nordic Capitalism: The Business History of a Competitive Periphery*, edited by Susanna Fellman, Martin J. Iversen, Hans Sjögren, and Lars Thue. 265–91. New York: Palgrave Macmillan.

Iversen, Torben. 1996. "Power, Flexibility and the Breakdown of Centralized Wage Bargaining: Denmark and Sweden in Comparative Perspective." *Comparative Politics* 28: 399–436.

Iversen, Torben, and Jonas Pontusson. 2000. "Comparative Political Economy: A Northern European Perspective." In *Unions, Employers, and Central Banks: Macroeconomic Coordination and Institutional Change in Social Market Economies*, edited by Torben Iversen, David Soskice, and Jonas Pontusson. 1–37. New York: Cambridge University Press.

Jackson, Gregory, and Richard Deeg. 2005. "How Many Varieties of Capitalism? Comparative Institutional Analyses of Capitalist Diversity." Max Planck Institute for the Study of Societies Discussion Paper 06/02. Cologne: Max Planck Institute for the Study of Societies.

Jacobsen, John K. 1994. *Chasing Progress in the Irish Republic: Ideology, Democracy and Dependent Development*. Cambridge: Cambridge University Press.

Jacobsson, Staffan, Cecilia Sjöberg, and Marie Wahlström. 2001. "Alternative Specifications of the Institutional Constraints to Economic Growth: Or Why Is There a Shortage of Electronic Engineers and Computer Scientists in Sweden?" *Technology Analysis and Strategic Management* 13: 179–93.

Jamison, Andrew. 1991. "National Styles in Technology Policy: Comparing the Swedish and Danish State Programmes in Microelectronics/Information Technology." In *State Politics and Techno-Industrial Innovation*, edited by Ulrich Hilpert. 305–27. London: Routledge.

Jochem, Sven. 2003. "Nordic Corporatism and Welfare State Reforms." In *Renegotiating the Weflare States: Flexible Adjustment through Corporatist Concertation*, edited by Frans van Waarden and Gerhard Lehmbruch. 114–41. London: Routledge.

Johnson, Chalmers. 1982. *MITI and the Japanese Miracle*. Stanford: Stanford University Press.

Kalela, Jorma, Jaakko Kainder, Ullamaija Kivikuru, Heikki A. Loikkanen, and Jussi Simpura. 2001. Introduction to *Down from the Heavens, Up from the Ashes: The Finnish Economic Crisis of the 1990s in Light of Economic and Social Research*, edited by Jorma Kalela, Jaakko Kainder, Ullamaija Kivikuru, Heikki A. Loikkanen, and Jussi Simpura. 3–21. Helsinki: Government Institute for Economic Research.

Kasvio, Antti. 1994. "The Social Infrastructure of Innovation in Finland." In *Explaining Technical Change in a Small Country: The Finnish National Innovation*

System, edited by Synnöve Vuori and Pentti Vuorinen. 57–78. Heidelberg, Germany: Physica-Verlag.

Katz, Richard. 1998. *Japan: The System That Soured*. Armonk, NY: M. E. Sharpe.

Katzenstein, Peter J., ed. 1978. *Between Power and Plenty: Foreign Economic Policies in Advanced Industrial States*. Madison: University of Wisconsin Press.

——. 1984. *Corporatism and Change: Austria, Switzerland, and the Politics of Industry*. Ithaca: Cornell University Press.

——. 1987. *Policy and Politics in West Germany: The Growth of a Semi-Sovereign State*. Philadelphia: Temple University Press.

Kennedy, John. 2009. "Modest Cut in STI Investments in 2010 Budget." *SiliconRepublic*, September 12. http://www.siliconrepublic.com/news/article/14641/government/modest-cut-in-sti-investments-in-2010-budget.

Kennelly, James J. 2001. *The Kerry Way: The History of the Kerry Group, 1972–2000*. Dublin: Oak Tree Press.

Kessler, Wolfgang, and Rolf Eicke. 2008. "The Emergence of R & D Tax Regimes in Europe." *Tax Analysis* 50: 845–47.

Kiander, Jaakko, and Jaakko Pehkonen. 1999. "Finnish Unemployment: Observations and Conjectures." *Finnish Economic Papers* 12: 94–108.

Kitschelt, Herbert, Peter Lange, Gary Marks, and John D. Stephens. 1999. "Convergence and Divergence in Advanced Capitalist Societies." In *Continuity and Change in Contemporary Capitalism*, edited by Herbert Kitschelt, Peter Lange, Gary Marks, and John D. Stephens. 427–59. Cambridge: Cambridge University Press.

Kitschelt, Herbert, and Wolfgang Streeck. 2004. "From Stability to Stagnation: Germany at the Beginning of the Twenty-First Century." In *Germany: Beyond the Stable State*, edited by Herbert Kitschelt and Wolfgang Streeck. 1–34. London: Frank Cass.

Kjær, Jakob Sorgenfri, and Kåre Pedersen. 2011. "Economists: Best to Stay Out of Euro." *Politiken*, July 13. http://politiken.dk/newsinenglish/ECE1335085/economists-best-to-stay-out-of-euro/.

Koski, Heli, Liisa Leijola, Christopher Palmberg, and Pekka Ylä-Anttila. 2006. "Innovation and Education Strategies and Policies in Finland." In *Finland as a Knowledge Economy: Elements of Success and Lessons Learned*, edited by Carl J. Dahlman, Jorma Routti, and Pekka Ylä-Anttila. 39–62. Washington, DC: World Bank Institute.

Koski, Heli, and Pekka Ylä-Anttila. 2006. "Structural Changes in the Finnish Economy: From Agriculture to High-Tech." In *Finland as a Knowledge Economy: Elements of Success and Lessons Learned*, edited by Carl J. Dahlman, Jorma Routti, and Pekka Ylä-Anttila. 17–24. Washington, DC: World Bank Institute.

Krantz, Olle. 2001. "Industrialization in Three Nordic Countries: A Long-Term Quantitative View." In *Convergence? Aspects on the Industrialization of Denmark, Finland and Sweden 1870–1940*, edited by Hans Kryger Larsen. 23–66. Helsinki: Finnish Society of Sciences and Letters.

Kristensen, Peer Hull. 1995. "Denmark: An Experimental Laboratory of Industrial Organization." PhD diss., Copenhagen Business School.

——. 1996. "On the Constitution of Economic Actors in Denmark: Interacting Skill Containers and Project Coordinators." In *The Changing European Firm*, edited by Richard Whitley and Peer Hull Kristensen. 118–58. London: Routledge.

——. 1999. "When Labor Defines Business Recipes." In *Mobilizing Resources and Generating Competencies: The Remarkable Success of Small and Medium-Sized Enterprises in the Danish Business System*, edited by Peter Karnoe, Peer Hull

Kristensen, and Poul Houman Andersen. 74–112. Copenhagen: Copenhagen Business School Press.

——. 2011. "The Co-evolution of Experimentalist Business Systems and Enabling Welfare States: Nordic Countries in Transition." In *Nordic Capitalisms and Globalization: New Forms of Economic Organization and Welfare Institutions*, edited by Peer Hull Kristensen and Kari Lilja. 1-46. Oxford: Oxford University Press.

Kristensen, Peer Hull, and Jørn Levinsen. 1983. *The Small Country Squeeze*. Roskilde, Denmark: Forlaget for Samfundsøkonomi og Planlægning.

Kristensen, Peer Hull, Maja Lotz, and Robson Rocha. 2011. "Denmark: Tailoring Flexicurity for Changing Roles in Global Games." In *Nordic Capitalisms and Globalization: New Forms of Economic Organization and Welfare Institutions*, edited by Peer Hull Kristensen and Kari Lilja. 86–140. Oxford: Oxford University Press.

Kristensen, Peer Hull, and Glenn Morgan. 2007. "Multinationals and Institutional Competitiveness." *Regulation and Governance* 1: 197–212.

Kristensen, Peer Hull, and Jonathan Zeitlin. 2005. *Global Players in Local Games: The Strategic Constitution of a Multinational Corporation*. Oxford: Oxford University Press.

Krugman, Paul. 1994. "The Myth of Asia's Miracle." *Foreign Affairs* 73: 62–78.

Kuisma, Markku. 1999. "We Have No Rockefellers but We Have Cooperatives." In *The Pellervo Story*, edited by Markku Kuisma, Annastiina Henttinen, Sami Karhu, and Maritta Pohls. 9–24. Helsinki: Pellervo.

Labanyi, David. 2011. "Ireland to Receive 85 Billion Euro Bailout at 5.8% Interest Rate." *Irish Times.* November 28. http://www.irishtimes.com/newspaper/breaking/2010/1128/breaking1.html.

Landesmann, Michael. 1992. "Industrial Policies and Social Corporatism." In *Social Corporatism: A Superior Economic System?* edited by Jukka Pekkarinen, Matti Pohjola, and Bob Rowthorn. 242–79. Oxford: Clarendon.

Lange, Knut. 2009. "Institutional Embeddedness and the Strategic Leeway of Actors: The Case of the German Therapeutical Biotech Industry." *Socio-Economic Review* 7: 181–207.

Lassila, Aki, Jani-Pekka Jokinen, Janne Nylund, Petru Huurinainen, Markku Maula, and Jyrki Kontio. 2006. *Results of the National Software Industry Survey 2006*. Espoo: Center of Expertise for Software Product Business.

Lee, Kwang-Suk. 2009. "A Final Flowering of the Developmental State: The IT Policy Experiment of the Korean Information Infrastructure, 1995–2005." *Government Information Quarterly* 26: 567–76.

Lee, Yeon-ho. 1997. *The State, Society and Big Business in South Korea*. London: Routledge.

Lehmbruch, Gerhard, and Philippe C. Schmitter, eds. 1982. *Patterns of Corporatist Policy-Making*. Beverly Hills, CA: Sage.

Lehtonen, Heikki, Simo Aho, Jarmo Peltola, and Mika Renvall. 2001. "Did the Crisis Change the Welfare State in Finland?" In *Down from the Heavens, Up from the Ashes: The Finnish Economic Crisis of the 1990s in Light of Economic and Social Research*, edited by Jorma Kalela, Jaakko Kiander, Ullamaija Kivikuru, Heikki A. Loikkanen, and Jussi Simpura. 102–29. Helsinki: Government Institute for Economic Research.

Lemola, Tarmo. 1994. "Characteristics of Technology Policy in Finland." In *Explaining Technical Change in a Small Country: The Finnish Innovation System*, edited by Synnöve Vuori and Pekka Vuorinen. 184–200. Heidelberg, Germany: Physica-Verlag.

———. 2004. "Finnish Science and Technology Policy." In *Embracing the Knowledge Economy: The Dynamic Transformation of the Finnish Innovation System*, edited by Gerd Schienstock. 268–84. Cheltenham, UK: Edward Elgar.

Leslie, Stuart W. 2000. "The Biggest 'Angel' of the Them All: The Military and the Making of Silicon Valley." In *Understanding Silicon Valley: The Anatomy of an Entrepreneurial Region*, edited by Martin Kenney. 48–70. Stanford: Stanford University Press.

Levy, Jonah D. 1999. *Tocqueville's Revenge: State, Society, and Economy in Contemporary France*. Cambridge: Harvard University Press.

Levy, Jonah D., Robert Kagan, and John Zysman. 1997. "The Twin Restorations: The Political Economy of the Reagan and Thatcher 'Revolutions.'" In *Korea's Political Economy: An Institutional Perspective*, edited by Lee-Jay Cho and Yoon-Hyung Kim. 3–57. Boulder, CO: Westview.

Levy, Jonah D., Mari Miura, and Gene Park. 2006. "Existing Etatisme? New Directions in State Policy in France and Japan." In *The State after Statism*, edited by Jonah Levy. 93–136. Cambridge: Harvard University Press.

Lijphart, Arend. 1968. *The Politics of Accommodation: Pluralism and Democracy in the Netherlands*. Berkeley: University of California Press.

Lilja, Kari. 1997. "Bargaining for the Future: The Changing Habitus of the Shop Steward System in the Pulp and Paper Mills of Finland." In *Governance at Work: The Social Regulation of Economic Relations*, edited by Richard Whitley and Peer Hull Kristensen. 123–38. Oxford: Oxford University Press.

———. 1998. "Continuity and Modest Moves toward Company-Level Corporatism." In *Changing Industrial Relations in Europe*, edited by Anthony Ferner and Richard Hyman. 171–93. Oxford: Blackwell.

Lilja, Kari, Juha Laurila, and Raimo Lovio. 2011. "Finland: Innovating the Global Positioning of Flagship Companies and Foreign-Owned Subsidiaries." In *Nordic Capitalisms and Globalization: New Forms of Economic Organization and Welfare Institutions*, edited by Peer Hull Kristensen and Kari Lilja. 47–85. Oxford: Oxford University Press.

Lilja, Kari, Keijo Rasanen, and Risto Tainio. 1992. "A Dominant Business Recipe: The Forest Sector in Finland." In *European Business Systems: Firms and Markets in Their National Contexts*, edited by Richard Whitley. 137–54. London: Sage.

Lim, Chaisung. 2008. "Towards Knowledge Generation with Bipolarized NSI: Korea." In *Small Country Innovation Systems: Globalization, Change and Policy in Asia and Europe*, edited by Charles Edquist and Leif Hommen. 113–55. London: Edward Elgar.

Lim, Paul J. 2009. "Hints of Which Sectors Will Weather the Storm." *New York Times*, February 14. http://www.nytimes.com/2009/02/15/your-money/mutual-funds-and-etfs/15.fund.html.

Lindmark, Sven, Eric J. Andersson, Erik Bohlin, and Mattias Johansson. 2006. "Innovation System Dynamics in the Swedish Telecom Sector." *Info: The Journal of Policy, Regulation and Strategy for Telecommunications, Information and Media* 8: 49–66.

Lodovici, Manuela Samek, and Renata Semenza. 2008. "The Italian Case: From Employment Regulation to Welfare Reforms?" *Social Policy Administration* 42: 160–76.

Lorenz, Edward, and Antoine Valeyre. 2005. "Organisational Innovation, Human Resource Management and Labour Market Structure: A Comparison of the EU-15." *Journal of Industrial Relations* 47: 424–42.

Lovio, Raimo. 1993. "Evolution of Firm Communities in New Industries: The Case of the Finnish Electronics Industry." PhD diss., Helsinki School of Economics and Business Administration.

Lovio, Raimo, and Liisa Välikangas. 2010. "The National Innovation System of Finland." In *Encyclopedia of Technology and Innovation Management*, edited by V. K. Narayanan and Gina Colarelli O'Connor. 391–400. New York: Wiley-Blackwell.

Lubanski, Nikolaj, Jesper Jesper Due, Jorgen Steen Madsen, and Carsten Stroby Jensen. 2001. "Denmark: Towards Multi-Level Regulation." In *European Labor Relations*, edited by György Széll. 26–45. Burlington, VT: Gower.

Lundvall, Bengt-Åke, ed. 1992. *National Systems of Innovation: Towards a Theory of Innovation and Interactive Learning.* London: Pinter.

——. 2009. "Why the New Economy Is a Learning Economy." In *Techno-Economic Paradigms: Essays in Honor of Carlota Perez*, edited by Wolfgang Drechsler, Erik Reinert, and Rainer Kattel. 221–38. London: Anthem Press.

Lyall, Sarah. 2011. "Ireland's Governing Party Ousted in Historic Loss." *New York Times*, February 26. http://www.nytimes.com/2011/02/27/world/europe/27ireland.html.

MacSharry, Ray, and Padraic White. 2000. *The Making of the Celtic Tiger: The Inside Story of Ireland's Economic Boom.* Dublin: Mercier Press.

Madsen, Per Kongshoj. 2003. "Flexicurity through Labour Market Policies and Institutions in Denmark." In *Employment Stability in an Age of Flexibility*, edited by Peter L. Auer and Sandrine Cazes. 59–105. Geneva: International Labour Organization.

Magnusson, Lars. 2000. *An Economic History of Sweden.* London: Routledge.

Mahoney, James, and Kathleen Thelen, eds. 2009. *Explaining Institutional Change: Ambiguity, Agency and Power.* Cambridge: Cambridge University Press.

Manow, Philip, and Eric Seils. 2000. "Adjusting Badly: The German Welfare State, Structural Change and the Open Economy." In *Welfare and Work in the Open Economy: Diverse Responses to Common Challenges*, edited by Fritz Scharpf and Vivien Schmidt. 264–307. Oxford: Oxford University Press.

Marshall, F. Ray. 1958. "The Finnish Cooperative Movement." *Land Economics* 34: 227–35.

Martin, Cathie Jo. 2005. "Reinventing Welfare Regimes: Employers and the Implementation of Active Social Policy." *World Politics* 57: 39–69.

Martin, Cathie Jo, and Kathleen Thelen. 2008. "The State and Coordinated Capitalism: Contributions of the Public Sector to Social Solidarity in Postindustrial Societies." *World Politics* 60: 1–36.

Maula, Markku, and Gordon Murray. 2003. *Finnish Industry Investment Ltd: An International Evaluation.* Helsinki: Ministry of Trade and Industry.

McCarthy, Desmond. 2001. *Social Policy and Macroeconomics: The Irish Experience.* Washington, DC: World Bank.

Mjøset, Lars. 1987. "Nordic Economic Policies in the 1970s and 1980s." *International Organization* 41: 403–56.

——. 1992. *The Irish Economy in a Comparative Institutional Perspective.* Dublin: National Economic and Social Council.

Moen, Arild. 2011a. "Finland Lawmakers Still Split on Portugal Bailout." *Wall Street Journal*, May 10. http://online.wsj.com/article/SB10001424052748037308045763 15443832330746.html.

——. 2011b. "Nokia Stays Finnish, but Economy, National Pride Hit " *Wall Street Journal*, February 11. http://online.wsj.com/article/SB100014240527487037868045766138214187256354.html.

Moen, Eli. 2011. "Norway: Raw Material Refinement and Innovative Companies in Global Dynamics." In *Nordic Capitalisms and Globalization: New Forms of Economic Organization and Welfare Institutions*, edited by Peer Hull Kristensen and Kari Lilja. 141–82. Oxford: Oxford University Press.

Molina, Oscar. 2006. "Trade Union Strategies and Change in Neo-Corporatist Concertation: A New Century of Political Exchange." *West European Politics* 29: 640–44.

Morris, Damon C. 2005. "State Power and Institutional Challenges to Coordinating Industrial Adjustment: Industrial and Labor Market Politics in Denmark in the 1990s." PhD diss., City University of New York.

Natali, David, and Philippe Pochet. 2009. "The Evolution of Social Pacts in the EMU Era." *European Journal of Industrial Relations* 15: 147–66.

NESC (National Economic and Social Council). 1999. *Opportunities, Challenges and Capacities for Choice*. Dublin: National Economic and Social Council.

———. 2009. *Ireland's Five-Part Crisis: An Integrated National Response*. Dublin: National Economic and Social Development Office.

NID (National Informatics Directorate). 2006. "Software Industry Statistics for 1991–2004." Dublin: National Informatics Directorate. http://www.nsd.ie/htm/ssii/stat.htm.

Nikulainen, Tuomo, and Mika Pajarinen. 2010. "Is the Innovative Dominance of Nokia in Finland Unique in International Comparison?" In *Nokia and Finland in a Sea of Change*, edited by Jyrki Ali-Yrkkö. 69–90. Helsinki: Taloustieto Oy.

Nölke, Andreas, and Arjan Vliegenthart. 2009. "Enlarging the Varieties of Capitalism: The Emergence of Dependent Market Economies in East Central Europe." *World Politics* 61: 670–702.

O'Connell, Larry, Chris van Egeraat, and Patrick G. Enright. 1997. *Clusters in Ireland: The Irish Dairy Processing Industry*. Dublin: National Economic and Social Council.

O'Connell, Philip J. 1999. "Astonishing Success: Economic Growth and the Labour Market in Ireland." *ILO Employment and Training Papers* 44. Geneva: International Labour Organization.

O'Doherty, Dermot. 1998. "Networking in Ireland: Policy Responses." In *Sustaining Comparative Advantage: Proceedings of the NESC Seminar*, edited by NESC. 89–115. Dublin: National Economic and Social Council.

O'Donnell, Rory. 1998. "Ireland's Economic Transformation: Industrial Policy, European Integration, and Social Partnership." Pittsburgh: University of Pittsburgh Center for West European Studies.

———. 2001. "Towards a Post-Corporatist Concertation in Europe?" In *Interlocking Dimensions of European Integration*, edited by Helen Wallace. 305–22. London: Palgrave.

O'Dwyer, Conor, and Branislav Koval ík. 2007. "And the Last Shall Be First: Party System Institutionalization and Second-Generation Economic Reform in Postcommunist Europe." *Studies in Comparative International Development* 41: 3–26.

OECD (Organization for Economic Cooperation and Development). 1999. *OECD Economic Surveys, 1998–1999: Ireland*. Paris: Organization for Economic Cooperation and Development.

———. 2001. *OECD Economic Surveys, 2000–2001: Ireland*. Paris: Organization for Economic Cooperation and Development.

———. 2003. *OECD Economic Surveys, 2002–2003: Ireland*. Paris: Organization for Economic Cooperation and Development.

———. 2003 *Science, Technology and Industry Scoreboard*. Paris: Organization for Economic Cooperation and Development.

——. 2004. *Employment Outlook*. Paris: Organization for Economic Cooperation and Development.

——. 2005. *Science, Technology and Industry Scoreboard*. Paris: Organization for Economic Cooperation and Development.

——. 2009. *Economic Survey of Denmark*. Paris: Organization for Economic Cooperation and Development.

——. 2011. "OECD Statistics." OECD. http://stats.oecd.org/.

Ó Grada, Cormac. 1997. *A Rocky Road: The Irish Economy since the 1920s*. Manchester, UK: Manchester University Press.

Ó Grada, Cormac, and Kevin O'Rourke. 1996. "Irish Economic Growth, 1945–1988." In *Economic Growth in Europe since 1945*, edited by Nicholas Crafts and Gianni Toniolo. 388–426. Cambridge: Cambridge University Press.

O'Hearn, Dennis. 1998. *Inside the Celtic Tiger: The Irish Economy and the Asian Model*. London: Pluto.

Ohmae, Kinchi. 1990. *The Borderless World*. New York: Harper Collins.

Okamoto, Yumiko. 2010. "A Comparative Study on Biotechnology Companies in Sweden and Denmark: Why Do They Perform Differently?" *Donshisha University Policy Studies* 4: 139–57.

O'Malley, Eoin, Nola Hewitt-Dundas, and Stephen Roper. 2008. "High Growth and Innovation with Low R & D: Ireland." In *Small Country Innovation Systems: Globalization, Change and Policy in Asia and Europe*, edited by Charles Edquist and Leif Hommen. 156–93. Cheltenham, UK: Edward Elgar.

O'Malley, Eoin, Kieran A. Kennedy, and Rory O'Donnell. 1992. *The Impact of the Industrial Development Agencies*. Dublin: Stationary Office.

Ó Riain, Seán. 1999. "Remaking the Developmental State: The Irish Software Industry in the Global Economy." PhD diss., University of California, Berkeley.

——. 2000. "The Flexible Development State: Globalization, Information Technology, and the 'Celtic Tiger.'" *Politics & Society* 28: 157–93.

——. 2004. *The Politics of High Tech Growth: Developmental Network States in the Global Economy*. Cambridge: Cambridge University Press.

Ó Riain, Seán, and Philip J. O'Connell. 2000. "The Role of the State in Growth and Welfare." In *Bust to Boom? The Irish Experience of Growth and Inequality*, edited by Brian Nolan, Philip J. O'Connell, and Christopher T. Whelan. 310–39. Dublin: Institute of Public Administration.

Orlowski, Andrew. 2011. "Nokia's 15-Year Tango to Avoid Microsoft." *Register*, February 11. http://www.theregister.co.uk/2011/02/11/nokia_microsoft_history/.

Ornston, Darius. 2013. "Creative Corporatism: Explaining HighTechnology Competition in Nordic Europe." *Comparative Political Studies*. 46

Ornston, Darius, and Olli Rehn. 2006. "An Old Consensus in the 'New' Economy? Institutional Adaptation, Technological Innovation, and Economic Restructuring in Finland." In *How Revolutionary Was the Revolution? National Responses, Market Transitions, and Global Technology*, edited by John Zysman and Abraham Newman. 78–100. Stanford: Stanford Business Books.

O'Rourke, Kevin. 2006. "Late Nineteenth-Century Denmark in an Irish Mirror: Land Tenure, Homogeneity, and the Roots of Danish Success." In *National Identity and the Varieties of Capitalism: The Danish Experience*, edited by John L. Campbell, John A. Hall, and Øve K. Pedersen. 159–95. Montreal: McGill-Queen's University Press.

Ost, David. 2000. "Illusory Corporatism in Eastern Europe: Neoliberal Tripartism and Postcommunist Class Identities." *Politics & Society* 28: 503–30.

O'Sullivan, Mary. 1995. "Manufacturing and Global Competition." In *The Economy of Ireland: Policy and Performance in a Small European Country*, edited by J. W. O'Hagan, 363–96. London: Macmillan.

Paija, Laura. 2001. "ICT Cluster: The Engine of Knowledge-Driven Growth in Finland." ETLA Discussion Paper 733. Helsinki: Research Institute of the Finnish Economy.

Palier, Bruno, and Kathleen Thelen. 2010. "Institutionalizing Dualism: Complementarities and Change in France and Germany." *Politics & Society* 38: 119–48.

Palmberg, Christopher. 2002. "Technological Systems and Competent Procurers: The Transformation of Nokia and the Finnish Telecom Industry Revisited?" *Telecommunications Policy* 26: 129–48.

Palmberg, Christopher, and Erik Bohlin. 2006. "Next Generation Mobile Telecommunications Networks: Challenges to the Nordic ICT Industries." *Info* 8: 1–9.

Park, Insub. 2007. "The Labour Market, Skill Formation and Training in The 'Post-Developmental' State: The Example of South Korea." *Journal of Education and Work* 20: 417–35.

Parker, Andrew. 2011. "Google's Android Overtakes Nokia's Symbian." *Financial Times*, January 31. http://www.ft.com/cms/s/0/17433c60–2d31–11e0—9b0f-00144fe ab49a.html.

Pedersen, Christian, Michael Dahl, and Bent Dalum. 2006. "The Danish ICT Sector in an International Perspective: A Mismatch between Demand and Supply." *Info* 8: 85–99.

Pedersen, Christian R., and Bent Dalum. 2004. "Incremental Versus Radical Change: The Case of the Digital North Denmark." Paper presented at the DRUID Conference on Industrial Dynamics, Innovation and Development, June 14–16. Elsinore, Denmark.

Pedersen, Øve K., Niels A. Andersen, and Peter Kjær. 1992. "Private Policies and the Autonomy of Enterprise: Danish Local and National Industrial Policy." *Journal of Economic Issues* 26: 1117–44.

Pederson, Peder J. 1996. "Postwar Growth of the Danish Economy." In *Economic Growth in Europe since 1945*, edited by Nicholas Crafts and Gianni Toniolo. 541–75. Cambridge: Cambridge University Press.

Pekkarinen, Jukka, Matti Pohjola, and Bob Rowthorn, eds. 1992. *Social Corporatism: A Superior Economic System?* Oxford: Clarendon.

Pempel, T. J., and Keiichi Tsunekawa. 1979. "Corporatism without Labour? The Japanese Anomaly." In *Trends toward Corporatist Intermediation*, edited by Philippe Schmitter and Gerhard Lehmbruch. 231–70. London: Sage.

Perez, Sofia. 2000. "From Decentralization to Reorganization: Explaining the Return to National Bargaining in Italy and Spain." *Comparative Politics* 32: 437–58.

Piñera, José. 1995. "Chile." In *The Political Economy of Policy Reform*, edited by John Williamson. 225–31. Washington, DC: Institute for International Economics.

Pisani-Ferry, Jean, and André Sapir. 2006. "Last Exit to Lisbon." Bruegel Policy Brief 2006/3. Brussels: Bruegel.

Pizzorno, Alessandro. 1978. "Political Exchange and Collective Identity in Industrial Conflict." In *The Resurgence of Class Conflict in Western Europe*, edited by Colin Crouch and Alessandro Pizzorno. 277–98. London: Macmillan.

Pollert, Anna. 1997. "From Acquiescence to Assertion? Industrial Relations in the Czech Republic, 1989–1995." In *Industrial Relations between Command and Market: A Comparative Analysis of Eastern Europe and China*, edited by Gerd Schienstock, Paul Thompson, and Franz Traxler. 73–121. New York: Nova Science Publishers.

Pontusson, Jonas. 1984. *Public Pension Funds and the Politics of Capital Formation in Sweden*. Goteborg, Sweden: Tryckt av Graphic Systems AB.
———. 2005. *Inequality and Prosperity: Social Europe vs. Liberal America*. Ithaca: Cornell University Press.
Pontusson, Jonas, and Peter Swenson. 1996. "Labor Markets, Production Strategies and Wage Bargaining Institutions: The Swedish Employer Offensive in Comparative Perspective." *Comparative Political Studies* 29: 223–50.
Porter, Michael E. 1990. *The Competitive Advantage of Nations*. New York: Free Press.
Prondzynski, Ferdinand von. 1998. "Ireland: Corporatism Revived." In *Changing Industrial Relations in Europe*, edited by Anthony Ferner and Richard Hyman. 55–73. Oxford: Blackwell.
Rantanen, Miska, and Juha-Pekka Raeste. 2010. "Country Brand Working Group Sets Tasks for Finland." *Helsingin Sanomat*, November 11. http://www.hs.fi/english/article/Country+brand+working+group+sets+tasks+for+Finland/1135262030290.
Raumolin, Jussi. 1992. "The Diffusion of Technology in the Forestry and Mining Sector in Finland." In *Mastering Technology Diffusion: The Finnish Experience*, edited by Synnöve Vuori and Pekka Ylä-Anttila. 321–78. Helsinki: Taloustieto Oy.
Raunio, Tapio, and Matti Wiberg. 2008. "The Eduskunta and the Parliamentarisation of Finnish Politics: Formally Stronger, Politically Still Weak?" *West European Politics* 31: 581–99.
Regini, Marino. 1984. "The Conditions for Political Exchange: How Concertation Emerged and Collapsed in Britain and Italy." In *Order and Conflict in Contemporary Capitalism: Studies in the Political Economy of Western European Nations*, edited by John H. Goldthorpe. 124–42. Oxford: Oxford University Press.
Regini, Marino, and Ida Regalia. 1997. "Employers, Unions, and the State: The Resurgence of Concertation in Italy?" *West European Politics* 25: 210–30.
Regling, Klaus, and Max Watson. 2010. "A Preliminary Report on the Sources of Ireland's Banking Crisis." Dublin: Government Publications Office.
Rhodes, Martin. 1998. "Globalization, Labour Markets and Welfare States: A Future of Competitive Corporatism? " In *The Future of European Welfare: A New Social Contract?* edited by Martin Rhodes and Yves Mény. 178–203. London: Macmillan.
Rönkkö, Mikko, Eero Eloranta, Hanna Mustaniemi, Olli-Pekka Mutanen, and Jyrki Kontio. 2007. *Finnish Software Product Business: Results of the National Software Industry Survey 2007*. Espoo: Center of Expertise for Software Product Business.
Rönkkö, Mikko, Juhana Peltonen, and Dani Pärnänen. 2011. *Software Industry Survey 2011*. Espoo: Center of Expertise for Software Product Business.
Rose, Caspar, and Carsten Mejer. 2003. "The Danish Corporate Governance System: From Stakeholder Orientation towards Shareholder Value." *Corporate Governance* 11: 335–44.
Royo, Sebastian. 2002. *A New Century of Corporatism? Corporatism in Southern Europe*. Westport, CT: Praeger.
Saari, Juho. 2001. "Bridging the Gap: Financing Social Policy in Finland, 1990–1998." In *Down from the Heavens, Up from the Ashes: The Finnish Economic Crisis of The1990s in Light of Economic and Social Research*, edited by Jorma Kalela, Jaakko Kiander, Ullamaija Kivikuru, Heikki A. Loikkanen, and Jussi Simpura. 189–214. Helsinki: Government Institute for Economic Research.
Saarinen, Jani. 2005. "Innovations and Industrial Performance in Finland 1945–1998." PhD diss., Lund University.

Sabel, Charles. 1996. *Ireland: Local Partnerships and Social Innovations*. Paris: Organization for Economic Cooperation and Development.

Sabel, Charles, and Annalee Saxenian. 2008. *A Fugitive Success: Finland's Economic Future*. Helsinki: Finnish National Fund for Research and Development.

Sala, Vincent Della. 1997. "Hollowing Out and Hardening the State: European Integration and the Italian Economy." *West European Politics* 20: 14–33.

Salovaara-Moring, Inka. 2009. "Mind the Gap? Press Freedom and Pluralism in Finland." In *Press Freedom and Pluralism in Europe: Concepts and Conditions*, edited by Andrea Czepek, Melanie Hellwig, and Eva Nowak. 213–28. Bristol, UK: Intellect Books.

Sandberg, Åke, and Fredrik Augustsson. 2002. "Interactive Media in Sweden 2001: The Second Interactive Media, Internet and Multimedia Industry Survey." Stockholm: Arbetslivsinstitutet.

Sands, Anita. 2005. "The Irish Software Industry." In *From Underdogs to Tigers: The Rise and Growth of the Software Industry in Brazil, China, India, Ireland and Israel*, edited by Ashish Arora and Alfonso Gambardella. 41–71. Oxford: Oxford University Press.

Scharpf, Fritz W. 1984. "Economic and Institutional Constraints of Full-Employment Strategies: Sweden, Austria and West Germany, 1973–1982." In *Order and Conflict in Contemporary Capitalism*, edited by John H. Goldethorpe. 257–90. Oxford: Clarendon.

——. 1988. "The Joint Decision Trap: Lessons from German Federalism and European Integration." *Public Administration* 66: 239–78.

Schienstock, Gerd, and Timo Hämäläinen. 2001. *Transformation of the Finnish Innovation System: A Network Approach*. Helsinki: Finnish National Fund for Research and Development.

Schmidt, Vivien. 2002. *The Futures of European Capitalism*. Oxford: Oxford University Press.

Schmitter, Philippe C. 1974. "Still the Century of Corporatism?" *Review of Politics* 36: 85–131.

Schwartz, Herman. 1994. "Small States in Big Trouble: The Politics of State Reorganization in Australia, Denmark, New Zealand and Sweden in the 1980s." *World Politics* 46: 527–55.

——. 2001. "The Danish 'Miracle': Luck, Pluck or Stuck?" *Comparative Political Studies* 34: 131–55.

Schybergson, Per. 2001. "Large Enterprises in Small Countries" In *Convergence? Industrialization of Denmark, Finland and Sweden, 1870–1940*, edited by Hans Kryger Larsen. 97–155. Helsinki: Finnish Society of Sciences and Letters.

Seppelä, Timo. 2010. "Transformations of Nokia's Finnish Supplier Network from 2000 to 2008." In *Nokia and Finland in a Sea of Change*, edited by Jyrki Ali-Yrkkö. 37–68. Helsinki: Taloustieto Oy.

Sexton, J. J., P. J. O'Connell, J. Fitzgerald, J. Geary, T. Lalor, B. Nolan, and E. O'Malley. 1997. *Labor Market Studies: Ireland*. Brussels: European Commission.

Sherwood, Monika. 2006. "Unemployment in Austria: Low But . . ." *ECFIN Country Focus* 3: 1–6.

Shukla, Madhukar. 1997. *Competing through Knowledge: Building a Learning Organisation*. New Dehli: Response Books.

Siegel, Nico A. 2005. "Social Pacts Revisited: Competitive Concertation and Complex Causality in Negotiated Welfare State Reform." *European Journal of Industrial Relations* 11: 107–26.

Simpson, Glenn R. 2005. "Irish Subsidiary Lets Microsoft Slash Taxes in U.S. and Europe. *Wall Street Journal*, November 7.

Sinko, Pekka. 2002. "Labour Tax Reforms and Labour Demand in Finland, 1997–2001." *Government Institute for Economic Research Discussion Papers* 273. Helsinki: Government Institute for Economic Research.

Smyth, Emer, and Damian F. Hannan. 2000. "Education and Inequality." In *Bust to Boom? The Irish Experience of Growth and Inequality*, edited by Brian Nolan, Philip J. O'Connell, and Chistopher T. Whelan. 109–26. Dublin: Institute for Public Affairs.

Soskice, David. 1990. "Wage Determination: The Changing Role of Institutions in Advanced Industrialized Countries." *Oxford Review of Economic Policy* 6: 36–61.

———. 1999. "Divergent Production Regimes: Corodinated and Uncoordinated Market Economies in the 1980s and 1990s." In *Continuity and Change in Contemporary Capitalism*, edited by Herbert Kischelt, Peter Lange, Gary Marks, and John D. Stephens. 101–34. New York: Cambridge University Press.

Steinbock, Dan. 2000. *The Nokia Revolution: The Story of an Extraordinary Company That Transformed an Industry*. New York: Amacom.

———. 2004. *What Next? Finnish ICT Cluster and Globalization*. Helsinki: Ministry of the Interior.

Steinmo, Sven. 2010. *The Evolution of Modern States*. Oxford: Oxford University Press.

Sterne, John. 2004. *Adventures in Code: The Story of the Irish Software Industry*. Dublin: Liffey Press.

Stoerring, Dagmara, and Bent Dalum. 2007. "Cluster Emergence: A Comparative Study of Two Cases in North Jutland, Denmark." In *Creative Regions: Technology, Culture and Knowledge Entrepreneurship*, edited by Philip Cooke and Dafna Schwartz. 127–47. London: Routledge.

Stokke, Torgeir Aarvaag, and Christer Thornqvist. 2001. "Strikes and Collective Bargaining in the Nordic Countries." *European Journal of Industrial Relations* 7: 245–67.

Stråth, Bo. 2001. "Nordic Capitalism and Democratization." In *The Democratic Challenge to Capitalism: Management and Democracy in the Nordic Countries*, edited by Haldor Byrkjeflot, Sissel Myklebust, Christine Myrvang, and Francis Sejersted. 51–86. Bergen, Norway: Fagbokforlaget.

Streeck, Wolfgang. 1991. "On the Institutional Conditions of Diversified Quality Production." In *Beyond Keynesianism: The Socio-Economics of Production and Full Employment*, edited by Egon Matzner and Wolfgang Streeck. 21–61. Cheltenham, UK: Edward Elgar.

———. 1992. "Productive Constraints: On the Institutional Preconditions of Diversified Quality Production." In *Social Institutions and Economic Performance*, edited by Wolfgang Streeck. 1–40. London: Sage.

———. 1997. "The German Economic Model: Does It Exist? Can It Survive?" In *Political Economy of Modern Capitalism: Mapping Convergence and Diversity*, edited by Colin Crouch and Wolfgang Streeck. 33–54. London: Sage.

Streeck, Wolfgang, and Kathleen Thelen. 2005. "Introduction: Institutional Change in Advanced Political Economies." In *Beyond Continuity: Institutional Change in Advanced Political Economies*, edited by Wolfgang Streeck and Kathleen Thelen, 1–39. Oxford: Oxford University Press.

Sturgeon, Timothy J. 2003. "What Really Goes On in Silicon Valley? Spatial Clustering and Dispersal in Modular Production Networks." *Journal of Economic Geography* 3: 199–225.

Swenson, Peter. 1991. "Bringing Capital Back In, or Social Democracy Reconsidered." *World Politics* 43: 513–44.

Tainio, Risto, Mika Huolman, and Matti Pulkkinen. 2001. "The Internationalization of Capital Markets: How International Institutional Investors Are Restructuring Finnish Companies." In *The Multinational Firm: Organizing across Institutional and National Divides*, edited by Peer Hull Kristensen, Richard Whitley, and Glenn Morgan. 153–71. Oxford: Oxford University Press.

Tainio, Risto, and Kari Lilja. 2003. "The Finnish Business System in Transition: Outcomes, Actors and Their Influence." In *The Northern Light: Organization Theory in Scandinavia*, edited by Barbara Czarniawska and Guje Sevon. 69–87. Copenhagen: Copenhagen Business School Press.

Tainio, Risto, Matti Pohjola, and Kari Lilja. 2000. "Economic Performance of Finland after the Second World War: From Success to Failure." In *National Capitalisms, Global Competition and Economic Performance*, edited by Sigrid Quack, Glenn Morgan, and Richard Whitley. 277–96. Amsterdam: John Benjamins.

Taylor, George. 2002. "Negotiated Governance and the Irish Polity." In *Issues in Irish Public Policy*, edited by George Taylor. 28–51. Dublin: Irish Academic Press.

Tekes. 2005. *Business Cycle Effects on Start-up Finance in Finland*. Helsinki: Finnish Funding Agency for Technology and Innovation.

Telesis Consultancy Group. 1982. *A Review of Industrial Policy*. Dublin: National Economic and Social Council.

Teubal, Morris, and Terttu Luukkonen. 2006 "Venture Capital Industries and Policies: Some Cross-Country Comparisons." ETLA Discussion Paper 1006. Helsinki: Research Institute of the Finnish Economy.

Thelen, Kathleen. 1991. *Union of Parts: Labor Politics in Postwar Germany*. Ithaca: Cornell University Press.

Thomas, Damian. 2003. "The Irish Social Partnership 1987–2000: An Evolving Economic and Social Governance." PhD diss., Newcastle University.

Thun, Eric. 2008. "Globalization and Production." In *Global Political Economy*, edited by John Ravenhill. 346–72. Oxford: Oxford University Press.

Toivonen, Hannes. 2000. "Software Innovation in Finland." Technical Research Center of Finland Working Paper 52/00. Espoo: Technical Research Center of Finland.

Torfing, Jacob. 1999. "Workfare with Welfare: Recent Reforms of the Danish Welfare State." *Journal of European Social Policy* 9: 5–28.

Vaekstfonden. 2005. *Benchmarking the Market for Innovation Finance*. Hellerup, Denmark: Vaekstfonden.

Vail, Mark I. 2010. *Recasting Welfare Capitalism: Economic Adjustment in Contemporary France and Germany*. Philadelphia: Temple University Press.

Vartiainen, Juhana. 1998a. *The Labour Market in Finland: Institutions and Outcomes*. Helsinki: Prime Minister's Office.

——. 1998b. "Understanding Swedish Social Democracy: Victims of Success?" *Oxford Review of Economic Policy* 14: 19–39.

Verspagen, Bart. 2008. "Challenged Leadership or Renewed Vitality? The Netherlands." In *Small Country Innovation Systems: Globalization, Change and Policy in Asia and Europe*, edited by Charles Edquist and Leif Hommen. 319–54. Cheltenham, UK: Edward Elgar.

Veugelers, Reinhilde. 2009. "A Lifeline for Europe's Young Radical Innovators." Bruegel Policy Brief 2009/01. Brussels: Bruegel.

Viebrock, Elke, and Jochen Clasen. 2009. "Flexicurity and Welfare Reform: A Review." *Socio-Economic Review* 7: 305–31.

Visser, Jelle, and Anton Hemerijck. 1997. *A Dutch Miracle: Job Growth, Welfare Reform and Corporatism in the Netherlands.* Amsterdam: Amsterdam University Press.

Vogel, Steven K. 2003. "The Re-Organization of Organized Capitalism: How the German and Japanese Models Are Shaping Their Own Transformations." In *The End of Diversity? The Prospects for German and Japanese Capitalism,* edited by Kozo Yamamura and Wolfgang Streeck. 306–33. Ithaca: Cornell University Press.

Vuori, Synnöve, and Pentti Vuorinen. 1994. "Outline of the Finnish Innovation System: The Institutional Setup and Performance." In *Explaining Technical Change in a Small Country: The Finnish National Innovation System,* edited by Synnöve Vuori and Pentti Vuorinen. 1–42. Heidelberg, Germany: Physica-Verlag.

Wade, Robert. 1990. *Governing the Market: Economic Theory and the Role of the Government in East Asian Industrialization.* Princeton: Princeton University Press.

——. 2000. "Wheels within Wheels: Rethinking the Asian Crisis and the Asian Model." *Annual Review of Political Science* 3: 85–115.

Weishaupt, J. Timo. 2010. "After the Crisis Is before the Crisis? European Labor Market Responses in Comparative Perspective." Paper presented at the annual meeting of the American Political Science Association, September 2–5. Washington, DC.

Whelan, Karl. 2010. "Policy Lessons from Ireland's Latest Depression." *Economic and Social Review* 41: 225–54.

White, Tony. 2001. *Investing in People: Higher Education in Ireland from 1960 to 2000.* Dublin: Institute of Public Administration.

Wicken, Olav. 2009. "Policies for Path Creation: The Rise and Fall of Norway's Research-Driven Strategy for Industrialization." In *Innovation, Path Dependency and Policy: The Norwegian Case,* edited by Jan Fabergberg, David C. Mowery, and Bart Verspagen. 89–115. Oxford: Oxford University Press.

Woll, Cornelia. 2008. *Firm Interests: How Governments Shape Business Lobbying on Global Trade.* Ithaca: Cornell University Press.

Wong, Joseph. 2011. *Betting on Biotech: Innovation and the Limits of Asia's Developmental State.* Ithaca: Cornell University Press.

Wood, Stewart. 1997. "Capitalist Constitutions: Supply-Side Reform in Britain and West Germany, 1960–1990." PhD diss., Harvard University.

World Economic Forum. 2012. *The Global Competitiveness Report 2011–2012.* New York: Oxford University Press.

Ylä-Anttila, Pekka, and Christopher Palmberg. 2005. "The Specifities of Finnish Industrial Policy: Challenges and Initiatives at the Turn of the Century." ETLA Discussion Paper 973. Helsinki: Research Institute of the Finnish Economy.

Zahariadis, Nikolaos. 2002. "Asset Specificity and State Subsidies in Industrialized Countries." *International Studies Quarterly* 45: 603–16.

Ziegler, J. Nicholas. 1997. *Governing Ideas: Strategies for Innovation in France and Germany.* Ithaca: Cornell University Press.

Zysman, John. 1983. *Governments, Markets, and Growth.* Ithaca: Cornell University Press, 1983.

——. 1994. "How Institutions Create Historically Rooted Trajectories of Growth." *Industrial and Corporate Change* 3: 243–83.

——. 2006. "Creating Value in a Digital Era: How Do Wealthy Nations Stay Wealthy?" In *How Revolutionary Was the Revolution? National Responses, Market Transitions, and Global Technology,* edited by John Zysman and Abraham Newman. 23–52. Stanford: Stanford University Press.

Index

Aalborg, Denmark, 89, 95, 108n21, 112–119, 121, 124, 203
Aalborg University, 112
advertising industry, 185
aerospace industry, 14, 170
Agrarian Union Party, Finland, 32
Agricultural Advisory Service, 44
agriculture, 45, 194, 204; in Denmark, 9, 18, 32, 40, 43–47, 93–94, 98, 109; in Finland, 32, 59; in Ireland, 47, 137, 144–146, 158–159
Aho, Esko, 63–64, 163
Alliance for Jobs, 170
An Foras Áiseanna Seothair (FAS), 141
Apple, 58, 84, 87–89, 128, 149
apprenticeship system, 170
Arbejdsmarkedets Tillaegspension (ATP), 106
Austria, 2, 9, 13t, 24t, 32, 167–168, 193–194, 202; conservative corporatism in, 24, 171–173, 186, 188–190, 195, 200
automotive industry, 9, 173, 185, 190, 192

Bank of Denmark, 41, 106
Bank of Finland, 41, 72
banking blocs, in Finland, 31–34, 55, 63–64, 72, 198; in Sweden, 31, 72
banking system, 9, 17, 171, 193; in Denmark, 15, 28, 39–40, 96, 99, 120–123; in Finland, 15, 28, 31–32, 37, 72–76; in Germany, 168; in Ireland, 28, 47–48, 51, 135, 146–147, 160; in Norway, 172; in the United Kingdom, 48. See also universal bank
Belgium, 13t, 24t, 88n75
Bildt, Carl, 182–183
biotechnology industry, 186n4; in Denmark, 1, 12–13, 54, 92–96, 109–112, 118–119, 122, 171, 194; in Finland, 1, 56–58, 74, 83–89; in Germany, 171; in Ireland, 126, 144, 155; in Norway, 172; in Sweden, 85, 171, 184, 199; in the United Kingdom, 194
Bluetooth, 95, 112, 116–118
Britain. See United Kingdom
Business Development Fund. See Vaekstfonden

Business Expansion Scheme, 147
business-angels, 75, 117, 148

cable industry, 33, 36, 58, 122
capital flight, 30, 133, 142
cartels, 19, 28, 32, 44, 202; in Finland, 28, 55, 63, 66, 198
CDMA standard, 116, 118, 124
center contracts, 101, 110–111, 123
Center Party, Finland, 62, 69
Center for Personal Communications, 117
Center for Teleinfrastructure, 117, 121
Central Association of Finnish Wood Processing, 32
Central Laboratory, 32
Cetelco, 58, 112–116
chemicals industry, 35, 37, 41, 192
China, 82, 116, 186
civil war, Ireland, 50
Civil War of 1918, Finland, 28, 33–35, 50, 162
Common Market, European, 99, 109
communications. See telecommunications
Communists, 34–35, 60, 69, 177–178, 189–190, 195
competitive corporatism, 66, 166–167; adjustment, 19–20, 178; adoption of, 189; bargains, 19–20, 126, 152, 161–162; definition of, 2–4, 16, 19–21; in Denmark, 103; and fiscal policy, 197; and institutional innovation, 196; in Ireland, 3, 54, 104, 125, 132, 138, 148, 152, 163; limitations of, 179, 201; and market policy, 197; in the Netherlands, 166, 174; resurgence of, 175; risks of, 173; stability of, 197; successes, 175; and tax policy, 174
computer industry, 10–11, 50–52; in Finland, 56, 80, 87; in Ireland, 1, 6, 12, 46, 50, 52, 126, 149, 155; in Sweden, 181
concertation, and competitive corporatism, 194–197; and conservative corporatism, 189–193; and coordination, 2–3, 8, 18–21, 166; creating, 54, 201–202; and creative corporatism, 54, 197–200; definition of, 2–3, 8; in Denmark, 51–54; in East